LAND USE

Professor Denman is the sole or joint author of:

Tenant-Right Valuation
Tenant-Right Valuation and Current Legislation
Origins of Ownership
Estate Capital
Farm Rents
Bibliography of Rural Land Economy and Land Ownership
Land Ownership and Resources
Contemporary Problems of Land Ownership
Land in the Market
Land and People
Commons and Village Greens
Rural Land Systems
Land Use and the Constitution of Property

LAND USE

An Introduction to
Proprietary Land Use Analysis

by D. R. Denman
Professor of Land Economy, University of Cambridge

and S. Prodano
Lecturer in Land Economy, University of Cambridge

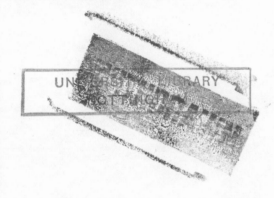
UNIVERSITY LIBRARY
NOTTINGHAM

London. George Allen & Unwin Ltd
Ruskin House   Museum Street

First published in 1972

This book is copyright under the Berne Convention.
All rights are reserved. Apart from any fair dealing for the
purpose of private study, research, criticism or review,
as permitted under the Copyright Act, 1956, no part of this
publication may be reproduced, stored in a retrieval system,
or transmitted in any form or by any means, electronic,
electrical, chemical, mechanical, optical, photo-copying,
recording or otherwise, without the prior permission of the
copyright owner. Enquiries should be addressed to the
publisher.

© George Allen & Unwin Ltd 1972

ISBN 0 04 333013 4

Printed in Great Britain
in 10-point Times Roman type
by Unwin Brothers Limited
Woking and London

Foreword

Landowners take decisions which are critical for the use of land and natural resources. This book is concerned with why and how they do so, and to draw the attention of planners operating at national and regional levels to the positive contribution from the proprietary land side. Landownership and land tenure take their colour from the land law of places and periods. Proprietary land use analysis introduces a new approach to the decision-making framework of land ownership, with the objective of confining local variations to standard categories and avoiding the ambiguities associated with juridical notions of ownership and the peculiarities of land tenure systems.

Over the last ten years or so, in lecture rooms and conference halls, in corridors and cafés, and wherever else we have met colleagues and pupils, the ideas and principles of this analysis have been debated, modified and consolidated. The upshot is the introduction offered here to a new analytical philosophy. The text has been deliberately kept to the bare essentials required of an introduction but the resilience of the analysis lends itself to the discovery of new depths of interpretation and the refinement of concepts; and its range of practical application is almost boundless. As a method of enquiry it is proving an invaluable tool in the hands of consultants and others who need to comprehend what is pertinent to a practical understanding of the forces and institutions which determine the use of land and natural resources in the developed and in the developing world.

To single out two or three among the countless contributors who have helped to bring these thoughts to print would be invidious and wholly inadequate in the light of the sincere gratitude which we feel towards the innumerable partners in discussion who have made the book possible. The final version is ours alone, with what is worthy and what is unworthy.

D. R. D.
S. P.

Cambridge, 1971.

Contents

Chapter I

A FORGOTTEN DIMENSION

Authority for taking decisions about the use of land operates at two levels. Government executives devise plans for regional and national purposes and the general principles and criteria which guide them have added a new department of knowledge to social and economic studies. But the development of the new knowledge has tended to obscure the lower level at which the decisions taken are more critical in one sense than the global decisions of the planners. Both are necessary, but the one should not be eclipsed by the other.

The lower level of authority is provided by those who hold property rights over the land and who, in consequence, take positive decisions for the use of it. The process of decision-making at this level can be studied and analysed by identifying the fundamental unit within which decisions are taken. This unit we shall call the proprietary land unit and in later chapters define its standard forms and expound the analysis of which it is the focus.

At this stage, we must show why this forgotten dimension should not be overlooked.[1] It is proposed, therefore, to take a brief look at some familiar ideas and procedures associated with the use of land resources and to see what new insights the identification of the proprietary land unit provides.

Rent and the Land Market. From the time of the classical economists to the present day the theory of rent has inevitably been linked with the name of Ricardo. For Ricardo, rent was a residuum, a surplus remaining to land after capital and labour had each received their respective rewards of interest and wages. Land was given; it lay passive, to have rent bestowed upon it.

Later and modern theories of rent see it more as reward for the services rendered by land to the production process or to some

[1] D. R. Denman, *Property, The Forgotten Dimension in Planning*, Occasional Paper No. 4 (Faculty of Commerce and Administration, University of British Columbia, 1969).

other purpose.[2] Although they come closer to reality than the Ricardian theory ever did, the modern theories like the classical ascribe to land as a form of wealth a homogeneity which, as a commodity on the land market, it does not possess. Rent does not issue from land *per se* as the rent theories imply. It is not and cannot be a reward to virginity.

Rent is a differential. And differentials have no tangible form unless they lie within the bounds of exclusive property rights. The advantage measured by rent lies not in the land itself, but in the right to possess, occupy and cultivate the land to the exclusion of all others. The true source of rent is not virgin homogeneous land but land subject to property rights. As a reward to and output from land, rent cannot be properly understood or related to its true source without identifying the unit of exclusive possession in land wherein it is generated.

It is also this unit which in all economies, wherever a land market is admitted, is the commodity in which the land market deals. No land market deals in virgin land. No man buys land as such; he buys land-cum-property rights, that is, a proprietary land unit.

Place of Land in Social Accounting. Land in social and central economic planning tends to be looked upon as a homogeneous continuum; a chequer-board over which capital, labour and management move in interaction. Land is either left out of the analysis of national aggregates,[3] or if it is fed into the accounts as an input, it is quantified in superficial measures (acres, hectares)—as if it had a uniform consistency and a value which was a linear function of the number of units available.

In the real world the association of capital needs and equipment with land is critically dependent upon the nature, scope and duration of property rights. Bottle-necks checking the input of capital can be created by a particular type of proprietary land unit. The value which the land market places on a superficial unit of land is a function of the character of the proprietary land unit within which the land lies. Land as an input in a social accounting matrix cannot be evaluated without relating it to a structure of proprietary land units. It is not land as such which is the true input. A crucial question therefore in making any evaluation is whether the existing proprietary

[2] See for instance W. S. Jevons, *Theory of Political Economy* (Macmillan, 1871), p. 205 *et passim*; L. Walras, *Elements of Pure Economics*, trans. Jaffé (Allen and Unwin, 1954).

[3] A. Shonfield, *Modern Capitalism* (Oxford University Press, 1965), p. 223.

structure of the land is to be taken as permanent, or whether change is to be postulated, and if so, in what fashion it should be conceived.

Social Evaluation of Land and Development Projects. When alternative schemes for the use of land are evaluated from what is called a social standpoint, land costs and values are frequently left out of the calculations on the plea that the land factor is common in extent and therefore in value to all the alternatives.

Thinking along these lines divorces the calculations from reality. A development scheme for land cannot be carried out unless the public or private agencies executing the development have the legal sanction over the land to pursue their intentions; in other words, all development schemes must and can only take place on the land within a given and appropriate proprietary framework. What has to be costed is not the sum of so many superficial units of land, but the value of an array of interrelated proprietary land units. Logically, the proprietary structure of the land must accommodate and be appropriate to the land use scheme, otherwise the scheme will be still-born. The physical development pattern presupposes an appropriate proprietary structure and alternative schemes demand differing proprietary structures. As we have seen above, the value of the so-called land element is the value of the proprietary land units as such and cannot be constant for all schemes.

In those economies where a land market exists, the cost of a proprietary land unit can be calculated at market price. From the social standpoint, the price would be a measure in monetary terms of the amount of public resources which would need to be exchanged in a transfer of the title to the proprietary land unit to a public agency. If interests in land were not to be acquired by a public body, the value of each proprietary land unit would have to be taken into account on the input side of the social cost account, and the sum of the values before the scheme compared with the sum of the values resulting from the proprietary structure devised to meet the needs of the new scheme. If the balance between the latter and the former were positive, the difference could be regarded as a measure of the value of new wealth generated by the development scheme. In this sense, it would represent a social benefit. And such would also be the case where the interests in the land were acquired by the public agencies prior to the development.

Sometimes cost-benefit accounts for land development schemes calculated from the social standpoint regard acquisition costs of the proprietary land units as a cost item and the money paid to

13

the vendors of the units as a benefit which offsets the cost.[4] Knowledge of the character of a proprietary land unit and of the critical part played by motive[5] in the internal economy of a unit would illuminate the falsity of a calculation of this kind. The market value of a proprietary land unit handed over in cash, as payment for the title to it on a forced sale to an acquiring public authority is not a sure measure of the benefit reaped by the vendor. It is a benefit of a kind. Only if the motive of the holder of the proprietary land unit at the time was to acquiesce in the purchase of the unit could the compensation paid for compulsory purchase be regarded as a full compensatory benefit. A true statement of account would probably be impossible, because frequently the value of the proprietary land unit to the current owner (the benefit then existing) is higher than any figure the land market would give for the unit.[6] If the value to the holder of the unit were measurable in money terms, the difference between it and the compensation money would need to be counted among the costs, not among the benefits.

Positive Planning. In the Western world, particularly in Britain and the USA, national and regional planning of the use of land and natural resources have been mainly undertaken through the imposition of public controls on the use of land and have in this sense been negative. Land use and development plans are the basic documents depicting by zonal reference the directions in which development on the initiative of holders of property rights in the land would be permitted. At most, the state planners could only achieve the execution of their intentions indirectly by prohibiting the use of land for purposes unacceptable to them. Legislation empowering the public control of land use by prohibition from the early days to the present time struck an allocatory note. It was required of a development plan under the Town and Country Planning Act 1947 in Britain, for example, to do no more than impose from above designations of use, as if the planner had executive power of disposition over the land. Specification on these lines implies that the planner making a plan need not concern himself with the proprietary land structure.

Planning by prohibition has culminated in a universal sense of ineffectiveness and a desire to strike a positive note. Neither the planners nor the planned are content. The planner is denied the

[4] N. Lichfield, *Cost-Benefit Analysis in Urban Redevelopment*, Research Report 20 (Berkeley: Real Estate Research Program, Institute of Business and Economic Research, University of California, 1962).
[5] Below, Ch. IV ff.   [6] Below, p. 178.

power of positive planning and the holders of the property rights are discouraged from thinking daringly.

Remedy lies in bringing the proprietary land unit into the planning process. By identifying and studying the proprietary land unit, planners will come to know and perhaps appreciate the motives and powers of the holders of the units and hence what lies behind the decision-making which issues in positive action for the use of land. Working with the planners, the holders of proprietary land units will see their own problems and the significance of the decisions they take within the social and economic framework of an entire planning district or region and even against the background of the national economy.[7]

Thresholds in Land Use Planning. Town and country planning schools have recently fashioned a new technique to aid land use analysis, a device which Hughes and Kozlowski,[8] the pioneers of it, have designated threshold analysis. Threshold analysis, as perfected so far, recognizes the contribution to aggregate patterns made by the concourse of decisions within separate and identifiable decision-making units, and that barriers (thresholds) exist which limit the degree of manœuvrability in decision-making. Recognition of the proprietary land unit as a seat of thresholds peculiar to it would greatly extend the range of threshold analysis and enrich the rewards to be won from the pursuit of it.

Land Tenure and Land Use. Economists, scientists and others concerned with the problems of natural resource development in developing countries have become almost parrot-like in the repetition of declarations and even of protestations on the need to come to grips with the problems of land tenure as a preliminary step towards the implementation of any systematical policy for the use of land and natural resources. What is true of developing countries is no less true, though less immediately apparent, of the developed countries.

Land tenure is the creation of land law and cannot escape the complexities and confusions created by local and national juridical distinctions, customary usages and colloquial terminology. General

[7] D. R. Denman, *Land Use and the Constitution of Property.* An Inaugural Lecture (Cambridge University Press, 1969), p. 20.

[8] J. T. Hughes and J. Kozlowski, *Threshold Analysis—An Economic Tool For Town And Regional Planning*, Urban Studies (Glasgow University, June 1968), p. 132.

15

studies[9] of the proprietary land unit, as a universal concept and criterion of land use, have shown the way towards overcoming the obstacles of local terminology and the nice distinctions drawn by differing juridical systems—thus reducing the study of land tenure and land use to general categories and universal concepts.

Feasibility Studies. What has come to be known as a feasibility study of development potential has of recent years emerged from the combination of land use planning and economic planning. On the land side, feasibility studies make much play of what the technicians who produce them call land restraints.[10] A restraint suggests more a psychical obstacle than a physical one. In the jargon of feasibility studies, however, the land restraint denotes some physiographical formation to which planners of the use of resources are required to give heed. It would be more in keeping with the dictates of semantics to use the term land restraint to denote the restraints imposed on action by property obligations and the sanction of the land law. No feasibility study is worth serious consideration unless attention is paid by it to restraints of this kind which condition the execution of decisions for the use of land and natural resources.

Motives for Land Use. Since property power over land is the seat of positive action for the use of the land, the study of land use is incomplete unless it takes cognizance of the motives which move men to hold and use that power. Motives always take a predicate. Motive cannot exist as a pure notion in itself but must have an object towards which it acts. Motives which determine the use of land and resources are invariably expressed towards the holding and exercise of property rights in land and hence are focused on the proprietary land unit.

[9] D. R. Denman, *Rural Land Systems* (International Federation of Surveyors, Commission 4, 1968).

[10] See for instance, *The Moray Firth—A Plan for Growth in a Sub-region of the Scottish Highlands* (J. Holmes Planning Group, Glasgow, March 1968).

Chapter II

A FUNDAMENTAL UNIT

Its Recognition

Uses of land and other factors of production in an economy are the outcome of numerous decisions taken within a calculus of decision-making units. To isolate the proprietary land unit for study and analysis is not to abandon the consideration of the public ownership and use of land resources for the study of private interests. No emphasis is too heavy to hammer home this fact. The emphasis is necessary because whenever one speaks of the interests of holders of property rights in land or of landowners, the common assumption is to suppose that sides are being taken between the private and the public sectors of an economy and that the speaker is concerned only with the former. Let it be abundantly clear: the study of the proprietary land unit is the analysis of the character and functioning of the decision-making unit within which positive decisions are taken about the use of land and such a unit may be held by a private citizen, by trustees, by an institution of any kind or by a department of central or local government.

Holders of interests in land, whoever they may be, should find that this attempt to identify the form and to study the functioning of the decision-making units within which they exercise their land rights is an analysis of practical value. Experience has shown that not too infrequently it is the holders of property rights in land who have the vaguest notions of the nature and potentialities of the decision-making units they possess. They are unaware of the criteria by which one policy for the use of them can be compared with possible alternatives; of the place a particular unit occupies within the national honeycomb of units; and of the relationship which the policy-making within the unit bears to national and regional plans and to the powers and intentions of those who make them. The key to a better understanding is the ability to see each unit and its inherent potentialities as a component of a national or regional framework of decision-making units, the land use pattern of which

B

and the distribution and employment of resources within which, are dependent upon the decisions taken and executed by the holder of each individual proprietary land unit.

Land is a resource of primary consequence in the economy of any country, especially if we permit the definition of land to include water. Whether we regard it in pure form as one of the given things of nature or as manipulated by the hand of man by developments of various kinds, land has about it a static quality which by its uniqueness has a significant bearing upon the manner in which decisions can be made about the use of it. An owner of an interest in land cannot pocket his possession. To use it he must go to it and work upon it, or permit others duly authorized to do so.

Land is no different from other forms of wealth in that decisions about its use are made within the calculus of the decision-making units. Its static quality however, gives a particular character to the decision-making unit within which all positive decisions are taken for the use of it. Legal authority for taking decisions will lie in the property rights over the land which in themselves will largely be fashioned by the local land law. Because the subject matter, the physical *solum* and its fixed improvements are co-ordinate in geographical space, the property rights which authorize positive land use can be related to a particular place on the map and extent of land surface. And these two elements, the run of property rights and the area of physical land to which they pertain together constitute the decision-making unit which is fundamental to all positive decisions about land use and which is referred to as *the proprietary land unit*.

The proprietary land unit is not the unit within which local and central Government planners take decisions for land use planning, as planners. Planning at this level, indeed, has been more or less oblivious of the fundamental dimension and of the significance of the proprietary land unit in the ultimate determination of land use. The present analysis of the character and function of the proprietary land unit will, it is hoped, encourage and enable Government planners to embrace the fundamentals and take them into account in future planning. The proprietary land unit also puts the place of land in economic analysis in a somewhat different perspective from the view of it taken by the classical economists and their successors. The analysis, however, should be of especial interest and value to the holders of interests in land, whether as private citizens or public bodies concerned to organize the use of their land and its fixed equipment.

18

Its Land Element

Economists have held differing opinions regarding the nature of land. Some regard it as one of the basic factors of production, along with labour, capital and management. In that context it is usually considered as the natural source of raw materials such as food, minerals and energy resources. Land in the orthodox definition of it held by economists[1] is distinguished from capital and labour because as a factor of production it exists in the natural order of things and no labour has been expended on its production. This concept of land is essentially analytical. The analysis divides the virgin, given thing, the natural resource, from all that has been done upon it to exploit its inherent wealth and make it more productive. In theory, the analysis holds good whether land as the natural resource is confined to the narrow view of the physical soil or has a wider connotation to include surface and subterranean waters, minerals and natural forests. This abstract, analytical definition of land is valid enough for the theory of economic analysis. But land under the foot of human settlements, primitive and sophisticated, is so inextricably admixed with the works of men upon it that to identify the virgin substance is impossible.

Land to the lawyer, especially if he follows the schooling of the English jurists, does not conform to the abstract concept of the economist. The land lawyer looks at the whole thing, improved, developed, worked upon. Land for him is far more than the natural surface and the virgin depths. It includes land as a natural resource, and includes it in its fullness, all that nature gives of soil, water, minerals, trees and vegetation and, in addition, all the works of man upon the natural resource. Thus to the lawyer land means not only the natural soil or waters, the *solum*, but all buildings, roads, fences, shafts, ditches and all erections and excavations which are physically attached to or identified with the soil. This includes all things superjacent and subjacent above and below the earth's surface.

From the very nature of the concept, the land element in the proprietary land unit cannot be land in the virgin, natural state of the economist's definition. To create the unit property rights have been conceived in the land. The proprietary land unit is a practical way of looking at the wholeness of things and the land element within it must inevitably satisfy the lawyer's notion of land rather than the abstract virgin resource of economic analysis. Land within the meaning of a proprietary land unit is always land as the natural

[1] A. Marshall, *Principles of Economics* (Macmillan, 8th edn, London, 1964), p. 66.

19

resource together with all the works of man upon it as they are known and manifest at the moment of identification of the unit.

Although more will be made of the particular point later on, it is not too early in the text to point out that land within the definition of a proprietary land unit as it stands at a given stage of development is, unlike the virgin resource of economic analysis, not fixed in supply. The buildings, roads, terraces and fences which together with the natural resource on which they stand compose the land element and give to it a particular conformity of character. It is this character and conformity which is not fixed and static. It can be altered to meet demands for land of a different conformity and character. Having made this point, it is relevant to note than the land element in the pattern in which it exists at any moment of time within a particular proprietary land unit is absolutely fixed in supply. To multiply supply could at best mean creating similar units conforming exactly with the original. To do so would not increase the supply of land within the original. The original is the soil with the buildings and other fixtures upon it as it stands at a given moment within the confines of a particular proprietary land unit and this entirety is unique and cannot be repeated or multiplied.

Its Property Element

Some care has been exercised in introducing the notion of a proprietary land unit to speak of property rights in land as the seat of the power which sanctions the decision-making activities within the unit. The concept of ownership has been avoided. The purpose of this work is to present ideas in the form of an analytical method having a more or less universal relevance throughout human communities and to avoid the differences which spring from national and local customs and juridical systems. It is an exercise in reaching after standard forms. 'Property rights in land' is a less ambiguous term than 'ownership'.

The term itself, however, requires a brief consideration of the notions of ownership to define it for our purpose. Law codes such as those prevalent in Western Europe, which take their cue from the *dominium* of Roman law conceive ownership as resting in a thing of which land in the purely physical sense is an example. A man has rights of property over land because he is the owner of it. He can use it, enjoy it and dispose of it 'de la manière la plus absolue'.[2] It follows from this that the owner has an absolute title and may enter into agreements and contracts with others to give

[2] *Code Civil de Napoléon (1804). Article 544.*

them permission to use the land in various ways, agreements which bind the parties person to person but which do not burden the land with rights of ownership other than those vesting in the owner who initiates the agreement. Ownership of land thus attaches to the land itself.[3] These ideas differ radically from those familiar to the common law of England and Anglo-American jurisprudence. In English law, for example, the doctrine of tenures and the doctrine of estates provide the basic principles of the law of real property. The concept of property in rights over land and not in land itself is fundamental to English law and the early lawyers were adamant that the king, of whom all estates were derived was never the owner of the land but merely the paramount seigneur over every acre.[4] A subject cannot own land, but only an estate in it, giving him the right to hold it for some period of time. A man does not have property rights over land because he owns the physical thing—the soil; he owns an interest or estate in the land because he owns a bundle of property rights over it. Ownership is in the rights and is not the origin of them. It follows from this that in any one parcel of land a number of persons can each own an interest having a specific range of rights. Hence it is not repugnant to an English lawyer to think of a parcel of land as being criss-crossed by an intricate weave of rights which are the property of each individual holder of them. The English lawyer, observed Kahn-Freund,[5] does not find it incongruous to say that the claim for the repayment of a loan, a mortgage on another's land, or a share in a limited company, belongs to a person's property.

In the modern world of commerce and industry, the power to decide and do has become more and more widely separated from the seat of ownership; the classical example of this is the division of powers between the shareholders of a company who own share certificates and have as a consequence certain voting powers over the affairs of the company and the powers of execution and management which in the interests of the company must vest in the members of the board of directors. The business world of the continental codes is more acutely aware of the separation than is the business world within the common law camp. In the strict view of the French code, for example, a tenant who by English notions would be the

---

[3] G. Ripert and T. Boulanger, *Traité de Droit Civil* (Paris, 1957–9), Vol. 2, no. 2227.

[4] A. W. B. Simpson, *An Introduction to the History of the Land Law* (Oxford University Press, 1961), p. 44.

[5] Kahn-Freund, *Introduction to Renner, The Institutions of Private Law and Their Social Functions* (1949), p. 19.

21

owner of a term of years absolute giving him certain rights of action against the reversioner to safeguard in some measure capital investments made by the tenant in the demised premises, would have no more than a personal claim against *le bailleur*. Movements are afoot on the Continent to give a greater resemblance to property rights to these personal rights and claims; the French lawyers have coined the phrase '*propriété commerciale*' to give a tenant a greater sense of property in his claims against *le bailleur*; and the German law schools have been for some time speaking of *Konnexinstitut* as the critical power to take and carry out decisions – use assets, make profits, create loans, take rent – and contrasting it with the arid right of ownership.

The modern world is coming to accept, even among the most doctrinaire jurists of the continental schools, that property has a generic status, is not exclusive to one absolute form of power and action as was the notion of ownership under the *dominium*, but is descriptive of the general powers of action and control which a person, real or fictitious, may have over a thing—and in particular land in the widest sense.[6] It is this modern emancipated notion of property rights which underlies the notion of property rights in land as the seat of sanctions within the proprietary land unit.

To be more precise we can say that property rights as conceived for the purpose of defining and identifying a proprietary land unit are: all rights vested in a person, persons or corporate bodies to do, or to forbear from doing, positive acts on, or in relation to, a specific parcel or area of land. This definition takes no notice of ownership. In the eyes of the land law rights satisfying the definition may or may not convey ownership to the holder of them. The definition is wider than the range of the rights which at common law in England would amount to the ownership of an interest or estate in land. The owner of a fee simple estate in possession grants to a farmer a right to graze a particular field under the terms of an agistment licence, the rights enjoyed by the farmer would meet with the definition of property rights used here.

Although the definition is very general it is careful to relate the property rights it defines to a specific parcel of land. This is a critical feature of the definition which excludes from it powers of a universal kind exercised by central or local government departments to order and compel the doing of prescribed actions on land; as, for example, war agricultural executive committees were empowered to do in wartime by statutory authority which gave them power to order landowners and tenants to crop their lands in a certain way. The

[6] Below, p. 19.

powers of town and country planning authorities to restrain and prohibit the use of land for specified purposes are excluded from the definition on two counts: in the first place these powers are negative and the property powers which satisfy the definition are sanctions to do positive acts or to forbear from doing them; and secondly, the planning authorities' powers are universal and do not as given relate to a specific parcel of land.

There is a border-line case which might lead to uncertainty and debate. In some places, Sweden for example, rights to enter upon land are vested in members of the public at large—an *allemansratt*. Similar rights are given to the public under the authority of access agreements or access orders authorized by the provisions of the National Parks and Access to the Countryside Act 1949 in Britain. The privileges have a universality about them. It is submitted, however, that this should not bar them from the reaches of the definition of the property rights which may constitute a proprietary land unit. The access rights satisfy the definition because they give sanction to do a positive act—to enter upon land for recreation and exercise; and also although the area of land over which the rights are exercisable may be very extensive, it is nonetheless identifiable by specific boundaries. Clearly this is so in Britain where the land involved is clearly delineated in the terms of the access agreement or order, and in Sweden the *allemansratt* is not indiscriminate as it is limited to open land beyond specified distances from buildings. The land over which such rights were exercised would constitute the physical component of a proprietary land unit which those benefiting from the rights would be said to enjoy for the purposes of the right in common with each other and the holders of other interests in the land.

A Definition

The proprietary land unit is a particular variety within the genre of decision-making entities or units that provides the structural frame of an economy. The firm and the household are notable examples of other varieties. Fortunately the concept of the proprietary land unit as an identifiable, *sui generis*, unit within the economy is a novel one and in attempting a definition of it we are not faced with the difficulties of sorting out clashing and ambiguous definitions culled from a large literature, a tiresome exercise only too well known to authors handling themes on the firm or the household.

Comparison of a firm and a proprietary land unit can be helpful

23

LAND USE

here as an aid to draw the distinction between them. The firm has been defined as an autonomous administrative unit, the activities of which are interrelated and are co-ordinated by policies which are framed in the light of their effect on the enterprise as a whole.[7] This is the guise in which the firm can best be compared with the proprietary land unit. The firm in the empirical world is a unit co-ordinator of organized capital, the marshalling ground on which the agents of production are arrayed, grouped and set about their business of generating or attempting to generate incomes and services. Simply, it is the production unit of a modern economy. As such, firms need land for factories, warehouses, communications, offices, dwellings and so on. The firm becomes a proprietor of land or of interests in land. The proprietary interest of a firm in land may coincide with or extend beyond what is essential to the discharge of the firm's purpose and function. Land owned by a railway company, for example, in the vicinity of its stations and bridges, if not actively serving the rail enterprise, is available for hotels, shops and other subsidiary uses. Where a railway company runs a hotel on its land, the hotel is another firm, another enterprise, quite distinct from the rail enterprise. The railway enterprise and the hotel business, however, operate on land owned by the railway company; there is an affinity in the landownership, both hotel and railway company operate within one and the same proprietary land unit. There is a fundamental distnction and difference to be drawn between the production units, the firms, and the proprietary land unit. A more general example is the farm. A farm is a firm in the entrepreneurial sense. Agricultural economists concentrate attention upon it as the production unit but like any other production unit the farm must operate within and on a proprietary land unit if the farmer is not to be guilty of wanton trespass. The farmer as entrepreneur running a production unit usually dwells in the farmhouse with his family. When this happens the proprietary land unit which accommodates the production unit provides the land used by a household for purposes peculiar to a household as another variety of decision-making unit. Whilst the proprietary land unit accommodates the firm and the household as autonomous entities in themselves, it is nonetheless to be distinguished from either.

Reduced to simplicity and precision, the proprietary land unit can be defined as an area of land used as a single entity and coextensive in its physical dimensions with vested rights of property, to use, to dispose and to alienate. Land in its context is the lawyer's defini-

[7] E. T. Penrose, *The Theory of the Growth of the Firm* (Blackwell, Oxford, 1963), p. 15.

24

tion of the soil and all that is affixed thereto on the surface and beneath. Rights of property more particularly are rights to do and to forbear from doing positive acts on or in relation to the land in the unit.

Its Physical Attributes

No one proprietary land unit can, by definition and nature, be like another. Yet, their features are cast in a common mould. Firms and households are likewise plastic and protean. Alfred Marshall,[8] however, was not daunted in his attempt to define the representative firm, admittedly a move towards the abstract and away from the empirical realities; an attempt, nevertheless, to reach after the general from an infinite maze of particular variations.

We shall not attempt to specify a representative proprietary land unit. From the maze of possible variations, an attempt will be made to define and delimit the nature and the boundaries of the individual attributes common to all proprietary land units—the general standards to which in some measure each variation will conform.

The common attributes fall into two main categories: the physical and the abstract.

The primary physical attributes are the given things of nature, the features of the natural order—the soil formation itself, the subsoil and rock formations, natural waters and vegetation. Because we are working with the lawyer's notion of land we must include among the physical attributes all of a secondary order which for simplicity and ease of expression can be caught up in the development use pattern of the natural resources—buildings, erections, workings, excavations inclusive of the superficial and the subterranean. Size and shape of a proprietary land unit may at first sight appear to belong to the physical categories. As principal features of a proprietary land unit, however, for reasons given later it would be more consistent to regard them as belonging to the abstract attributes.

The physical attributes of a proprietary land unit put a stamp upon its outward form. In a rough and ready way one can distinguish homogeneous from heterogeneous units. A clearly perceptible universality of physical character marks the homogeneous character. Homogeneity does not mean a single type of physical feature occupying the unit to the exclusion of all others; but rather a complementarity of function and form that displays a unity. Take for example, a fee simple estate of 200 acres given up entirely to

8 A. Marshall, *op. cit.*, p. 285.

dairy farming by he who is owner and occupier. The primary physical attributes show little or no variation and although the development use pattern includes houses, a farmstead, roads, fences and ditches, each and every several physical feature serves a common function and purpose with the others—there is a homogeneity about the general physical form and attributes and we can speak of the unit as an agricultural proprietary land unit given (if we wish to be more specific) to dairy farming.

Heterogeneous proprietary land units are of two types: one has a high degree of variation patent in all or in the majority of its attributes; the other is not multi-featured but has two, perhaps three, outstanding attributes which challenge one another for dominance.

Proprietary land units thus can be classified by reference to their physical attributes. The broadest classification and one perhaps we should be content with for the general case is:

homogeneous
heterogeneous:
    (*a*) multi
    (*b*) simple.

The classification is capable of subdivision. Proprietary land units which are homogeneous can be sub-classified by choosing suitable descriptive adjectives—upland, agricultural, residential and so on. The multi-heterogeneous must be left to occupy the primary sub-class. The simple-heterogeneous require the identification of dominance in the physical attributes for further sub-classification. Dominance may be either areal or evaluated in some other way—in money terms perhaps. Imagine 8,000 acres of a fairly uniform natural topography and inherent soil conditions wholly given to mixed arable farming, with the exception of 800 acres of hardwoods indifferently managed on silvicultural lines; with the farm land let on yearly tenancies to 50 tenants and the woodland kept in hand to the owner of the fee simple. The areal domination of the mixed arable land, albeit liberally and adequately supplied with houses, farmsteads, roads and other specific fixed equipment would stamp the general physical character of the fee simple estate, part in reversion contingent upon the yearly tenancies and part in hand, as an agricultural proprietary land unit. By contrast, take an upland fee simple estate in hand to the owner of the fee extending to 16,000 acres of heather given to sheep runs and eight miles of lucrative salmon and trout fishing; the capitalized value of the shooting and fishing rights well outruns the capital value of the land for sheep

26

run and gives the proprietary land unit the character of a sporting unit despite areal dominance of the sheep farming land.

Its Abstract Attributes

The abstract attributes of the proprietary land unit are those characteristics of the general form which are conceptual and cannot be discerned without some form of descriptive explanation. There are three types of abstract attribute, each of which in one form or another is to be found in every proprietary land unit:

   i. size and shape;
  ii. duration; and
 iii. a bundle of rights.

Size and Shape. Frequently, what the uninformed eye would take to be the boundary of a proprietary land unit is not the boundary at all. A hedge, a ditch, a roadside, a river bank, are examples of physical features commonly mistaken as boundary markers. The boundaries of any proprietary land unit are set by the reach of the property rights over the land. In certain circumstances, for example, the common law of England runs the boundary of a proprietary land unit not along the river bank, as the layman might suppose, but *usque ad media acqua*; not along the roadside hedge as would appear obvious, but *usque ad media via*. The size and shape of a proprietary land unit, although fully apparent to the eye, cannot be known unless and until the reach of the property rights of which the unit is in part composed is explained and pointed out with reference to the physical conformity of the land. For this reason the size and shape of proprietary land units are properly classified among the abstract attributes and despite appearances to the contrary should not be regarded as physical attributes. The logic of the classification is reinforced if we realize that a proprietary land unit may be composed of lateral rights augmenting the total autonomy of the unit, yet in themselves being of a lesser degree of sanction than the rights of property peculiar to the body of the unit they serve; a right of way over neighbouring fields is a simple example of what is meant. The right of way may to the lawyer be an easement, an incorporeal hereditament, a servitude—it matters not: for the purposes of this general analysis it adds to the sum of the rights peculiar to a particular proprietary land unit. The existence of the right of way would not be apparent to the uninformed observer; essentially it is an abstract attribute of the unit which needs to be defined for anyone who would comprehend the full compass of the

27

unit. Moreover, property rights in land can penetrate *ad inferos*. How deep is down? No eye can tell. The law must say, as indeed it must *ad caelum*, to the heavens above.

Where a person has two or more parcels of land holdings or estates the question arises whether he has one scattered proprietary land unit or a number of intact separate units. This problem of shape is best solved by applying the test of managerial co-incidence.

All proprietary land units are subject in some degree to what may be thought of as management; the holder of the property rights in them must take decisions about the use of the rights. Even if the decision is negative and he decides to do nothing, the decision-maker holds in his mind's eye the subject of his deliberations. When one reduces possibilities down to generalities what becomes significant is not the degree of efficiency or the mode of management, but the relationship between the administrative area and the proprietary area.

When the area over which administrative decisions are taken, the managerial area, coincides with the proprietary area, the land over which run the rights of property vesting in the holder of the unit, we can speak of there being one unit, not two or more. Each proprietary land unit then has managerial and proprietary coincidence. The land subject to the coincidence may be an intact block lying in a ring fence or it may lie in scattered parcels; in the former event, the proprietary land unit would be intact and in the latter event it would be a scattered unit. Managerial conformation is the test to apply in order to determine whether the holder of a proprietary land unit has one scattered unit or many discrete units. Managerial in this context for the purposes of determining the shape of the proprietary land unit may or may not be the subject of highly sophisticated decision-making techniques; at least, no more than the organization of resources to satisfy a motive in respect of the proprietary land unit; the motive might be the making and maximizing of financial gains or the perfection and participation of recreational, residential or sporting pleasures or the reaching after some other objective. For classification purposes, therefore, a proprietary land unit is either intact or scattered as determined by the test of managerial coincidence.

Duration. A proprietary land unit has a time as well as a space dimension. The rights of property enjoyed in land today may be the same as those of yesterday and the same as will be enjoyed tomorrow. There is no final limit to the time dimension of a proprietary land unit. The rights which contribute to its composition may continue for a day, a week, months or years, for the life of the present holder of them or for the life of some other person. Or they may bridge the passage of generations and endure, generation by generation, down a long line of heirs. The time dimension of a proprietary land unit runs from any one moment in time backwards into the past and forwards into the future. It is in the very nature of rights of property to have a life span. An instantaneous right is a non-event. If we take a particular proprietary land unit as it exists in a given moment of time, the property rights which pertain to it will determine at that moment its potential future life span. It may be indeterminate – for ever and ever – or its continuity may be contingent on the happening or not happening of an unpredictable event – the discontinuation of a line of heirs, the marriage of a named person; or the duration may be definite and predictable – seven years from the inception of the unit.

Measurements into the past involve the problem of the continuity of indentity. A landowner in England may boast of his estate that it has existed since the time of the Domesday Survey, 1086. What does he mean? Is the continuity he is so proud of in no more than a name, known to the historians, recorded in the archives? Does he mean that the acres are all there, just as when William the Conqueror gave it to a Norman baron? Or is it that our landowner has the title to the land in mind and can trace a devolution of title from an unbroken line of heirs, generation by generation, from his Norman forbears? And if he means this, what if the physical features and other characteristics have changed over the years out of all recognition. These are the questions which confront us when we try to measure in retrospect the duration of a proprietary land unit. The answer must be an arbitrary one, but it need not be an irrational one. It would be reasonable to say of a proprietary land unit in the present that it remained intact from the past, intact that is in identity, if today it is held in hands which are those anyone at any time in the past looking forward into the future and knowing the future duration of the unit as it would have appeared at that moment of foresight would have expected to hold it today. An actual example will help to clarify the somewhat complicated proposition. Shortly after the conquest, William of Normandy gave a manor on the banks of the Dee in Cheshire to Hugh Lupus, the Conqueror's great huntsman. His title, 'The great huntsman', became over the ensuing years an eponym; and the Grosvenors have held that manor on the Dee from the date of the original gift, in unbroken succession, to the present day. We can say of the particular proprietary land unit as it exists today, that it has continued in existence for nearly

29

900 years. Originally the gift was a gift in fee; and this to a lawyer of the thirteenth century would have meant that at that time the estate in fee would continue down the line of the Grosvenor heirs to the last decades of the twentieth century and beyond, as it has done. If, however, by some event, a sale, a gift over, a failure of the line of heirs the fee had passed into other hands than those of the true heirs, we should conclude that at that moment of change the duration of the original unit had ended and the life of a new unit had begun.

If we take this criterion for establishing the continuity of identity of a unit from the past, we must allow change to take place without loss of identity. Duration is a function of the fulfilment of expectation of devolution of title and is not affected by changes in the physical or other attributes of the proprietary land unit. The broad acres within the Grosvenor fee simple on the Dee are not identical with the hides William gave, point for point, and grass-dryers and self-feed racks stand where the baulks and gore acres ran in medieval days, but the proprietary unit is the same unit—the unit that William gave.

Bundle of Rights. We have thought of the rights of property which contribute to a proprietary land unit as a bundle of rights. Like sheaves in a wheat field, the bundles can be plump or slim. The larger the bundle the greater the degree of power and of sanction in the hands of the holder of the proprietary land unit. If we imagine Robinson Crusoe on his island before Man Friday came, we see him a law unto himself, a man of absolute power to do what he would or could with the land of the island. After the fateful day when he found the footprint, he had to come to terms with another human. To live amicably together he had to surrender some, however little, of his rights to Man Friday. To permit this new neighbour to have a booth or sleeping place was meagre enough but the arrangement and gift would have been meaningless if Crusoe had not respected it and given up some of the rights abstracted from the total of what he previously had. It follows that no one can hold a proprietary land unit of absolute power in a civilized society. A bundle of rights is always an abstraction from the absolute power.

The various devices used under the law to abstract from and reduce the size of the bundle of rights remaining in the hands of a holder of a proprietary land unit can be classified in four comprehensive categories, as follows:

i. universal restrictions imposed by the positive laws of a state;

ii. restrictions arising from the contiguity or proximity of one proprietary land unit with or to another;
iii. restrictions imposed on an inferior proprietary land unit in the interests of a superior unit, derived from it; and
iv. restrictions imposed on a superior proprietary land unit in the interests of an inferior unit derived from it.

Its Proprietary Character Form

The physical and abstract attributes of a proprietary land unit are important because they have an immediate bearing upon what can and what cannot be done within the unit. They are, however, not the only factors which predetermine policy. What may be thought of as the constitutional form of the holder of the property rights exerts a similar influence which needs to be recognized. The constitutional form of the owner of the rights cannot logically be an attribute of the unit itself. While recognizing them, we must keep the two sources of influence apart. There is, however, no reason why the constitutional form should not be regarded as a distinctive and distinguishing feature of the unit itself. Consequently this feature will be added to those already described and we shall refer to it as the proprietary character form of the proprietary land unit. To think of a charity will help us to understand the significance of the proprietary character form. A charity is set up for a particular purpose. A charity which holds a proprietary land unit must use the resources of the unit to fulfil its charitable commitments. To act otherwise would be to deny its own character. Thus the proprietary character form predetermines policies.

Proprietary character forms in the sense of the term used here are moulded and fashioned by social, economic and juridical considerations. Human history down the ages has displayed innumerable instances and the future will add to their numbers. It is, however, feasible to reduce the exceedingly wide range of actual and possible varieties to three categories of a primary order. The items of the primary order are not mutually exclusive and the proprietary character form of a proprietary land unit can be a combination of any two or of all three of them. The three categories of the primary order are:

i. the simple;
ii. the fictitious; and
iii. the fiduciary.

The Simple. Simple is used here to denote the single and uncom-

31

plicated. Amongst proprietary character forms it is the fully adult individual person, competent under the law to hold property rights in land, to enter fully upon the privileges they offer and to exercise the rights of use, disposition and alienation. Appearances can mislead, and as with the abstract attributes descriptive information is required to identify the proprietary character form. A man or woman may appear to hold property rights unconditionally when in reality each holds them as a beneficiary of a fiduciary relationship. In these circumstances the proprietary character form – illustrated by the bankrupt, the minor, the lunatic – is fiduciary and simple.

The Fictitious. The fictitious proprietary character form is a compound, standing at the other pole from the simple. It is created by and out of a fiction. Two or more persons are for the purposes of ownership or for some other reason regarded as one person and are assumed to have a unity, bodiliness, a selfhood over against and distinct from each constituent member. A common form created by the jurists of Christendom in western Europe in the fifteenth century is the body corporate—the corporation. The modern western world is populated by whole genera of bodies corporate of various kinds—joint stock companies, local government authorities, collegiate and ecclesiastical followships. The fictitious *personae* belong by nature to the immortals. Human frailty and death have no claim upon them—the Bishop of London has had being for nearly a thousand years. The immortality provides an interesting and clear illustration of how the proprietary character form can affect the function of a proprietary land unit and the uses to which its assets are put—an immortal can do what no mortal can. The immortality is a liberalizing influence upon the use of the rights of property. The criterion of the fictitious is not exclusively the legal fiction of a body corporate. Social systems and customary laws too primitive or too unsophisticated to devise so subtle a transformation of the many into the one, adopt attitudes towards groups, families, communities as if to imply that the many were the one—the extended family is owner of the family land.

The Fiduciary. The fiduciary proprietary character form is conditional. He whose proprietary character form it is, is by nature under an obligation of faith to use and dispose of what he holds for the benefit of another or others or to the fulfilment of a purpose not of his own choosing. In the history of English landownership a classical example is the early English *use*. Property rights at common law would vest in the *feoffee to uses*, the forerunner of the modern

32

trustee, who was required in equity to hold and employ the rights on behalf of another, the *cestui que use*, the equivalent of the modern beneficiary. The feoffee must keep faith and act in fiduciary capacity in the interests of the *cestui que use*. The fiduciary proprietary character form is cast in different moulds throughout the world and throughout history. It exists wherever the holder of property rights is under an obligation to use them for the benefit of another. Consider again the charity. Under English law, a charity holds property rights for a definite purpose and must act with due fiduciary responsibility in the use of them. The continuing obligation to direct resources to fulfil a definite need for the benefit of others or the achievement of a specified purpose must affect what can be done with proprietary land units owned by the charity; in short, the proprietary character form sets limits within which plans for the use of the land assets of the proprietary land units must be made. The fiduciary relationship frequently involves two parties each of whom holds a proprietary land unit in the same parcel of land, one as a beneficiary enjoying the benefits and fruits of the wealth of the unit and the other as responsible to see that such enjoyment is facilitated. For the purpose of our analysis and following the definition of property rights adopted, each party would hold a proprietary land unit.

Combinations. Proprietary character forms are not mutually exclusive. Instances often occur when two of the forms are simultaneously present in the one proprietary land unit and sometimes there are all three forms. A bishop is a good example: the real man by virtue of his office is a *persona ficta*, enjoying *ex officio* immortality, in the language of western jurisprudence—a corporation sole. And it is incumbent upon him as *persona* incorporate to act in a fiduciary manner and use and plan proprietary land units held by the bishopric in good faith as becomes his office. The units are held by him as an individual person and in this respect their proprietary character form is simple. The real person, however, is concealed behind the face of the present living incumbent of the corporate office with its fiduciary obligations. Thus, at one and the same time, the proprietary character form is simple, fictitious and fiduciary. Ministers of state who hold proprietary land units *eo nomine* and are answerable to Parliament and the public for their use and management are further examples of the trinitarian proprietary character form.

Its Universality
The characteristic features discernible in each proprietary land unit

c

33

TABLE I

Possible Variants of the Characteristic Features of a Proprietary Land Unit

CHARACTERISTIC FEATURES

Index Nos.	Physical	Attributes				Proprietary Character Form
	I	II	III	IV	V	VI
				Abstract		
1	Heterogeneous—simple	Intact	Determinate duration	Contiguous and lateral rights	Derivative	Simple
2	Heterogeneous—multi	Scattered	Indeterminate	Entire	Non-derivative	Fictitious
3	Homogeneous					Fiduciary
4						Simple/fictitious
5						Simple/fiduciary
6						Fictitious/fiduciary
7						Simple/fictitious/fiduciary
Nos. of totals	3	2	2	2	2	7

Total possible combinations = 336

differ in a variety of ways; the development use pattern, for example, may be heterogeneous or homogeneous. Differences are displayed by six features which are mutually exclusive; a scattered proprietary land unit cannot at the same time be intact. Table I sets out the mutually exclusive variants of each of the characteristic features. At any time any one proprietary land unit will be a combination of six of the variations, each variation representing one of the six characteristic features. The number of combinations that is mathematically possible is 336.[9] In other words if we select any proprietary land unit anywhere at any time we shall find that its anatomy conforms to one of the 336 possible patterns and for the purposes of analysis we can slot it into a descriptive pigeonhole using the numerical notation of Table I to give it an identification tab. Take an example of a 50-acre in-bye farm in a Cumberland valley where the farm is held by a working farmer as a fee simple absolute in possession with rights of common pasture on the adjoining fell and having the 50-acre in-bye scattered over the valley in 5 lots within a mile of each other. The appropriate identification notation would be: I(3); II(2); III(2); IV(1); V(1); VI(1).

The generalities used here to define and describe the characteristic features of the proprietary land unit and the variations of them are an attempt to handle the analysis of land tenures and to provide a frame of reference of universal relevance throughout the world. Tenurial systems everywhere and each in its different way forge proprietary land units peculiar to themselves. These are the fundamentals. To them we must turn in the last analysis to understand the land use patterns of a nation and to guide aright the development of the land resources.

[9] The number of possible combinations is given by the product
$3 \times 2 \times 2 \times 2 \times 2 \times 7 = 336$.

Chapter III

PROPRIETARY LAND RESOURCES

The physical attributes of a proprietary land unit consist of a land mass disturbed in its natural order by erections and excavations of various kinds. Within the circumference of the unit, the land and the works upon it make up the sum of what we shall call the proprietary land resources. The pattern of these resources is constantly changing; indeed it is the objective of decision-making and management in general to effect changes. As will appear later, ordered change pre-supposes conscious motive.[1] The next stage in our analysis is to look at the components of a proprietary land unit, the morphology of the pattern of its resources, as a step to understanding how and why the pattern changes at the instance of the holder of the property rights.

Proprietary land resources are a particular arrangement of wealth. We shall refrain from calling them capital and thus avoid the difficulty of trying to fit the conception of this form of wealth into the orthodox theories of capital in the literature of economics. Of those theories from the classical days of Ricardo and Mill to Keynes and the moderns, the theory which comes closest to the way in which we intend to look at and study the use and arrangement of proprietary land resources is the one which sees capital as a physical construct and has been elaborated by Lachman as the morphological theory of capital.[2] It is the stage-management view of capital: items and effects are moved from place to place, interchanged with one another and exchanged for replacements as the patterns alter under the kaleidoscope of management. The morphological theory is a clue, no more, to the way we should scrutinize proprietary land resources. In order to analyse and comprehend in a systematic way the forces of change within a proprietary land unit it is not necessary to present the land resources in a guise which fits an accepted theory of capital, nor indeed to devise an *ad hoc* theory. The study

[1] Below, p. 57.
[2] L. M. Lachman, *Capital and its Structure* (London, 1956).

36

and the explanation of change and decision-making within the proprietary land unit do, however, require the adoption of a method of analysis. What this will be will become apparent as we proceed. At this stage we acknowledge our debt to the mode of thought which inspired the morphological theory of capital. The form of our own analytical method owes much to it, so much in fact that an outline description of the theory will in itself provide a logical and useful lead to the method of analysis which is the central theme of our text.

The Morphological Theory of Capital

The primary tenet of the morphological theory of capital is the proposition that capital is not a homogeneous mass to be handled in the lump. As Schumpeter[3] has observed when treating of the fundamentals of economic choice, a start must be made with a given stock of goods which is neither homogeneous nor an amorphous heap—the goods complement each other in a way readily understood as soon as we hear of buildings, equipment, raw materials and land. Capital in a narrower sense is a collection of things related to each other according to a plan designed to provide services essential to economic survival. By looking at capital in this way, the morphological theory of capital avoids the perplexing problems associated with the value of capital and the relationship of capital to income flow. Measurements of capital and of the income it generates demand the postulates of the neo-classical theories and the accountant's outlook on capital.

The morphologists are concerned with what capital does and how it does it. Each item of wealth has a distinctive part to play, hence their stress on the heterogeneous character of capital. Lorries and lettuce frames are not homogeneous either in form or function, yet both may be essential components of the capital stock of a nurseryman. At the same time all is not higgledy-piggledy. There is a pattern and a plan which, like the run of a crazy paving, binds together the separate, irregular parts into a single cohesive whole. The key to the cohesion is purpose or motive. For the entrepreneur the purpose is the maximization of output at minimum cost, the greatest possible profitability. For the householder the motive is different; effects which correspond to the entrepreneur's capital goods in a business sense are accumulated and arranged to satisfy that motive. Whether it is the inventories of the assets of a firm or the effects of a house-

[3] J. A. Schumpeter, *History of Economic Analysis* (Oxford University Press, 1954), p. 631.

37

hold, the contents of them are chosen and set in definite orders and the pattern of the order depends upon the purpose or motive to be achieved. Firms and households manipulate arrays of goods linked together in distinct combinations. The structure of national wealth is built up from these combinations.

Heterogeneity central to the morphological theory of capital lies not only in the physical differences between capital goods. If all capital goods were made of some ingenious, standard substance, says Lachman,[4] the critical heterogeneity would not be removed. Capital goods may differ from each other in physical forms and land in particular has its own inherent characteristics. What are vital for the morphological theory are the differences in the respective functions of the capital items. Heterogeneity is essentially functional heterogeneity. Land and every other form of capital asset has a function peculiar to itself, expressed in a pattern of variations which Lachman calls multiple specificity.

Functional heterogeneity is significant for every capital combination. The differences between the constituents of the combination are functional and if the several functions are at variance with one another, the aim and purpose which prompts the making of the combination will be in jeopardy. Lone wolves and ugly ducklings must be eliminated. Unity of purpose makes each capital component essential to the proper functioning of each of the others in the combination—railway lines cannot provide the transport service expected of them unless rolling stock is available to run on them.

Success requires harmony; and harmony can only be rooted in complementarity. Complementarity is essential to the successful employment of capital goods and land. As an ideal or perfection to be reached after, it may differ in the degree in which it is present throughout the range of the components of a combination of capital goods. Moreover, one item can be more dependent upon the presence and proper functioning of a particular item of plant or stock, than it is upon the provision and performance of other capital resources.

In the history of economic thought, Edgeworth[5] and Pareto[6] first recognized the phenomenon of complementarity and illustrated it by reference to the marginal utilities of consumer goods. Pareto found difficulty in taking his theory far in practical application because of his profound mistrust of all attempts to measure marginal utilities quantitatively. Hicks[7] has argued that Pareto had overlooked

[4] L. M. Lachman, *op. cit.*, p. 2.
[5] F. Y. Edgeworth, *Papers Relating to Political Economy* (1925), Vol. 1, p. 117.
[6] V. Pareto, *Manuel d'Economie Politique Pure* (Paris, 1909), p. 268.
[7] Sir J. R. Hicks, *Value and Capital* (Oxford University Press, 1957), p. 47.

the need for a third factor, a kind of measuring stick by which to determine the presence and degrees of complementarity. He replaces Pareto's marginal utility by the marginal rate of substitution of money and says: Y is complementary with X if the marginal rate of substitution of Y for money is increased when X is substituted for money. The need for a yardstick, a Hicksian third factor, is accepted as demonstrated if we are to handle complementarity to any purpose. But complementarity among the items of land and works making up the aggregate of the proprietary land resources of a proprietary land unit can be discerned by reagents other than the marginal rate of the substitution of money. As suggested later on[8] motive and the attainment of it is all that can and need be used.

The morphological theory as an analytical device introduces us to what has been labelled period and process analysis.[9] The grouping of capital goods and land in a combination, if it is logical, takes its cue in the first place from a preconceived plan drawn up to achieve a particular end and to do so within a definite period of time. The types of component and the amounts of each expressed by appropriate coefficients are arranged to attain the purpose in mind. If all goes well and at the time appointed the plan is fulfilled, a second plan will follow with such adjustments of the items and their coefficients as the planners may deem necessary—and so on *seriatim*. The second plan will take its lead from the successful completion of the first plan. Each successive plan will depend on the successful outcome of its predecessors. The comprehension and analysis of the concatenation of interlinked periods and the process within each leading to and influencing the process and timing of the successive plans is aptly designated period and process analysis. As an idea and tool of analysis it will prove most useful in the study of the process and procedures of decision-making within the proprietary land unit.

The key to the understanding of a morphological theory of capital resides in Walras'[10] words: *Les Capitaux proprement dits* ('The Capitals', as appropriately they ought to be called). The word capital is collective. It indicates genus; its species are manifold.

'Capital' is not measurable in absolute unitary dimensions since it is not homogeneous. A thing becomes a capital when the potentialities of its contribution, in whatever form, to the production of a yield have been discovered or recognized. The heterogeneity of capital which matters is, of course, not physical heterogeneity but

---

[8] Below, p. 62.   [9] L. M. Lachman, *op. cit.*, p. 13.
[10] L. Walras, *Eléments d'Economie Politique Pure* (Lausanne, 4th Edn, 1900), leçons 17–19.

functional heterogeneity. In theory, every capital good which, at any specific moment is devoted to a particular phase of a particular process contributes to it in a manner which reflects the most appropriate use to which that capital good can be put in the context of that particular activity. However, a change in circumstances may alter the position. Kinetic instability leads to a new dynamic equilibrium position. Consequently the various quanta of capital goods must be rearranged in a new order of allocation in the new capital combination. Obviously there is a limit to the number of ways in which one capital good may be combined with others, and in every combination, land is a component. 'Any capital combination is in fact a combination of land and other resources.'[11] The number of ways in which a capital good is capable of combining with others is a measure of its multiple specificity, and the degree to which it can be combined with others denotes their relative complementarity.

A capital in total isolation is but an inert quantum of potentiality. It is only in the dynamic interplay of needs, uses and effects that one capital, polygamously allied to others is capable of exhibiting creative momentum, thus identifying itself through its function. The combination of capital goods is not an arbitrary operation and the number of effective combinations cannot be assessed merely on a permutation principle. At any moment, the number of effective combinations is limited by the modes of complementarity which not only are practicable but usually economically viable as well. The selection of the optimum combination requires skill, effort and expertise. The onus rests with the operator.

Keeping clearly in mind the three basic concepts of heterogeneity, multiple specificity and complementarity, it is possible to integrate constituents into patterns to indicate the structure of a plan at a particular point in time through, for example, an explicit function such as:

$$P_{t_1} = f(\alpha_1 C_1, \alpha_2 C_2, \alpha_3 C_3 \ldots \alpha_n C_n)$$

where P = a plan at time t_1

$\alpha_1 \ldots \alpha_n$ = indices relating the various effective capital combinations

$C_n \ldots C_n$ = complementary forms of capital.

(In addition, C factors may be mutually variable.)

It must be remembered that the whole pattern is subject to the time element. A change from time (t_1) to time (t_2) may not only require changes in the relative values of quanta of the various

[11] L. M. Lachman, *op. cit.*, p. 11.

capitals but also cause certain types of capitals to become non-effective and thus necessarily to be deleted altogether from the new arrangement. The logical approach to planning the arrangement of capitals should therefore include provision for periodic revision. It may become necessary to relegate primary aims and uses to inferior positions and to effect the substitution and general redistribution of capital assets. Indeed, the very purpose of the initial plan may alter drastically with time.

When Robert Burns, the Caledonian Bard, ran a ploughshare into the homely nest of a field mouse, he commiserated with the 'wee, sleekit, timorous beastie' adding the thought that 'the best laid schemes o' mice an' men gang aft agley'. Experience in an Ayrshire cornfield finds its parallel in the world of planned capital combinations. Plans go astray. The unexpected happens. Unexpected change means revision, again and again, and revision upsets the timetable, the periodicity and the foreseen processes of the plans. The chain of plans and periods running out into the future from the initial capital combination is dismantled with every unexpected event. Users of proprietary land resources must be constantly on the alert, ready to review afresh the plans they have made and to recast them. Recognition of the stark indeterminacy of the combinations of capital goods marks off the morphological theory of capital from the static concepts implicit in the equilibrium analysis of the classical theories which conceive of capital as a homogeneous aggregate.

Combinations of Proprietary Land Resources

Although the proprietary land resources of a proprietary land unit would conform to the definition of capital as the stock of resources available at a particular date to satisfy or help satisfy future wants,[12] it is less confusing not to do so, and this for three reasons. In economic analysis concepts of capital are associated with the production processes and the generation of income, and capital is set over against land as a separate and wholly different agent of production. Proprietary land resources in the context of the proprietary land unit are combinations of land and the works upon land held under a common title to property rights. The property rights are the propretary sinews which bind the components of the functional combination in an indissoluble unity; a cowshed cannot be legally used without the land it stands on—the rights of user over the build-

12 *Everyman's Dictionary of Economics* (Compiled), A. Seldon and F. G. Pennance (London, 1965), p. 53.

ing serve the land also. Otheriwse he who uses the shed is *ipso facto* a trespasser on the land. The first reason for avoiding the use of the term capital, then, is the constitutional point that land and the works upon it must be seen as items of wealth in a functional and proprietary relationship for which the separation of the two is a contradiction of the unity consistent with the notion of a proprietary land unit.

The second reason for avoiding the use of the word capital for proprietary land resources is the confusion it can cause between the pragmatic world of landownership and tenure and the world of abstract economic theory. Landowners and other holders of property rights in land do not, in work-a-day business and decision-making, make distinctions between land as a factor of production and the works and fixtures upon the land. If they use the word capital, they use it of land and all that has been done upon it and of other forms of wealth besides—often of all their savings in whatever shape or form they may be. And as we are concerned with the proprietary land unit, its influence upon land use and the motives that move the holders of units to make decisions for the use of their land resources, it is well either to keep to the idioms of the pragmatic world of everyday decision-making or to devise designations, like proprietary land resources, to suit our own special ends.

The third reason like the first has to do with the functional side of the proprietary land unit. To the purist who would assign capital wholly to the production realms of an economy, the use of the term for proprietary land resources would cause confusion because at any one moment in time the proprietary land resources of a proprietary land unit are likely to be employed simultaneously as agents of production and to further and facilitate the satisfaction of domestic needs and the enjoyment of amenity.

Combination of capital goods, it will be remembered in the language of the morphological theory of capital, implies multiple specificity where the goods are combined to fulfil a particular plan; and multiple specificity points to functional complementarity. Complementarity, in its turn, needs a yardstick to test for its presence and the degree of its operation. Proprietary land resources are a combination of land and other forms of wealth. The fulfilment of plans for the use of them implies complementarity between the land and the other components of the combination.

Two items in a combination of proprietary land resources are in a relationship of functional complementarity when the contribution each makes to the fulfilment of a plan would not or could not be made either wholly or in part without the other. Fulfilment of

42

a plan is the satisfaction of the motive which inspires the plan. The contribution made by the joint function of the two items is a contribution towards the attainment of a motive. The attainment of motive is the yardstick to be used to test for functional complementarity. Pareto found difficulty in measuring the marginal utilities of two or more consumer goods to test for complementarity because what was marginal was the addition of a hypothetical increment of a consumer good which had no specificity in real existence. Consumer goods like goods of all kinds come in wholenesses and cannot be supplied in tiny marginal advances. The functional complementarity between proprietary land resources does not present us with a similar impasse because, following the thought form of the morphological theory of capital, we accept that each item in a combination of proprietary land resources is a whole thing in itself—a beer barrel, a ditch, a lettuce forcing frame. The test we apply asks the question how far, if at all, does each of a pair, or each member of a trio or greater grouping of whole things add to the contribution made towards the fulfilment of motive by each and every other component of the combination of proprietary land resources. The notion of the margin belongs to the realm of homogeneous existences. If in a combination of items there were a number of identical lettuce frames, we could with reason talk of the last additional frame as marginal to the group of frames. Within a combination of resources each playing its own part and making its own contribution to the achievement of motive and as a complement to one or more of the others no one item is marginal, no one item extends the margin of any other item, each is unique. Complementarity therefore is not associated with notions of the margin, but with the total contribution of specific items in a combination to the plan which has brought the combination into being. In the practical world of decision-making, each item is judged by the contribution it makes in association with its fellow items to the achievement of the motive which predetermined the plan for the combination. Motive, in short, is an adequate test for complementarity.

The significance of motive as a test for complementarity can be simply illustrated from the use of proprietary land resources for agricultural purposes. Imagine for a moment a 500-acre farm held in fee simple in possession by an individual landowner who farms the land with its farmhouse, farmstead and 3 cottages. The cottages are built of Cotswold stone, have historic interest and considerable architectural merit. In accordance with the present plan for the use of the proprietary land resources, the cottages are occupied by farmworkers and careful budgeting shows that so used they make the optimal contribution to the maximization of farm output at minimal cost.

If the motive directing the use of the land resources is primarily and solely to maximize farm output at minimal cost, it would be wise to leave the cottages as they are with their present occupants. In this event, the motive behind the use of the proprietary land unit would be agricultural and entrepreneurial. But the condition of the rural land market is such that forces generate demand for rural land, houses and cottages which take but secondary cognizance of the contribution which these resources make to farm output and profitability. The present demand for the Cotswold cottages on the farm in our illustration is such that a derivative interest in the form of a long lease can be created in each and sold for a premium which far outruns the cost of building a new bungalow for the worker and his family. If the motive inspiring the use-plan of the proprietary land unit is not simply agricultural and enterpreneurial but is concerned to maximize the total value of the wealth realizable in the proprietary land unit while farming it for maximum profit, the better plan would be to commit consociate funds[13] to the building of two new cottages thus leaving the old Cotswold cottages available for long leases. This change of plan would not have been apparent if the holder of the proprietary land unit had not clearly discerned the motive behind the planning of his land use and tested the existing lay-out of land and buildings for complementarity in the light of it. Under the second plan, the new bungalows would owe their ability to add to the attainment of the maximization of wealth and farming profitability to the presence of the Cotswold cottages. They could not have made the contribution which they did make but for the old cottages. The old cottages for their part could not have made the contribution to total market worth of the land resources which they did make, but for the new cottages whose existence enabled the old cottages to be vacated by the farmworkers and sold on a leasehold basis. Cottages and bungalows display a functional complentaritity easily discernible and demonstrated against the background of the motive to maximize wealth and promote farming profit.

Motives vary, affected by place, time and circumstances and by the attributes and proprietary character forms of the proprietary land units dominated by them. We can accept nonetheless the motive of landownership as a general criterion against which to test for complementarity in the particular case. Changes in motives are not changes of principle and hence in the driving force promoting

13 Below, pp. 145, 146.

land use decisions but in the direction of the force. The mere fact that motives change is not ground for arguing that to base complementarity upon them is to stand the test for it upon shifting sands.

Manœuvrability

Changes of mind and the unexpected turns of fortune precipitate reviews of plans and the regrouping of the constituents of combinations of proprietary land resources. On the practical plane what is actually done depends upon what can be done, in other words upon the capacity which the owner of a proprietary land unit has for manœuvre, on the mobility of the resources in the hands of the holder of them. It behoves us, therefore, in the next stage of our analysis to consider the factors which determine the degree of manœuvrability available to the holder of a proprietary land unit. Our consideration will follow the broad two-way division of the preceding chapter, dealing in the first place with the manner in which the physical attributes of a proprietary land unit affect manœuvrability and subsequently with the influence of the abstract attributes upon it.

Physical Attributes and Manœuvrability. Nature sets limits beyond which the works of man cannot go. He who plans to replace a hill by a natural plain is pipe-dreaming of the impossible. Our planner can bulldoze the hill off the face of the earth but the place where the hill once stood is a man-made surface and can never be a natural plain. Great strides in scientific and technical knowledge are overcoming natural obstacles which in the past have withstood the advance of man, but inherent in the *criterium ordinis* of nature is a point where physical conformities are the masters of circumstances. Here is the threshold where the power of manœuvrability over physical attributes comes to a dead end.

Inside that insuperable boundary, the degree of manœuvrability available to the holder of a proprietary land unit over the land resources of the unit is conditioned by a number of factors, factors which can be identified in the general case.

The first to engage our attention is cost. If in the natural order of things a physical attribute can be removed, manœuvrability is a potential state the actual degree of which will depend in a particular case on the cost of removal. Cost of removal must not be confused with the cost of replacement. Manœuvrability in the present context is definitive of the present condition of a proprietary land unit, of the power to use the existing land resources in a novel way; it has no relevance to other resources outside the proprietary land unit. Whether or not the holder of the proprietary land unit has means to meet the cost of removal and is willing to employ them to that end is a question touching the structure, amount and use of consociate wealth;[14] important, indeed, to the deployment of the total wealth of the holder of the proprietary land unit but collateral to the state of manœuvrability within the proprietary land unit. Removal cost is a factor governing the degree of manœuvrability and replacement cost is not, because the necessity to undertake removal is a condition imposed by the *status quo* on the making and execution of a new plan for the proprietary land resources.

In theory if a landowner can finance the cost of removal and wishes to do so, the physical attributes do not affect manœuvrability one way or the other. The natural limitations mentioned earlier preclude replacement, not removal. Physical attributes restrict manœuvrability when the cost of removal is beyond the fortune of the holder of the proprietary land unit to finance.

Financial resources can be extended by credit. Raising a loan, if the prospective return on investment will pay for the funding, is sound enough business. We must remember, however, that landowners are not always entrepreneurs. They are moved by other motives. There is, for example, a marked reluctance among rural landowners in Britain to borrow on their land titles.[15] We can say of them and possible of landowners in the general case, that their attitude to incurring expense on regrouping physical attributes is largely conditioned by the amount and nature of the consociate wealth of the owners of the proprietary land units. A landowner who is not holding land from a strictly commercial or industrial motive will be less inclined to be affected by cost and credit considerations. He will be moved, perhaps unwittingly, to take his cue for planning and re-planning the use of the proprietary land resources from the dominant physical attributes of his proprietary land unit. Although he could afford, for example, an architecturally more satisfactory residence or set of outbuildings, he never considers the cost of removing the present house or contemplates doing so. The existing physical form of the buildings with which he has become familiar has established a permanent image in his mind and planning. He plans for and about the thing as it is, not actually conscious of the fact that the attribute itself is setting the direction of his planning and affecting the operative manœuvrability.

14 Below, p. 150.
15 *Report of the Committee on the Working of the Monetary System*, Cmnd. 827 (H.M.S.O., 1959), para. 913.

The submerged influence draws its strength from the degree to which the attribute is physically identified with the *solum* of the proprietary land unit. This attachment or identity which we shall call the '*soil affinity factor*' depends on motive and circumstances. Other things being equal, light temporary erections have less affinity with the *solum* than have substantial structures standing on deeper foundations. On the other hand, the soil affinity factor is not simply another name for a demolition index. Time has something to do with it. An ancient structure physically infirm can have a higher degree of soil affinity, in the sense we mean, than a recently erected concrete and steel building unfamiliar and unknown to family or national tradition.

We might be accused here of dragging abstract thought into our discussion of the physical attributes: this is only true in so far as all interpretative thought is abstract. We have not turned our eyes from the physical attributes of the proprietary land unit. We are looking steadily at the natural formation of the land mass and the development use pattern and saying, in effect, that for a diversity of reasons some of the physical features we see have a greater soil affinity and potential longevity than others and influence future planning accordingly.

If the motive for holding a proprietary land unit is to preserve the ancient buildings, then the old buildings do not act as a restraint upon the plans of the holder and upon the manœuvrability of the other assets. Manœuvrability is not reduced or impaired since the holder of the unit is experiencing complete freedom to implement his plan. The ancient buildings constitute a soil affinity factor which like all such reduces the range of removals in re-planning but in a manner which openly, manifestly and deliberately affects the thinking and planning of the holder of the proprietary land unit.

Where the motive for the plan and use of a combination of proprietary land resources is centred upon the preservation or retention of certain of them – buildings or amenity features – these items will patently have a definite soil affinity. Functional complementarity, however, between items with a patent soil affinity and others will not infrequently inoculate the others to give them a soil affinity which of themselves and by themselves they would not have had. A feature of outstanding architectural merit beloved of its owner and acclaimed by public regard can exert a widespread ban over adjoining land against works of development; works which would not impinge upon and adversely affect the desired feature itself but which would render it less attractive and perceptible by altering the physical environment or blocking the approach vistas opening

47

upon its setting. The adjoining land and vistas enhance the aesthetic qualities of the architecturally desirable building. If they lie in one proprietary land unit and are among the land resources we can say of them that there is functional complementarity between them. Without the environmental approaches the now desirable building would have little attraction. Plans to preserve the architectural merits of the building should include in their ambit the associated buildings and approach vistas. In these circumstances, not only would the architecturally desirable building itself have a definite and patent soil affinity, but the adjoining and nearby buildings and approach ways and vistas would share it. To remove the latter would impair or destroy the former to which the central soil affiinty pertains. There is also a counter functional complementarity; without the desirable building the environmental complex of buildings and vistas would lose from their character the element which gives them a function in relation to the desired building and a soil affinity.

An interesting and outstanding example of the manner in which a soil affinity factor can determine the degree of manœuvrability open to the holder of a proprietary land unit and the direction and content of plans for the rearrangement of resources was recently manifest by the reconstruction of the Nash Terraces flanking the south-west approaches to Regent's Park in London. The owners of the freehold reversions wished to retain John Nash's original facades while remodelling and modernizing the entire structure of the eighteenth-century terraces. At a certain point in the reconstruction process, the facades, one stone thick, were standing gaunt and silhouetted awaiting the renovations to be fitted in behind them. The pattern, the costs and the ultimate ensemble of the reconstruction plan were set and predetermined by the soil affinity factor of the Nash facades.

So far, we can say of manœuvrability that it is a function of the cost of removal of physical features as existing under the prevailing plan and of the soil affinity factors. Removal, however, as a contributory factor to the degree of manœuvrability becomes progressively of less consequence as the chances of providing alternative sites increases within the proprietary land unit. Imagine an urban site totally occupied by an old warehouse and the land and freehold estate in it constituting a proprietary land unit. In these circumstances no alternative plan for the development of the unit could be carried out without the removal of the existing warehouse in whole or in part. Manœuvrability would be entirely dependent upon the cost of removal. If a similar warehouse were to occupy the land of a proprietary land unit which in itself had sufficient land surface of the right contour, condition and location to accommodate the

48

kind of development to make room for which removal would have been necessary in the previous case, manœuvrability would be less dependent upon the cost of removal. The greater the land surface within the proprietary land unit, the less the dependence. An example may serve to illustrate the point. Running down to the shore of the sea-girt Ring of Kerry in Ireland are peasant holdings, each in its order a proprietary land unit. Jarring with the natural beauty of the littoral is a repeated untidiness. On holding after holding, new white-washed cottages and bungalows stand alongside the abandoned cots of an earlier habitation. Inevitably, the holdings have an air of desolation about them, quite unjustified. The land area in each unit was ample enough to build a new dwelling alongside the old without replacing the latter. These ragged examples illustrate how the relationship of total land area to buildings within a proprietary land unit can affect its planning where through lack of consociate wealth or indifference, replacement of old buildings is unnecessary in order to provide new plans with substitute functions to replace existing plans.

We can state the proposition in the general case by saying that manœuvrability is a function of the ratio between the total land surface of the proprietary land unit and the area occupied by works and excavations to be removed as a prerequisite to the execution of a new plan. When the value of this ratio is greater than unity, the cost of removal is of less consequence as a variable affecting the degree of manœuvrability. The relationship can be simply expressed mathematically as:

$$B_m = f[c, L, (r - a)].$$

where: B_m = the degree of manœuvrability of the proprietary land unit.

c = the cost of removal.

r = the surface of land occupied by removable works.

a = the surface of land occupied by the soil affinity factors.

L = the total land surface of the proprietary land unit.

More precisely, the degree of manœuvrability is a function of the sum of the costs of removing each removable item and the sum of the areas of the specific sites occupied by the removable items less the sum of the areas occupied by each item affected by soil affinity and the total area of the land of the proprietary land unit. The independent variables (a) and (L) are within the competence of the holder of the proprietary land unit to alter. By changing his attitude towards certain erections and other works he can alter the

D

incidence of the soil affinity factors. It may be decided to remove what had hitherto been regarded as a building to be preserved. The change of attitude deprives the building of the protective soil affinity and deprives in the bargain and in a similar fashion all buildings and other works in a relationship of functional complementarity with the building of the first instance now to be removed. The magnitude of (L), the total land area of the proprietary land unit can be altered by selling off land or giving it away or by buying additional land or accepting gifts of land to add to the total area. The independent variable (c) changes with shifts in prices beyond the control of the holder of the proprietary land unit. The factor which remains is (r), the area taken up by the removable items. This is constant if one is judging the degree of manœuvrability at any one moment and the forces which can change the degree, up or down, before any move is made to take advantage of the potential manœuvrability by altering the lay-out and positions of the land, buildings, works and fixed equipment of the proprietary land unit.

An example of another kind may further help to illustrate the notion of the soil affinity factor. The manœuvrability of an interior wall of an old house might be quite positive but for a Tudor fireplace and chimney breast. The owner of the proprietary land unit of which the house is an integral feature wishes to preserve the fireplace and chimney breast but would destroy them if he dismantled the wall. Since they are embodied in the wall, the wall is affected by their static status and patent affinity factor. There is a functional complementarity between the fireplace, chimney breast and wall directly related to the motive of the house owner to preserve the fireplace as a purpose of the plan for the use of the land resources of the unit. At first sight it may seem that the functional complementarity is unilateral in the sense that, on simple constructional grounds, the wall is essential to the preservation of the fireplace and chimney breast but the fireplace and breast are not essential to the functioning of the wall. This, however, is a superficial way of looking at the relationship. The functional complementarity is the consequence of motive and its force and incidence must take their cue from motive. Motive creates an existential frame within which functional complementarity must be interpreted. In the existential frame the wall is the wall-supporting-the-fireplace and consequently the fireplace and chimney breast are essential to the existing function of the wall. Functional complementarity interpreted against motive is two-way between the fireplace and the wall.

Abstract Attributes and Manœuvrability. The rights of property which, as we saw in the last chapter, help to fashion the abstract attributes of a proprietary land unit are the positive rights to do, to act and to be. Inevitably they are not in sum absolute. The bundle of them pertaining to any one proprietary land unit is a residuum of power within which the holder of the rights may operate. The bundle has been cut down as it were from the unlimited power of absolute right. The pruning effect is experienced by the landowner and holder of property rights as a complex of restraints. The law gives but also takes away. At the opposite pole to rights of property lie the restraints upon the use of land resources. Liberties to plan and arrange the patterns and combinations of proprietary land resources within a proprietary land unit are sanctioned by the former and checked by the latter. The counterparts, the checking restrictions, cut down the areas of freedom for the holder of a proprietary land unit and thereby condition his manœuvrability. We must now pay attention to these restraints and restrictions.

We are now, as before, concerned with the general case, to find a universally valid scheme for the classification in broad and comprehensive categories of the restraints and prohibitions of various kinds which counteract the absolute power and cut down the size of the bundle of property rights. A lead to what we are looking for are extracting agencies mentioned previously.[16] Our classification of the types of restraint will follow this lead. It presents pigeon-holes, generous enough to gather up the niceties and differences of local laws into generic similarities while giving a breadth of arrangement which is articulate and not so broad as to be futile. There is a basic dichotomy to the classification dividing the restrictions into those which are derived from reciprocal relationships and those which are not so derived. The general scheme is as follows:

i. restrictions derived from reciprocal relationships consequent upon—
(*a*) contiguity of boundaries;
(*b*) superior and inferior privities; and
(*c*) *ad hoc* commitments.
ii. restrictions not derived from reciprocal relationships—
(*d*) universal restraints.

The holder of a proprietary land unit forced by lack of space to adopt a plan for a second best is not obstructed by a physical limitation. It may look like it and he may speak as if it were so, complaining of insufficient land or a plot of the wrong shape to fulfil his ideal purpose. He is restrained in fact by the faith he keeps

[16] Above, pp. 30, 31.

with his neighbours. He observes and honours their property rights. These restrain his actions. There is land enough. Broad acres run to horizons far beyond his boundary, flat, open, fertile, perfectly suited to the purpose in mind. They are of no avail because to use them would be to trespass over his neighbour's pale. The boundary, the march, is the line along which reciprocal restrictions meet and respect each other. The holder of our proprietary land unit forgoes his ideal plan, has regard for his neighbour's rights and the curtailment they impose on his own actions and bundle of rights and expects and receives from the neighbour a reciprocal respect and concern which restrain the neighbour within the contiguous unit. Such reciprocal restraints run true whether the law that requires their observance sees them as an English estate, a continental servitude or some other institution, for they are born of the contiguity of proprietary land units.

The restrictions derived from the reciprocal relationships of superior and inferior privities are not the consequence of contiguity. The word privity is used here because whenever an inferior interest in land is derived from the higher sanction of a superior interest a special relationship is created; both interests stand in the same parcel of land and the land is the link between the parties to the transaction. In English law the word has a narrower connotation[17] than the meaning implied by the use of it in the present context. Here it is doing the same job but to serve our general ends and we should not impute into its meaning the narrowness of the English legal nuance.

The privity created by the common physical attributes appropriated by superior and inferior interests in the same land is the ground for reciprocal restrictions limiting the powers of the respective units. An inferior unit appropriates land and land resources in which the holder of the superior unit retains an interest. Manifestly the holder of the inferior interest who is by virtue of the interest in occupation of the land must respect the land as wealth over which the holder of the superior interest has rights of property. What in any particular circumstances that respect may amount to and require of the holder of the inferior interest will depend upon the terms on which the inferior interest was granted. By nature an inferior interest is carved out of a superior interest. The owner of the superior is the initator of the arrangement. The holder of an inferior interest must know, therefore, that it is in the very nature of the inferior interest to be fashioned in a manner which will not

[17] See, for instance R. E. Megarry and H. W. R. Wade, *The Law of Real Property* (Stevens and Sons, London, 3rd Edn, 1966), pp. 725 ff.

damage without recompense the land resources of the superior interest. Hence, in the very nature of its origin the inferior interest is subject to restraints in favour of the superior interest. The holder of the inferior interest is restricted in his actions in favour of the holder of the superior interest—the restrictions are reciprocal, in that one man's fetter is another man's freedom. All this adds up to the curtailment of the powers of manœuvrability available to the holder of the inferior interest. Take an example from recent agricultural history in England. It used to be thought that to make a pasture would make a man, and to break a pasture would break a man and landlords of farm lands would draw leases which imposed severe penalties on a tenant who put the plough through a pasture. The lease clearly limited the manœuvrability of the tenant in planning the use of the proprietary land resources of his inferior unit. The legal assumption was, at that time, that retention of the permanent pasture was essential to the maintenance of the value of the landlord's reversion. The prohibition suffered by the tenant was the reciprocal of the landlord's right to have the pasture retained.

Privity between the holders of a superior and an inferior interest in the same land is, however, inevitably a two-way affair. When the holder of the superior interest carves out of it an inferior, he by his very action sets limits to what he can in future do on and over the land while the inferior interest remains in being. He must not derogate from his own undertaking. By carving the inferior interest out of the superior one, the holder of the latter undertakes to allow the holder of the inferior interest to occupy and use the land resources. In future he cannot use them himself in a manner which will prevent the holder of the inferior interest from enjoying the use of the rights granted to him by the very act of creating the inferior interest in the land. The reciprocal relationship between the holders of the respective interests in the land thus imposes restrictions on the use of the land resources by the holder of the superior interest in a manner which limits the manœuvrability within the superior interest and does so in favour of the holder of the inferior interest.

The *ad hoc* commitments which impose limitations on manœuvrability within proprietary land units are the consequence of agreements or covenants between the holders of units. The agreements are not contingent upon locational or proprietary circumstances, as with the reciprocal relationships born of contiguity or privities. The *ad hoc* committments are reciprocal in that the restraint imposed on and accepted by one of the parties to the arrangement is matched by a reciprocal benefit in favour of the other party. The restrictions are not inherent in the very location or constitution of the units,

53

inextricably the consequence of site or make up, so that the non-observance of them would jeopardize the existence of the units they condition. They are the outcome of agreements which are not pre-conditioned and there is no limit to the type and purpose of them. Modern examples, illustrative of the category, are the undertakings entered into by householders whose proprietary land units on which their respective houses stand have development use patterns which include unfenced, open lawns and pathways fronting the houses. Each householder enters into a covenant with the others to cultivate the flower-beds and maintain the lawns and pathways to a specified standard. The undertakings are positive obligations creative of reciprocal relationships—the observance of them imposes a burden on each householder to the benefit of all the others; each house-holder in turn enjoys a benefit in exchange for a burden. Manœuvra-bility is curtailed and contained. Each householder cannot plan to use his land resources in a way which would destroy the paths, flower-beds and lawns or cause them to be neglected or altered so as not to conform to the agreed pattern and lay-out.

The universal restraints which occupy the fourth division in our general classification scheme are such as might affect all holders of rights of property in land nationally or within a particular region. They differ from the restraints in the other categories in that there is no reciprocal relationship between those burdened by the restraints and other parties in receipt of counterpart benefits. Town planning laws which impose controls over the use of land in regions or national areas are examples. All holders of proprietary land units are subject to them. The benefits which spring from honouring the restraints are not held in hands that have imposed them in the first place either by *ad hoc* agreement or as a logical and inevitable act necessitated by locational or proprietary circumstances. An example from the common law in England is the maxim '*sic utere tuo ut alienum no laedas*'. The point might be that this general maxim governing the use of land and the town planning controls which in some measure are like unto it, dispense a wide-felt benefit to all holders of proprietary land units in the region or nation. But this presupposes a common consensus and experience. The beneficiaries have not been consulted about the actions of those who are burdened obstensibly on their behalf. It could well be that the restraints and the way in which they are interpreted impose burdens all round. The reciprocal polarities of burden and benefit are lost—there are burdens at both poles! It is safest not to postulate reciprocal relation-ships and to classify the restrictions imposed by the universal restraints in a class apart. At the burdened end they diminish the

54

bundle of rights within a proprietary land unit and reduce the degree of manœuvrability.

Consociate Wealth—a Note

At this juncture it is apposite to make a passing reference to consociate wealth. The concept will engage our attention for some time later on in the unfolding of the general analysis. Mention is made of it here because it is necessary in treating of manœuvrability to draw a distinction between the power a holder of a proprietary land unit has to rearrange the combinations of proprietary land resources within a proprietary land unit, the degree of manœuvrability within the unit itself, and the power to transpose the assets of his total fortune.

Analysis earlier on in this chapter has shown the critical role that the power and cost of removal plays in determining the degree of manœuvrability within a proprietary land unit. We deliberately excluded all consideration of replacement. Replacement involves bringing in resources from outside the proprietary land unit and in the earlier context was irrelevant, as at that time we were concerned only with manœuvrability within the proprietary land unit. Nevertheless, in nine cases out of ten the revision of a plan for the combination of the proprietary land resources of a unit where it involves the removal of one or more items is associated with the replacement of those items by others. The holder of the proprietary land unit reaches out beyond the confines of the unit to other wealth and makes a transposition. He takes from assets which are not items within the combination of land resources being re-planned, converts what he takes into money or some other form of liquidity and exchanges the money for replacements of the items removed from the combination being re-planned. The landowner or holder of the proprietary land unit cannot do this unless he has the power to make the necessary transpositions; in other words it depends upon the degree of manœuvrability conditioning his entire fortune. The magnitude of that degree of manœuvrability in its turn is dependent upon a number of factors, including motive for the use and disposition of the entire fortune, but equally upon the power of assimilation—that is, the right to hold property rights in all forms of wealth, land and goods, so that each may be assimilated with the others in a common bond of proprietorship.[18] Wealth consociate with a proprietary land unit is that wealth external to the unit which may

[18] V. Kruse, *The Right of Property*, trans. P. T. Federspiel (Oxford University Press, London, 1939), p. 108.

be assimilated with it by virtue of the holder of the proprietary land unit holding the unit and the external wealth to himself by titles which vest the unit and the external wealth in him with an equal right of property or ownership. Consociate wealth is vital to the power of the holder of a proprietary land unit to rearrange the combination of land resources in the unit. Go back for a moment to the earlier conclusions about the independent variables which determine the degree of manœuvrability within a proprietary land unit. One of them was cost of removal and another the amount of total land space in relation to the area occupied by removable items. While these factors indicate the degree of potential manœuvrability in the hands of the holder of the unit and within the unit, they have no practical significance unless the holder of the unit has sufficient consociate wealth to meet the cost or removal of the utilization of the open land as may be required to implement new plans for the combination of the land resources of the unit. Consociate wealth conditions the manœuvrability of the entire fortune without which the manœuvrability within the confines of the proprietary land unit is like an engine without fuel.

Chapter IV

MOTIVE AND COMPLEMENTARITY

Motive and Pursuits

An entrepreneur devoting all his energies to making a profit to pay high yields to capital and labour is a man with a single motive. The holder of a proprietary land unit may do the same and turn the entire resources of the unit towards achieving an entrepreneurial objective; or he may have some other motive. No one can explain the combination of the land resources of a proprietary land unit at a given time who is ignorant of the motive which has prompted the holder of the unit in his decision-making. Motive is the co-ordinating principle which enables functional complementarity to make sense of the multiple specificity of the array of land resources in a proprietary land unit. Motives are as varied and numerous as the whims and fancies in the minds of men. A survey[1] made in the 1950s of the motives which moved proprietors in Britain to become or to continue to be landowners, showed a remarkable diversity of intentions, with, incidentally, the aims of an entreprenur well down in the order of preferences. Where a man holds property rights in land there must be a motive to explain his holding of them. Our forebears used to say *nulle terre sans seigneur*—there is no land without a lord. That there is no proprietorship of land without a motive is an axiom no less true and of a far wider universality.

Motive, by definition, can be invariably regarded as a single-eyed posture; and must be so accepted for the purpose of analysis. What sometimes point to mixed motives are in truth ostensible activities covering a hidden single intent. One cannot make a clear decision unless, at the time of making it, one is moved by a dominant, single, overriding motive. Now, this is just what happens when the holder of a proprietary land unit follows two or more pursuits, co-ordinating each by reference to a single motive. Motive governs the distribution of resources between the multi-uses to which they

[1] D. R. Denman, *Estate Capital* (Allen and Unwin, London, 1957), Chapters 7, 8.

57

are put. We must make the distinction, a fine but a crucial one, between motive and pursuit. Authors of guides to eating and sleeping places find it difficult at times to tell whether the proprietor of an establishment is running a hotel or a restaurant. The proprietor himself is not confused. His motive in following two pursuits is not a contradiction but an essential arbiter of the distribution of resources between the two, an expression of a single-eyed intention to divide available resources in definite proportions. If the motive were not single and clear-cut but mixed, no decisions between the claims of the restaurant and the claims of the hotel would ever be made or if made would be unco-ordinated and inconsistent.

A motive can accommodate more than two pursuits simultaneously. A few years ago the owner of a country seat near the town of Diss in Norfolk announced his intention of building up the acreage of the estate piecemeal until it reached the boundaries boasted of in the centuries gone by. The estate was then and always had been residential and agricultural. The overall concern of the owner at the time was to extend the land area to satisfy a historical ideal. The motive in the mind of the owner of the fee simple of the core of 23 acres when he bought it in 1936 was unambiguous and single-eyed. He was intent upon developing the estate by following a trinity of pursuits: the restoration of a past image, the provision of a farming livelihood and the maintenance of a family residence. Doubtless, restoring the historical image had to be the dominant pursuit whenever land was available on the local market which when bought would bring a few more acres within the traditional boundary. Time would be when the additional acres bought for the historical pursuit would lower the marginal returns from the land and buildings. If the motive had been simply an entrepreneurial one, the extra land would not have been bought in these circumstances. Buying it was not the outcome of a mixed motive and waivering indecision but a logical step and judgement in fulfilling a single motive to use the land resources in the proprietary land unit for three distinct and simultaneous pursuits.

Motive the Criterion of Complementarity

The firm and the household are designations of decision-making units whose very connotations convey the motives behind the activities of each. The motive is imputed by the activity. It is not so with the holding of a proprietary land unit. Land resources can be put simultaneously to many uses and the mere holding of a

58

proprietary land unit gives no indication of the motive of the holder. Visual evidence is all the more unreliable when the proprietary land resources are used for two or more pursuits. In the case of the entrepreneur motive does not consciously concern those who would analyse his activities. Analysis knows what it is after and how to judge the outcome of the entrepreneurial enterprise—it is an analysis of inputs and outputs and marginal gross and net profits. Motive, as such, is disregarded. It cannot be so with the analysis of the use of land resources within the proprietary land unit. To understand anything, we must first know what the motive is of the holder of the unit.

Unless we introduce motive, we cannot define functional complementarity. Equipped with motive, we may define functional complementarity for the purpose of our general analysis as: the quality in one component which enables other components associated with it in a combination of proprietary land resources within a proprietary land unit to function more effectively in fulfilling the motive of the holder for holding the unit. Functional complementarity between two items in a combination is invariably mutual. Because A assists B in the fulfilment of motive, B is essential to A in the same context, otherwise A's special function could not be performed. We saw this earlier in the case of the Tudor fireplace and the supporting wall.[2] The wall is necessary for the fireplace and the fireplace is the *raison d'être* of the wall.

Perfect complementarity is the key to making a successful plan for a combination of proprietary land resources. A component which adversely affects the performance of other resources in a combination, or does not contribute to their performance in a way which a possible substitute could do is an obstacle in the path of fulfilment. The existing arrangement would need to be altered, and the obstacle removed in the case of optimal performance.

The presence of an obstruction may not be immediately discerned where components in a combination of resources have potential complementarity. Consider two garages on a house plot. One garage would adequately meet the requirements of the householder whose motive is to use his proprietary land unit for residential pursuits and to satisfy a desire for a residence set in a garden where no land is neglected and every corner contributes to the plantations or the flower gardens. Only one of the two garages can be used; the other will be disregarded. At first sight it might appear that each garage is the simple substitute for the other. A garage is essential to the fulfilment of the residential motive of the householder.

2 Above, p. 50.

Consequently, either garage has equally with the other potential functional complementarity. Actual complementarity is dependent upon use. Once a choice has been made, the potential complementarity of what will then be the disregarded garage will disappear and the garage will be seen as an obstacle in the path of the fulfilment of the residential motive of the householder. The unused garage does not assume a neutral role. It becomes a positive disturbance. It stands on land which is required to perfect the garden lay-out and the fulfilment of the residential motive of the householder. A component in the combination of resources having potential complementarity is now seen as an irritant and the cause of disequilibrium.

The notion that motive is the background against which we can demonstrate the existence of functional complementarity may seem too naive and vague when we remember the insistence of Professor Hicks[3] on the necessity for a third good for which the complementary things can each in turn be substituted. Hicks was trying to solve Pareto's problem of finding some measurable objective way of showing that items in a schedule of consumer goods were complementary. The substitution of each for money could provide the required yardstick. Pursuing somewhat analogous lines we might argue that functional complementarity between two components of a combination of proprietary land resources in a proprietary land unit could be demonstrated by reference to the interaction between the pattern of the resources and the assets which make up the consociate wealth of the unit.[4]

Consider, for the sake of the argument, the structure of the assets of an entire fortune, of which a proprietary land unit is part. To add a new component to the combination of land resources of the proprietary land unit, the holder of the fortune would need within its general framework to substitute the additional land resource in the proprietary land unit for an item or items within the asset structure of the consociate wealth of the unit. Following the Hicksian line, it could be said that functional complementarity between two components in a combination of land resources of a proprietary land unit would be demonstrated if the holder of the fortune were prepared to rearrange the structure of his fortune to provide for component A of the land resource combination a functional companion B and, but for the existence of A, B would not have been provided and the fortune rearranged. Suppose a householder wishes to build a garage to enhance the residential attractions of his dwelling. To finance the garage he must sell out

[3] J. R. Hicks, *Value and Capital* (Oxford University Press, 1957), p. 47.
[4] Below, Chapter IX.

certain equity holdings, and in terms of his total fortune substitute the garage for them. If the proprietary land unit had not had a house among the land resources, it may be assumed that the holder of the unit would not have restructured his fortune and realized equities to finance the erection of the garage. Because he was willing and able to do so, and in fact did make the substitution, it can be concluded that the house and the garage were in a relationship of functional complementarity such as would not have pertained between the garage and the bare land plot.

This approach suggests that the consociate wealth of a proprietary land unit, or rather the asset structure of the wealth and the items which compose it provide the third factor, in the Hicksian sense, by which the presence of complementarity among the land resources of the proprietary land unit can be demonstrated. But it does not get us very far. It can show in its own way, the presence of functional complementarity between the resources of the proprietary land unit and by implication point to a disequilibrium among the total assets of the fortune which the adjustment – the building of the garage and the sale of the equities in the illustration – was intended to rectify. But it does not explain why the demonstrated complementarity existed in the first place. And this is true also of the Hicksian attempt. Complementarity demonstrated by the rate of the substitution of two consumer goods for money is no explanation of the complementarity itself or of the force or forces which have generated it.

To go back to the illustration of the house and the garage: the garage would not have been substituted for the equities in the total fortune unless some wind of change had disturbed the equilibrium of the overall functional complementarity of the entire fortune including the place of the land resources of the proprietary land unit in it. But to put the conclusion this way, simply begs the whole question. We have answered the question about the cause and nature of complementarity by introducing the concept in the explanation. We have moved in a circle.

The circle can be broken. Once again we must realize that we are dealing with functional complementarity, measured in terms of the assistance given by two or more assets in relationship with each other and, as a consequence of the relationship, to the fulfilment of the motive for holding them. We are not harking back here to the utility theories which caused Pareto's dismay. We are dealing with preferences not of individual goods but of whole combinations of assets—the kind of geography we find among indifference curves. To say a man prefers one combination to another evokes the

61

question of why does he do so. What is his motive? By defining complementarity by reference to motive we are saying no more than this: a man prefers this combination of land resources before that combination because when the resources are arranged in the proportions and order of the first combination they come nearest to achieving the fulfilment of the motive which prompts his choice.

Coefficients of Combinations

The joint contribution of two or more resources in functional complementarity with each other to the achievement of motive can in a rough and ready way be indicated by coefficients of magnitude as percentages of an optimal contribution. It is not possible to give coefficients to each of the several resources individually, and plot in graph form a series of coefficients for one type of resource against the series for another and read off from the co-ordinates magnitudes indicative of the joint contributions. It is impossible to do this because the coefficients are indices of the percentage contributions to the achievement of motive of two or more resources in functional complementarity. We could not plot a series of coefficients for different types of a particular resource. It would not be possible to estimate what they were as the contributions we are handling are as much the yield of one of the resources in complementary relationship as it is of the other. If a farmer needs land and a house to fulfil his motive for holding an agricultural proprietary land unit, a house and land will operate in functional complementarity to fulfil the intention and it will not be possible to say how much the land contributed to the final result and how much was the share of the house; without the house the land's contribution to a residential-farming motive would have been nil; and likewise a house without land can make no contribution towards fulfilling such a motive. The coefficients we may use are magnitudes of the joint contribution of two or more resources which as contributors are inextricably united. Neither is it permissible to think of the contributions flowing as a continuous stream of infinitesimal marginal changes. One combination may give a greater contribution than another, but in each case what is given comes from two sets of resources each differing in its wholeness and physical conformity from the other. Where one contribution is greater than another, the distinction is represented by a definite step, usually a steep one. A sustained flow, rising and falling, like the marginal production curves dear to economic theory implies that whatever generates the flow increases and decreases by infinitesimally small increments of a homogeneous

62

substance. This is all right when we are dealing with hypotheses, abstract theories and models. In the real world changes in the supply of land resources are never, nor ever could be, the tiny gradations postulated by economic theory. Change does not mean a little bit more of the same thing; it is total structural rearrangement, a change in wholenesses, which cannot therefore be plotted as a line on a graph.

It follows that margins are not the creeping increments of marginal utility theory. Marginal analysis has become so closely associated in economic analysis with linear and curvilinear movements of infinitesimal increments that we hesitate to use the term in connection with the contributions to the achievement of motive from changing combinations of two or more types of land resource. It would, however, presumably not be incongruous to speak of a marginal contribution, albeit of wide proportions, of a particular combination of two types of resource when that combination is substituted for a different combination of the same resources.

Perfect complementarity does not always mean perfect fulfilment of motive. Two items in a combination of resources may be operating in complete functional complementarity without fully achieving the motive of the owner of them. One may have a higher potential magnitude than the other and be retarded in its contribution by the limitations inherent in the other. The highest achievement is reached by substituting for the weaker of the two an item whose potential is equal to that of the stronger of the original two.

The greater the number of resources in functional complementarity with one another, the more tedious and difficult the task becomes of judging and comparing the respective coefficients of each possible combination; and the exercise becomes more complex still when motive covers more than one pursuit. A series of possible combinations can be arranged in ascending order of magnitudes. The significance of motive is at once apparent if we compare the order of coefficients of a series of combinations of specific resources under a particular motive with the order of the coefficients of a series of combinations of exactly the same resources under different motives.

Suppose the following alternative choices are open to the holder of a proprietary land unit who wishes to use his resources as a farming enterprise to make and maximize a financial profit:

(a) 100 acres of fertile arable land and a large rambling house:
(b) 100 acres of the same land with the same house plus a cottage;
(c) 500 acres of similar land with a similar house and cottage;
(d) 500 acres equipped as (c) but with two cottages; and

(*e*) 500 acres of similar land with no house but two cottages.

Estimates and budgets indicate that the larger the operational unit the higher the marginal net profit per acre; the rambling farmhouse is a drain on current resources and a diseconomy unlike the cottages which are an asset to attract labour on to the farm. With his entrepreneurial motive in mind the holder of the proprietary land unit would probably judge the coefficients of each of the alternative possibilities in the order of Line I of Table II.

TABLE II: *Order of Combinations of House, Cottages and Land and Coefficients of Contribution to Motive*

MOTIVE		COEFFICIENTS AS % OF POSTULATED ACHIEVEMENT					
		20	40	60	80	100	
Farming	I	a	b	c	d	e	
Farming + residential	II	e	a	b	c	d	Order of preference
Farming + residential + sporting	III	a	e	b	c	d	

If, however, the motive of the holder of the unit was to follow with equal fervour the running of a commercial farming enterprise and a country residence, the order of his preferences and the corresponding coefficients of the alternative combinations would probably be as shown in Line II. The pattern would shift again if the motive had in addition to commercial farming and residence the use and development of the unit for sporting; the order could then be as shown in Line III.

It should be stressed again that the coefficients are those of the contributions to the achievement of motive from three types of land resource – farm land, house and cottages – in functional complementarity with each other. In practice the quantification of the respective coefficients would involve a high degree of subjective judgement. Much would depend upon motive. If the motive were to make a financial profit, the judgement of the holder would often be assisted by *ad hoc* budgets and by general statistics of profitability related to the types of resources being handled. In any event the coefficients can never be other than estimated forecasts of what he who makes the decision judges would be the outcome of adopting one of a range of available alternatives; not until the choice has been made and the combination of resources chosen set to work will it be seen how far the estimated coefficient was sound. Types of resources which by their very nature perform certain functions will obviously be afforded higher coefficients, in relation to motive whose fulfilment involves those functions, than are given to other resources. A residential motive, as in the above example, associated with a farming one would receive a greater contribution to its fulfilment from a combination of resources which included a farmhouse with the land than it would receive from a combination of land and cottages. A subjective element in the judgement on the quantification of the coefficients can never be entirely removed and in the practical world exerts a greater influence than the outward evidence might suggest. Take the entrepreneurial motive with its accepted emphasis on profitability: in the first place someone has to decide to use the resources at his disposal for profitable pursuits and as a secondary issue to decide whether to go for maximum surpluses or to draw the line at a lower level, as the owners of a proprietary land unit may do if they were operating as a housing association.

The world of applied economics has tended to overlook the role of land law and land tenure in providing a framework in which decisions are taken about the use of resources. The firm and the household have held first place. Hence there are very few statistics of a general kind available to help holders of proprietary land units to judge the probable outcome of combinations of resources devoted even to financial ends. A recent survey of the causes of differing levels of farm rents in England and Wales[5] did make some attempts to show the correlation between rent levels and specific combinations of land resources; Table III is compiled from the evidence to show the relationship between land, buildings, electricity services and rent. Evidence of this kind is directly concerned with land resources in a proprietary structure pattern of proprietary land units and not, as is so often the case, with production or commercial units and the input-output ratios of these in relation to gross and net margins. The evidence on the proprietary basis can be used almost without adaptation in certain circumstances when judging the probable consequences of using a combination of land resources of the kind to which the statistics relate.

Evidence of the kind used for Table III would be of practical value to the owner of a fee simple proprietary land unit in England and Wales whose motive is to carve derivative interests out of the

[5] D. R. Denman and V. F. Stewart, *Farm Rents* (Allen and Unwin, London, 1959).

E

fee simple, to let the inferior interests to tenants and retain the freehold reversion as an investment. The evidence will help him to judge the likely contribution to rent levels of combinations of land, farmhouses, farmsteads and electricity supplies. The evidence of the Table is related to combinations of resources—farmhouse, farm buildings, land (specific acreage) and electricity. From the Table

Table III: *Average Current Rent per Acre and Fixed Equipment with and without Electricity*

1957

| | WITH ELECTRICITY TO: | | | | | | NO ELECTRICITY | |
| | House and buildings | | House only | | Buildings only | | | |
FIXED EQUIPMENT	Rent per acre £	Average size of holding acres	Rent per acre £	Average size of holding acres	Rent per acre £	Average size of holding acres	Rent per acre £	Average size of holding acres
Farmhouse and buildings	2·12	182	1·83	121	1·23	248	1·50	155
Farmhouse only	—	—	2·14	61	—	—	1·53	61
Buildings only	—	—	—	—	2·23	183	1·51	128

it is not possible to tell precisely what contribution to rent levels electricity installation makes as the differentials could be partly explained on the ground that they reflect differences due to the provision of other equipment – buildings – to which the electricity is provided as much as to the provision of electricity itself. An attempt to analyse the evidence by showing the rent margins between combinations of resources similar in type but with or without electricity has been made and the results given in Tables IV and V. These Tables analyse the data further to show the influence of different land use patterns and acreages, rents of holdings with or without electricity. The figures are an interesting indication of the working of functional complementarity. There is a consistently higher rent differential when electricity is installed in farm buildings than in a farmouse only. This points to the functional complementarity between the buildings and the electricity; by putting the electricity in the buildings the latter enhance the value of the former to a degree greater than what would have emanated from the installation of electricity to the farmouse only—electricity and buildings together are worthy of a higher coefficient than are electricity and farmhouse together.

Because the general trend of official and other statistics is unrelated to the performances of proprietary land units, what are available

TABLE IV: *Difference in Average Current Rent per Acre on Provision of Electricity by Farming Type*

LAND USE	RENT PER ACRE DIFFERENCE ON PROVISION OF ELECTRICITY		TO HOLD-INGS WITH BUILDINGS ONLY
	TO HOLDINGS WITH HOMESTEADS		
	House and buildings	House only	
	£	£	£
Specialists	0·96	1·68	0·98
Mixed livestock (lowland)	0·42	0·10	−0·03
Mainly dairying	0·37	0·13	0·05
Mixed livestock (upland)	0·31	−0·06	0·67*
General mixed	0·30	0·14	0·29
Dairy and mixed (Grass)	0·28	−0·20	0·13
Heavy arable land	0·25	0·11	−0·12
Mixed with dairying	0·16	0·11	0·25
Corn, sheep and dairying	0·08	−0·66*	−0·44*
Alluvial arable and mixed	−0·06	−0·10	0·38
Light arable land	−0·08	0·11	0·33
All farming types	0·37	0·22	0·32

* Adjusted for rough grazings.

are as a rule related to data which from the view point of the holder of a proprietary land unit are extremely abstract and in consequence need to be handled with care if used to assist in making judgements about contribution coefficients of proprietary land resources. Average input-output figures in official agricultural statistics, for example, show marginal net profits in relation to acreages of land, as if the land factor in production were in itself homogeneous and unrelated or combined with other land resources and the size and shape of a proprietary land unit.

67

Complementarity and Predisposition

We must turn back for a moment to the morphological theory of capital and remember what it told us about period and process anaysis.[6] The systematic use of resources takes place as a series of plans, the earlier giving way to the later, and each occupying its own period in time. Destructible wealth could be destroyed as the

TABLE V: *Difference in Average Current Rent per Acre on Provision of Electricity by Farm Size-Groups*

UNIT SIZE-GROUP	RENT PER ACRE DIFFERENCE ON PROVISION OF ELECTRICITY		
	TO HOLDINGS WITH HOMESTEADS		TO HOLD-INGS WITH BUILDINGS ONLY
	House and buildings	House only	
acres	£	£	£
15–49	0·77	0·35	0·90
50–99	0·58	0·25	0·51
100–149	0·44	−0·06	0·38
150–299	0·40	0·11	0·29
300–499	0·37	0·23	0·49
500 and over	0·54	0·25*	0·33*
ALL SIZES	0·37	0·22	0·32

* Adjusted for rough grazings.

outcome of a final plan in a series; new plans would start again in a world where the old plans were lost to memory and influence. Where, however, land is among the constituents of a plan, the series to which the plan belongs can never stop; it goes on while the earth and the moon endure. New plans there can be, many and endless, but always, at least, the land, whatever its condition may be, is there to be handled under the new plan as the old had left it. Moreover, the past physical of the land set the stage within which the new plans must take shape. The old combination of resources in its final form exerts what we shall call a predisposing function upon present plans for the future. Later on much will be said about the principle of the predisposing function.[7] Just now, we shall do no more than introduce it as we are dealing with the notion of

[6] Above, p. 39.   [7] Below, pp. 96–123.

functional complementarity and the predisposing influence from the past has its own bearing upon the subject.

In planning the resources of a proprietary land unit we must start with what is given. It comes to us as a combination—of land as a natural resource and the works of man upon the land. Whatever new resources are provided either as additions or replacements of those removed, they have to be fitted into the existing combination as into a framework predetermined and set. The frame may consist of little else than the soil and derelict works and buildings; or it can be a highly developed complex of buildings, services and cultivated areas. However it is, the new plan must start with the old combination and so choose and distribute the new and additional resources that they dovetail into the existing framework to provide a general functional equilibrium and the degree of functional complementarity among the groupings of the resources to give expression to it. It is the need to ensure functional complementarity between the resources of the framework left by the old combination and resources to be provided under any new plan which underwrites the force of the predisposing influence from the past. The framework can predetermine the type of resources to be used in the new plan, the quantities and the placing of them so as to obtain as perfect an equilibrium and functional complementarity as possible between what will now be the total array of resources in the proprietary land unit. We are not in the present context concerned with consociate wealth, but it is opportune to point out that the framework of resources left when the old plan ended will determine also in some measure the number, type and disposition of the assets of various kinds which, as part of the consociate wealth of the unit, are used immediately in conjunction with it—such as the live and dead stock of a farming enterprise operated by the owner of the proprietary land unit within the unit. The pattern of a framework at the present time may be the consequence of earlier plans having to be fitted into even earlier frameworks and so on in a regressive series of frameworks down the past years.

The man with the new plan on his hands is robbed to some extent by the dictates of the framework into which he must fit his new resources. Fortune may smile on him and give him wisdom to find the combination of ideas and resources, to fit the new items neatly and comfortably into the old in a way which enables both together to achieve the fulfilment of the motive which moves the planner. In this event he will have engineered as high a degree of complementarity as he would have done if he were free from the beginning to choose what should be at his disposal.

More likely, however, the holder of the proprietary land unit faced with making new plans will be frustrated and blocked by the predisposing influence from the past and the framework of the old combination. To take an example: imagine a proprietary land unit consisting of an open building plot over which the owner of an adjoining unit has a right of light, which had been granted to him by the predecessor of the building plot. The easement of light cuts down the bundle of rights of property which otherwise would have constituted the abstract attributes of the proprietary land unit which is the building plot. The new owner of that unit must work and plan within the limited sanctions and this means he cannot build over a portion of the land of the unit which is completely sterilized by the easement of light. The motive of the holder of the unit is to erect a spacious residence on a plan which would infringe the easement of light. It is possible to build a house of lesser dimensions and respect the right of light or to put a small block of flats with a lower building to land ratio than the desired house would have had. The smaller house would be an independent residence and in this respect would conform more closely to the motive of the holder of the plot than the provision of a block of flats would but in itself would fall far short of the ideal. A block of flats on the other hand would fulfil the need for a residence and bring some financial rewards in the bargain. Using the device of a coefficient of contribution introduced above, we can say that there will be functional complementarity between the buildings and the land as grouped resources whatever plan is followed and that as a result of the predisposing function of the framework left by the old plan, the best that can now be done to satisfy the present motive is the provision of a house and land with, say, a 50 per cent coefficient or a block of flats with, say, a 20 per cent coefficient. The holder of the unit, however, might bow to the inevitable set by the framework in which he must now plan and allow the pressures from the past to change his mind and his motive. He now decides on the flats. At once the coefficients change: the land and flats will now contribute all that is required and the coefficient of achievement will be 100 per cent, that for the smaller house would drop back and the plans for the larger would probably be a non-event.

Derivation of the Predisposing Function

The term predisposing function carries the implication that one who is affected by it has no freedom of choice to avoid its consequences; it is a phenomenon that involuntarily induces an attitude and outlook in the mind of whoever is influenced by it. It behoves us at this stage in the development of our analysis to consider how this phenomenon may occur in the general case.

In the illustration just given of the inhibiting impact of the ease-ment of light, the predisposing influence arose from the contiguity of two proprietary land units, one with what English law calls the benefit of a dominant tenement – to impose the recognition of the right – and the other with the burden of a servient tenement – the obligation to respect the right – and also from a creative action undertaken at some time in the past by the then holder of the servient tenement in favour of he who at that time held the dominant unit.

The present holder of the unit in making plans for the future use of land resources has to contend with the easement of light and the attributes of the unit affected by it and by provisions of the earlier decision made by predecessors. He has to plan within a framework set by the past. The crucial question is how did he come to be under compulsion in this way? If he put himself into it of his own free will, is it right to say his mind has been predisposed by the action of a predecessor? Suppose for the sake of argument, he bought the building plot subject to the easement, knowing at the time of the restriction it imposed on the use of the land resources. He would have acted freely. In buying the plot, he would have voluntarily acquiesced in the dispositions already made and the consequential impact of them on future planning. The same could be said of one who entertains the offer of a derivative inferior proprietary land unit, as when a prospective tenant is negotiating the terms of a lease with a potential landlord. If the owner of the proprietary land unit subject to the easement of light had come to the plot by inheritance or by some other process of law over which he had no mandate of choice, there would have been no point in time when he would have been free to reject or accept what had been done, and in facing the problem of future plans he would have to embark from a state of affairs in which he had had no previous opportunity to acquiesce.

A predisposing function affecting the use of resources in a par-ticular proprietary land unit invariably arises from decisions taken by antecessors in title to the proprietary land unit's affected area or decisions taken over the use of resources in another proprietary land unit. One proprietary land unit will not affect another by exerting a predisposing function over it unless the two units are either in a relationship of a superior to an inferior unit or are con-tiguous with each other or in such close proximity that what is done in one affects what can be done in the other. In the following two

71

chapters, this theme will be more thoroughly examined. At this point of introduction of the concept of the predisposing function, we need only sum up our remarks so far by setting the general case that a proprietary land unit will be subjected to a predisposing function as a consequence of:

(a) inheritance; or
(b) the relationship of superior and inferior interests; or
(c) contiguity or close proximity of proprietary land units.

All causes of frustration turning the course of a plan in a particular direction or holding up the execution of proposals are not in themselves the result of predisposing functions. The holder of a proprietary land unit who has to trim his ideas to take account of items of fixed equipment, which are either on land resources with high soil affinity factors or which in the current circumstances are too costly to remove, is not affected by a predisposing function simply on account of the check on manœuvrability. He would only be so affected if items causing his present predicament were the provision of earlier demands over which he, the current holder, had no authority and in the outcome of which he had willy-nilly to acquiesce.

The items too costly to remove at present might become mobile in the future. The winds of fortune can change and if in the future they blow from a more congenial financial quarter they can liberate the present immobile resources and enable the holder of the proprietary land unit to plan in accordance with his wishes. The predisposing function of the proprietary land unit imposes restraints upon the powers of ownership and not economic restraints. The function immediately affects the abstract attributes of the proprietary land unit. Until the holder of the unit acquires it he cannot experience any predisposing force. If for any reason prior notice of restrictions has been given and a voluntary acquiescence of them made the predisposing function is rendered nugatory. The force of the predisposing function arises from decisions being taken at a time when he who is affected by the force is deprived of the power of property rights over the use of the resources affected.

Inheritance or bequest, the devolution of a past title upon a present holder, as such, does not exert a predisposing function. Inheritance may pass to the current holder of a proprietary land unit property rights over the resources of the unit which in every way are a passport to freedom over the use and the disposition of them. Once in possession of the unit, the heir is free to manœuvre his resources at will and he experiences no sense of frustration or setback. Inheritance principally determines the plans for the future use of resources when the inherited proprietary land unit has attributes, physical and abstract, which are at variance with those necessary to carry out what the heir would wish and thus they enforce him to plan the use of his resources in a way contrary to what he would have done but for the predisposing function and decisions made by predecessors in title. The successor in title may have burdened the land revenue of a proprietary land unit in perpetuity to meet an annuity. The annuity could cut into income and reduce the means of accumulating monetary reserves as consociate wealth and thus curtail the range of decisions about what could be done with the resources of the proprietary land unit. Or a dead hand from the past can deprive the present of all incentive to improve its lot not from lack of funds but through a prohibition censoring the use of them by limiting the range of rights of property over them. An example of this type found in Scotland from time to time is a fee within which a fiar has carved out an alimentary life rent. The holder of the life rent is positively discouraged from investing consociate wealth in the development of the land subject to it and he who stands in the shoes of the original grantor sees the land over which he is the fiar neglected and starved of capital and investment. Both would doubtless have done otherwise but the earlier decision of the original fiar to create an alimentary life rent has imposed restrictions in accordance with which they have to plan the use of the resources in their respective proprietary land units.

A predisposing function over a superior or inferior proprietary land unit is not an unavoidable consequence of the relationship between units of this type. Indeed, as we have just noted, one who freely negotiates a lease with the owner of an interest in land is not under coercion in any way. If he does not like the attributes of the inferior unit which the lease will create he will not take it. And so it is reciprocally with the holder of the superior unit: he takes the initiative and thus dictates the terms on which the inferior unit will be held. He is free to do so, no predisposing function forces his hand one way or another.

The power of a predisposing function can arise between a superior and inferior unit subsequently to the initial act of creation and as a consequence of the relationship between the units. The key to understanding how this can happen is the existence of two distinct units related to each other but complete in their respective autonomies. The holder of the inferior unit may act in a way contrary to the agreed terms and cause the holder of the superior unit to

73

react. His reactions must lead in themselves to unintended and unexpected changes of plan forced on him by a decision taken by the holder of another unit, in this case the inferior unit, which decision affects the circumstances within his own unit. A tenant who quits the land he hires, for example, and leaves it impoverished contrary to the terms of a lease which requires him to farm in a husbandlike manner and to leave the holding in working trim, puts the landlord, the holder of the superior unit, in a position from which he must take decisions for the use of the resources of the superior unit which he would not have had to take if the tenant had acted as he, the holder of the superior unit, had intended and expected him to act. And so it is reciprocally. Long ago the tenants of the honour of all England holding as tenants in capite under King John were forced to a campaign of defiance against the king, not because he was a weak and evil sovereign but because as holder of the paramount seignory out of which their fees were carved he had acted contrary to his agreement with them. His breach of faith caused them to change plans and to use the resources of the estates in fee they held of the king to ends they never intended. The action taken by the king as paramount siegneur over the lands of his seignory exerted a predisposing function over the fees of his tenants.

The predisposing function that can arise as a consequence of contiguity or proximity is again the result of decisions taken in one unit which affect what can and is done in another. The mere fact of contiguous boundaries is not the cause. The holder of a proprietary land unit who buys it or takes it as a gift does so with his eyes open and is clearly aware of the common boundaries with neighbouring units and of the location of units nearby. What he cannot foresee and what in the future may cause him to change plans unexpectedly and against his deepest wishes are actions taken by neighbours, contiguous or nearby, over the resources of their respective units which affect his circumstances, environmental, economic or social, and force him to re-plan his own resources in a way he would never have intended. Forced is not too strong a word here. It does not imply that the neighbours whose actions cause him to re-plan dictate in any way what he should do. His circumstances have changed as a result of their actions. He cannot avoid experiencing the change and cannot plan as if it had not happened; in this sense his mind is affected against his will to make a new plan and the novel circumstances predispose his thinking.

Chapter V

RECIPROCITY OF RELATIONSHIPS

Two of the three standard derivations of predisposing functions, described in the previous chapter, are specific relationships between proprietary land units. These and other relationships between proprietary land units are the sources not only of predisposing functions; they are the seats of other reciprocities whose inevitable give-and-take fundamentally affects what can be done with the land resources of the units and the attributes of the units themselves. These other reciprocities unlike the predisposing functions are the consequence of actions which all parties could have foreseen and any one party could have avoided by not voluntarily entering into the relationship with the other. The type and content of agreements which set up reciprocal relationships between the holders of proprietary land units are innumerable. What we are concerned with in this analysis are the relationships themselves and the issues which devolve from each in the general case. There are four basic relationships to which all relationships between independent proprietary land units can be reduced. They are the four simple alternatives which the very nature of a proprietary land unit postulates. A proprietary land unit can be sold, given away, bequeathed or inherited; it must lie somewhere on the map with boundaries which do not make sense except between neighbours; and smaller derivatives can always be carved out of it. Thus it is that we have our four relationships: as between superior and inferior units; as between parties to *inter vivos* transactions—vendors and purchasers, donors and donees; as between units which lie side by side or nearby each other; as between beneficiaries and a testator. It is our purpose now to examine these relationships and discover standard forms of the issues which emanate from them and hence how the very relationships themselves affect what is and what can be done with the resources of the proprietary land units involved.

Reciprocities Between Superior and Inferior Units
We will start with the relationship between the superior and the

inferior proprietary land unit. But prior to dealing with and trying to discover standard forms of the issues to which such a relationship gives birth, we must have a clearer notion of what is meant by a superior proprietary land unit and of its reciprocal, the inferior unit.

A superior proprietary land unit has an inescapable polar relationship with an inferior one. At this stage we shall only look in one direction, from the superior pole towards the inferior and deal with the issues which must arise from the very relationship of a lesser unit carved out of a greater. At any particular moment a superior proprietary land unit may have greater physical proportions than the inferior unit carved out of it and have a formidable power of control over the use made of the land resources of the inferior unit. Yet, superiority is not ascribed to it on account of these magnitudes. Superior units are often similar in physical size to the inferior unit and the boundaries of each coincide. Not infrequently the holder of the inferior unit enjoys for a time the lion's share of the property rights of user. The essential criterion of the superior units is its matrix form. It is the womb wherein the inferior was conceived and the source of its very life and being. So, there is no argument: it must be greater in duration than the inferior; for short periods cannot beget long periods. Furthermore, when the inferior unit is created, the superior unit must be adequate to endow the inferior unit with the particular bundle of rights[1] peculiar to its nature. An inferior proprietary land unit cannot have rights of property which the superior unit has no power to bestow. Rights bestowed upon the inferior at its inception flow back as it were to join the bundle of rights of the superior and do so at that moment of paradox when the life of the inferior unit ends and the superior unit loses its identity as a superior of another.

Because the superior proprietary land unit is the origin of the inferior unit the holder of it in the very process of creation moulds the attributes of the inferior unit and thereby engineers the framework within which the holder must make his decisions. At first sight this may look like a predisposing function and the framework set up thereby;[2] but as we have seen this is not really so, for he who will become the holder of the inferior unit and be limited in his actions by the creative intentions of the holder of the superior unit is still free, before he assumes a title to the inferior unit, to object to the ideas of the holder of the superior unit and decline the proposed inferior unit. It is possible from the very nature of the superior–inferior relationship to specify the ways in which, in the general case, a holder of a superior unit can set the frame within

[1] Above, p. 30. [2] Above, pp. 70–74.

which the inferior lies and which moulds in some measure the cast of the abstract attributes and the form of the land resources which the holder of the inferior unit will have to plan and re-plan. The ways are as follows:

  i. determining duration;
 ii. influencing the liquidity of assets;
iii. imposing monetary restraints;
 iv. imposing direct prohibitions;
  v. setting limits to possible motives;
 vi. determining proprietary character form; and
vii. meeting the predisposing function of the superior unit.

Determination of Duration. The duration of all inferior units is primarily determined by the life of the superior unit out of which they are carved, no matter what form the inferior unit takes. From its very nature and the relationship between the two units an inferior unit must always be contained within the time limits of the superior unit as they are foreseeable at the time when the inferior unit is formed. The key word here is 'foreseeable': the duration of the superior unit may be shortened by an unforeseeable contingency which because unforeseeable would not affect the potentialities of the superior unit at the time when the inferior unit was carved out of it. An owner of a superior unit of inheritance, for example, could shorten its duration by giving it away or selling it to another whose heirs will take after him and not after the vendor or donor. Such an event is unpredictable. Until it occurs, the proprietary land unit vesting in the superior holder is an inheritance out of which he has the power to carve any number of inferior units whose duration will fall just short of or exactly coincide with the passing of life of the last of the line of his descendants. Whether gift or sale or some other form of alienation of the inheritance by the holder of the superior unit will terminate the duration of an inferior unit carved out of it is a matter of particular law; it does not affect the original control of the superior unit over the duration and status of the inferior unit. The duration of an inferior unit at the time of its creation is set within the predictable and definable time limits of the superior unit as these time limits are known at the instant when the inferior is created.

Turn to the particular for the moment and look at the leasehold within the idiom of English land law. One who holds a 60-year lease cannot grant a sublease of 99 years out of it; he can sublet for 40 years and carve a term of 40 years out of the 60 years. We

77

LAND USE

have then an hierarchical order; two derivatives, one, the shorter, immediately derived from the other and both carved out of a common superior unit which could be a fee simple. The holder of the larger of the two derivatives, the lessee of 60 years, could assign at any time his reversion contingent upon the 40-year sublease. The assignment may or may not terminate the 40-year sublease; the issue depending upon the circumstances and the state of the law at the time. However, this is irrelevant, for the point we are making is that at the time when the sub-term of 40 years was carved out of the 60 years, the holder of the latter had a title to a term long enough to accommodate comfortably the 40-year sub-term—the foreseeable duration of the superior unit was sufficient to sustain the granting of the sub-term. Or, again, the longevity of a superior unit of inheritance may end unexpectedly upon the line of heirs running out; at any time before the last of the line was beyond the stage of having issue (itself a problematical determinant) there could be carved out of the inheritance inferior units of any length of fixed term, for the accepted future of a line of heirs is always longer than a determinate period of years.

The duration of the term of an inferior proprietary land unit has a reciprocal action: it sets the boundaries of time within which the holder of the unit has to contain the periods and process[3] of his planning of the land resources of the unit; and as a reciprocal, the length of time within which the holder of the superior unit suffers voluntarily a curtailment of rights of property to enter and use the land resources for his own purposes. Planning of proprietary land resources within both the inferior and the superior land units must come to terms with these time thresholds. Yet, the setting of the drama is from the beginning in the hands of the holder of the superior unit; he decides just how long a duration the inferior unit shall have from its start. How he decides will invariably have a significant bearing upon the manner in which the holder of the inferior unit uses his resources. A tenant who has the means to make capital improvements to the land will not do so if the duration of his tenancy falls short of the expected span of useful life of the improvements. Much of the backwardness of rural Ireland in the early nineteenth century was due to the uncertainty of the duration of tenancies held by the tenants; the yearly and shorter tenancies provoked the best of them to 'farm to quit' rather than to 'farm to sit'. Duration is an attribute of the proprietary land unit of primary importance to the planning and use of its resources. And time is in the gift of the holder of the superior unit.

[3] Above, p. 39.

78

There are no standard periods of duration in the general case. Under different juridical systems the time limit of an inferior interest recognizable at law differs widely. Under English land law, for example, there is only one person who is never tenant and always paramount owner of the superior interest[4]—the Sovereign, of whose supremacy all interests are held. All estates and interests are derivatives. The range of rights, however, is exceedingly wide from the unconditional inheritance of a fee simple absolute[5] to the transient right of agistment of pasture.[6] In less sophisticated societies there is a tendency for the life of the holder to be the determinant of the period of an inferior unit. Certainly it was so in Old England until the learned prelates of the early Church taught the kings, the earls and lesser men to know the advantages of inheritance, of the *jus perpetuum*,[7] over the grant of occupancy under folk-right.

Can we, then, faced with numerous possibilities of duration for inferior proprietary land units, find any common categories in which to cast universal standard types? There is a useful and affirmative answer. In the general case all inferior units are either determinate or indeterminate in duration. Determinate units are those whose duration is certain and predictable from the moment of inception or has become so at a later date. Indeterminate units can be sub-classified according to the following contingencies:

   i. a specific event;
   ii. action at the instance of the holder of the superior unit;
   iii. action at the instance of the holder of the inferior unit.

Units in the first sub-class are held on conditional terms. The duration continues so long as a specified contingency does not happen; when it does the interest terminates. The contingency is usually specified at the initiation of the inferior unit but it can be so determined at a later date. Under trust arrangements in English law, for example, life interests in equity were often created with gift over to a named beneficiary in the event of a specified happening, such as marriage of the holder of the inferior unit. An interesting

[4] F. Pollock and F. W. Maitland, *The History of English Law Before the Time of Edward I*. Vol. 1 (Cambridge, 2nd Edn, 1952), Vol. 1, p. 234.

[5] R. E. Megarry and H. R. Wade, *The Law of Real Property* (Stevens and Sons, London, 3rd Edn, 1966), p. 68.

[6] J. Muir Watt, *Agricultural Holdings* (Sweet and Maxwell, London, 11th Edn, 1959), p. 41.

[7] E. John, *Land Tenure in Early England* (Leicester University Press, 1960), p. 11.

example from the African tenancies is the *abusa*[8] principle whereby the inferior unit continues so long as buildings on the land remain standing.[9]

Units of the second sub-class are those whose duration can be cut short by the action of the holder of the superior land unit. The power of curtailment can be absolute or conditional; an example of the latter is the power of the landlord in English law to terminate a yearly tenancy by legally giving notice to quit.[10] The power of the holder of the superior unit may, however, be quite arbitrary; as is often found in traditional societies in the Middle East and Asia today where a derivative right of cultivation is held at the arbitrary will of the landowner, and was clearly seen in medieval times in England when the villein of a manor would hold his base tenement *ad voluntatem domini*.[11]

The third subclass covers those units where the power of termination of the duration of the unit is in the hands of the holder of the unit himself. This power is distinct from the power of assignment or sale when the present holder passes his inferior interest to another and pulls out of it himself. We are concerned here, not with the cessation of an interest through transfer or alienation but with an absolute termination and ending. Often, both in English law and elsewhere, the holder of an inferior interest, be he a tenant or in the eyes of the law one with a different status, will have power to terminate his tenancy or interest by a formal notice to quit. By giving notice to quit he terminates the interest for himself and for all other people and in this respect the termination differs from that which transpires when the holder of an inferior interest assigns it or sells it.

Duration can be immediately affected by changing the proprietary character form of the proprietary land unit. Whether or not the law recognizes derivatives or allodial forms of ownership of land and of interests in land, whenever the property rights are held by individual real persons – the essential criterion of the simple proprietary character form[12] – the longest duration such a proprietary land unit can have will be conterminous with the line of descendants from the original holder of the unit drawn in accordance with the principles of devotion under local land law. Because humans are mortal, the probability exists in such titles of an end, unpredictable,

---

[8] N. A. Ollennu, *Principles of Customary Land Law in Ghana* (Sweet and Maxwell, London, 1962), p. 81.

[9] *ibid.*, p. 91.   [10] R. E. Megarry and H. R. Wade, *op. cit.*, p. 641.

[11] P. Vinogradoff, *Villainage in England* (Oxford, 1892), p. 173.

[12] Above, p. 31.

but a certain contingency to be reckoned with. Future prospects change if the title to the proprietary land unit is held by one of the immortals from the world of fictitious persons[13]—a corporation or other *persona ficta* can never be an heir. An heir takes by birth and by blood. Neither can a corporation have heirs. But he who inherits a proprietary land unit as an heir can grant the inheritance to a fictitious person, a corporation. The effect would be to give an endless life to the proprietary land unit—duration, world without end. Where there are heirs, the title runs from he who holds it now to he who shall come after, as God deems wise to draw the line of heirs; but if he who holds can never die or pass away no one can nor ever shall come after. The corporation or other fictitious person can be dissolved, wound up or terminated in some other way but such an event is not predictable *ab initio* at the time when the grant to the body corporate or fictitious person was made; what is foreseeable at that time is an interminable life, a duration without end.

Incorporation of communal holding is an aspect of modern land reform in many parts of the world and is often resorted to to gain the advantages of large-scale economies over the disadvantages of fragmented holdings held by individual peasants. An interesting variety of these reforms is the establishment of corporations within which the erstwhile holders of simple but tiny proprietary land units become shareholders of the body corporate. The great land reforms of the last ten years in Iran are now experimenting with this kind of change and land is passing into the hands of giant immortals in the form of farm corporations.[14]

If, therefore, the holder of a superior proprietary land unit is one of the immortals and holds the unit by a title which together with the proprietary character form of the holder establish a proprietorship of endless duration, it is within the realms of logical possibility for the holder of the superior unit to carve out of his superiority an inferior unit to be held itself by a body corporate and thus to grip the future in a dead hand that can never die.[15]

Complications and contradictions arise in the real world when the holder of a superior land unit whose proprietary character form is not fictitious but simple grants an inferior land unit from his inheritance to a fictitious holder or allows the holder of the inferior unit to assign his interest to a corporation or fictitious person. No contradictions develop when the body corporate holds an inferior

---

[13] Above, p. 32.

[14] D. R. Denman, 'Land Reform in Iran' (Part 2), *Agriculture*, Vol. 77, No. 9, p. 437.

[15] F. Pollock and F. W. Maitland, *op. cit.* (Vol. 1), p. 334.

unit of fixed duration within the time span of the superior unit. Difficulties come when the inferior units are themselves contingent upon death. Then, by assigning them or giving them to an immortal, the duration become endless and this would be a contradiction if the superior unit were held in a simple proprietary character form continuing at most until the line of heirs runs out. The principles of law could take care of this situation either by causing the inferior unit carved out of the simple superior proprietary land unit to cease when the superior unit terminated or by requiring whoever comes by the land which erstwhile belonged to the terminated superior unit to recognize the inferior unit vesting in the fictitious holder of it. In this event there would be no contradiction at the time when the inferior unit was first granted to the fictitious holder of it because at that moment the foreseeable duration of the superior unit was no longer than the line of heirs or descendants of the grantor, and the duration of the inferior unit would be presumed to run for no longer than the life of the superior unit—the arbitrary interference of the law at some future date was unforeseeable at the moment of creation of the inferior unit.

Grave disadvantages can develop for the holders of superior units when, by some transaction, inferior units carved out of the superior fall into the hands of immortals. This grave possibility was the grounds for the mortmain statutes of medieval England. The modern example is the creation of practically endless inferior land units in agricultural holdings in the United Kingdom as happens when a tenancy of an agricultural holding is granted or assigned to a joint stock company. Statute law[16] authorizes a landlord's notice to quit issued on a tenant to be vetoed by the Agricultural Land Tribunal except when the tenant dies. Corporations never die and when they are tenants the one chance of avoiding the veto of the Tribunal is lost.

Influences Affecting the Liquidity of Assets. A holder of an inferior proprietary land unit who erects buildings on the land and invests in other forms of improvement and fixed equipment faces the problem of liquidity. Money has been sunk in the land. The duration of the inferior land unit is likely to be determinate and perhaps short; how can the capital be recovered? Equipment with an effective economic life shorter than the duration of the inferior unit provokes no problem. Problems arise when the effective life of the fixed equipment and improvements is likely to outrun the duration of the inferior proprietary land unit. Two of the fundamentals of tenancy

16 See S. 3 of the Agriculture Act, 1958.

reforms[17] are, indeed, security of tenure and compensation for unexhausted capital improvements. The shorter the tenure the greater the need for liquidity provisions in the lease. Tenants are discouraged from providing the services of fixed equipment to continue after the termination of tenancy without some promise of compensation for the lost value. Services that continue into the future can be valued and capitalized at the end of the tenancy. To the holder of the inferior unit the value of any investments he makes in the land is the sum of the right to receive the future income from them during the continuation of the inferior unit plus the value of the right to receive the equivalent of the capital value of them at the end of the tenancy. Total value is a function of potential liquidity. If the buildings and equipment cannot be converted into money or some other form of liquidity, they have no value to the holder of the inferior unit at the end of the duration of the unit.

It follows that the use a holder of an inferior land unit makes of his land resources and consociate wealth[18] will greatly depend upon the terms made by the holder of the superior land unit concerning the duration of the inferior unit and compensation for unexhausted improvements and fixed equipment. If the compensation provisions are right, the holder of the superior unit will not be out of pocket in having to meet the claims of the holder of the inferior unit for, when the compensation provisions are fair, the compensation to the inferior holder measures the value of the reciprocal benefit enjoyed by the holder of the superior unit at the time he comes into possession at the end of the duration of the inferior unit. The holder of the superior unit, however, can deter the holder of the inferior unit from making the best use of it by refusing either to grant him duration sufficient in time to see out the effective life of any improvements made by him or to compensate him fairly for what he does. Inadequate provisions for liquidity are likely to have an adverse reciprocal effect upon the fortunes of both the holder of the superior unit and the holder of the inferior unit.

These general observations would be somewhat pointless for the purpose of our analysis if it were not possible to reduce to simple standard form the means of solving the liquidity problem of inferior proprietary land units. The holder of an inferior proprietary land unit can be given opportunities to exchange for cash investments made by him in the form of land resources of the unit. Right of

---

[17] D. R. Denman, 'A Classification of Universal Land Problems', *Contemporary Problems of Land Ownership* (Cambridge, 1962), p. 13.
[18] Below, Ch. IX ff.

exchange, in the general case, can be fashioned in one of the following three ways:

    i. removal of the fixed asset;
    ii. sale of the asset *in situ*;
    iii. compensation in money to the value of the asset.

While it is possible to solve the liquidity problem by any one of the three expedients, the holder of the superior proprietary land unit may withhold the power of exchange; in which event whatever the holder of the inferior unit has affixed or attached to the land he must leave in the land at the end of the duration of his unit—*quicquid plantatur solo solo cedit*. That such an insensitive attitude can prevail is written clear enough in the tragic history of Irish tenant-right.[19] Where the attitude obtains, the holder of the inferior unit has little inducement to develop the land resources of his unit by long-term capital investment and land improvement. Whether he does so or not, will be governed by the state of the market for inferior units. At the end of the eighteenth century in Britain the land hunger was so insatiable that farming tenants were willing to take holdings on six months' security and spend large sums of money in erecting farmsteads, fences and roadways—those were the days of the improvement leases.[20]

The practical virtue of the right of removal is more dependent than any of the other alternatives on the age and the condition of the fixed asset. A fixture whose useful life is nearly over is not likely to be worth the trouble and cost of removal. As a practical expedient, removal is also a doubtful course when a fixture is deeply embedded in the soil or a structure, as with the installation of electrical wiring; the sheer act of physical removal can damage the asset to the point where its function and value are entirely lost.

The extension of the duration of the inferior unit either in its original constitutional status – for example, as a lease – or by taking on new rights – as in the case of emblements[21] – is not a solution of the liquidity problem at all. The liquidity problem springs from the inconsistency between the life of the proprietary land unit and the life of capital improvements in the soil; if the life of the unit is extended to coincide with the life span of the improvement, the problem is not solved but circumvented; the circumstances which provoke it are changed and it does not arise.

[19] C. Woodham-Smith, *The Great Hunger* (Hamish Hamilton, London, 1962).
[20] A. G. Ruston and D. Witney, Hooton Pagnell: *The Agricultural Evolution of a Yorkshire Village* (Edward Arnold, London, 1934), p. 321.
[21] R. E. Megarry and H. R. Wade, *op. cit.*, p. 111.

There are in the general case questions which must always be answered if the holder of the inferior unit is to be given the right of removal. Is the right to be unconditional? Conditions may be laid down on the cautionary principle of Portia and Shylock – only a pound of flesh to be removed – which so restricts the right as to make it virtually nugatory. Another general question is whether the right shall be limited to the assets actually provided by the holder of the inferior unit himself or whether it should extend to other assets acquired by him from predecessors. And a third general question asks whether the right of removal shall be supplementary or alternative to some other form of liquidity provision – can the holder of the inferior unit choose whether to claim compensation for or remove what he has provided, or must he be content with following only one of the two courses, either removal or compensation?

Sales *in situ* raise questions concerning the purchaser. Who or what is he? There are three answers in the general case:

  i. the holder of the superior unit;
  ii. the holder of the inferior unit immediately following; and
  iii. the assignee of the holder of the inferior unit.

Purchase by the holder of the superior unit differs little in the practical event from the payment of compensation. At law there could be a distinction between allowing a man to buy and requiring him to pay compensation. As we shall see, compensation raises awkward questions of value concepts while a sale would not take place unless both parties were satisfied with the market transaction. Where the holder of a newly created inferior land unit buys a fixture or improvement from the holder of a unit that has just ended, the holder of the superior unit may have to be a party to the transaction if the purchaser wishes in future to have a subsequent right of disposal or compensation.[22] Under an assignment, the holder of the inferior unit steps out of this title and the assignee steps in. Where money consideration passes, it is usually in part a payment for improvements and other capital investments made by the assignor in the land resources of the unit. The purchase price which will be paid will depend upon what rights to eventual removal or compensation the assignor had to convey. If he had none, the assignee would only be willing to pay for the present value of the right to the future benefits from the improvements over the certain duration the inferior unit.

Compensation, unlike the receipts from a sale, is conventional and has to be defined and formalized. The holder of any inferior

[22] J. Muir Watt, *op. cit.*, Ch. 6.

land unit who has a right of compensation has some means of forecasting what amount of liquid cash he might eventually receive for his improvement or fixture, but he who intends to sell out has no sure yardstick by which he can predict what the amount might be. The holder of an inferior unit who, because of his rights to compensation, has some knowledge of what he might receive can plan his affairs and the disposition of the land resources of his unit with a surer hand than one who has to rely on a sale.

Universal law governing the relationship between the parties may intervene and give to the one the power to enforce the other party to sell to him the coveted asset.[23] With improvements and fixed assets this is unusual. In the general case, like all compulsory acquisition arrangements, it will be dependent upon a legal formula of compensation should he who owns the right to the coveted possession be unwilling to volunteer its sale. In these circumstances there is little to distinguish sale from outright payment of compensation. The viewpoints, however, are divergent: compensation can, as we shall see, be looked at in a number of different ways; while a sale is essentially a market transaction and some reference to costs and prices in the market must be incorporated in the price formula.

Compensation is even more likely to be a subject for which the legislator makes provision. Nevertheless, the experience of landlord and tenant relationships in England shows that the naked forces of economic expediency and social justice do move the holders of superior units to compensate voluntarily the holders of inferior counterparts, and to do so with such consistency that the law creates and deduces usages and customs from their attitude.[24] In passing, we should remind ourselves of the recent development under the continental codes where economic forces have carried the day and jurists are formulating new notions of property rights between parties so as to give the holder of an inferior proprietary land unit a property in compensation—*la propriété commerciale*.[25]

Law which gives into the hand of the holder of an inferior proprietary land unit the power to claim compensation from the holder of the superior counterpart does not as a consequence of the provision dissociate the two units and separate the inferior altogether from the influence of the superior. The holder of an inferior unit authorized by law to make a claim against the holder of the superior cannot avoid the attitudes and moods of the latter. Up against one

[23] See S. 13 (3) of the Agricultural Holdings Act, 1948.

[24] D. R. Denman, *Tenant-Right Valuation* (Heffer, Cambridge, 1942), p. 37.

[25] D. Bastian, *La Propriete Commerciale en Droit Français*, Travaux de l'Association Henri Capitant (1950).

who is unscrupulous, litigious and cunning, the holder of the inferior unit is likely to be more cautious and careful in committing his capital to finance long-term improvements to the land than he would be if the holder of the superior unit were open-handed, liberal and sympathetic. Safeguarding the interests of the holder of the inferior unit does not insulate him and his decision-making processes from the predisposing function of the superior unit[26] or from the general influence of the attitudes and intentions of the holder of that unit.

Furthermore, provision in law of a right to claim compensation against the holder of the superior unit may in the allocation of rights between the parties tie the hands of both more firmly together. Compensation, for example, may be conditional upon the holder of the superior unit approving what is done on the inferior unit or demanding notice of intention.[27]

In the general case, therefore, compensation as a means of solving the liquidity problem of the holder of the inferior unit is either not provided at all and therefore admits no solution of it or, if it is advanced, depends on the sanctions of:

    i. *ad hoc* agreement;
    ii. local usage or custom;
    iii. unconditional statutory authority;
    iv. conditional statutory authority.

Where in the form of one of the four alternatives just mentioned compensation is provided, the rights and reciprocities between the parties must settle certain practical issues. In the general case these are:

    i. the procedures to be followed in making a claim;
    ii. the number and type of the fixed assets or improvements eligible for compensation; and
    iii. the measure of the amount of compensation.

Drawing the lines of give-and-take between the parties in thees matters can either aggravate or ease tensions. Too great a leniency towards the holder of the inferior unit will diminish the sense of managerial responsibility at the superior end of the transaction; while too restrictive a code binding the hand of the holder of the inferior unit will induce apathy and blunt the effectiveness of the law. Sometimes these nice points are the forum of political thrust and counter-thrust between reformers and traditionalists, especially over the measure and range of compensation. To the traditionalists

---

[26] Below, pp. 96–98   [27] J. Muir Watt, *op. cit.*, Ch. 6.

the measure can appear to give too much to the holder of the inferior unit. This can be redressed, however, by limiting the range of compensation. The measure of compensation loses some of its glitter when the occasions to gain by it are hedged about by knotty legal restrictions.

Imposition of Monetary Restraints. We have noted[28] how consociate wealth is a critical factor of influence upon the degree of latitude to plan and re-plan the asset structure of a total fortune and the combination of the land resources of the proprietary land unit. The status of the proprietary land unit is of no consequence and does not affect the validity of the principle. Hence anything that impinges upon the capacity of the holder of the inferior unit to accumulate the wealth has an indirect but important bearing upon his ultimate power to take advantage of such manœuvrability as may be inherent among the land resources of a proprietary land unit when planning or re-planning their combinations. The degree of autonomy enjoyed by the holder of an inferior land unit in relation to a superior[29] varies widely. Usually some form of render or payment is reserved by the latter and extracted from the former and, as a general rule, the greater the autonomy enjoyed by the holder of the inferior unit, the less in monetary value or its equivalent will the payment or render be. What is rendered may have an intrinsic value of its own and be of little monetary value; as when the vassal holding the fee of Glenormiston in Peeblesshire renders on request to the reigning monarch of Scotland, the immediate and paramount seigneur of the superior proprietary land unit, one red rose grown from the soil of Glenormiston.[30]

Between landlords and tenants current payments are usually some form of rent. Whatever form the payments, renders and extractions may take, if they are too severe they can cripple inferior unit holder's facilities for saving money and accumulating consociate wealth, and thus indirectly diminish the planning powers over the land resources of the unit.

The impact of rent or other current payments as consideration for the rights of property over an inferior land unit upon the finances of the holder of the unit and his ability to accumulate capital is more patent, presented as it is in capital terms, when the holder of the superior unit does not demand full rack value of the current

[28] Above, p. 55.   [29] Above, p. 76.

[30] Her Majesty Queen Elizabeth II asked the proprietor of the Glenormiston Estate for the payment of one red rose, on July 1, 1967. This was presented to Her Majesty at the gates of Glenormiston.

payments (rent, etc.) but reduces it in consideration of a premium or lump sum paid by the holder of the inferior unit, usually when the latter takes possession. Premiums are the aggregate of the discounted values of future sums receivable over the duration of the inferior unit; the sums represent the difference between the expected gross payments (rack rents) and the payments actually demanded.

Rents and similar current payments are sometimes deliberately reduced below market value by the holder of the superior unit so as to enable the holder of the inferior unit to have the means of accumulating funds to finance capital for long-term improvements. In the general case, it is to the advantage of the holder of the superior unit to reduce rent which he could otherwise demand when the difference discounted to the present time between full payments (rent) and the reduced payments for each year over the duration of the inferior unit is less than the value of the improvement to be made by the inferior holder discounted over a similar period.[31]

In societies where a money economy is not fully developed, as in parts of Africa today subject to customary tenures, and as prevailed over much of England until the fifteenth century, renders to the holders of superior units are made in kind or in services. In practical terms the upshot is the same as if rent were paid in money. He who makes the renders, the holder of the inferior unit, is using land resources to produce what is rendered instead of using them to his own advantage, or is giving service to the advantage of the holder of the superior unit and neglecting to cultivate, manage or improve his own resources. Labour on the superior unit is labour lost to the inferior unit. Piers Plowman after William Langland laments over his lot and complains of the labour extractions of his lord (holder of superior unit) that leave his own crops to the mercy of weeds, pests and an ill-prepared tilth. Clearly it is in the interests of the holder of the superior unit not to press the imbalance too far and so burden the inferior unit that the holder of it cannot support himself and render his just dues and other predial payments.

Imposition of Direct Prohibitions. The property rights which mould abstract attributes of inferior proprietary land units can be curtailed by the holder of the superior unit imposing specific restrictions on the use of the land resources of the inferior proprietary land unit. In the general case these prohibitions are either:

---

[31] Note: This would not be so if, as is the case under S. (48) of the Agricultural Holdings Act, 1948, the amount of compensation to be paid for a new improvement is the increase attributable to the improvement in the value of the agricultural holding as a holding.

    i. express; or
   ii. induced.

In the former category they are embodied in the terms of a bargain struck between the parties when the inferior unit is carved out of the superior; the alternative prohibitions are induced by the very process of creating an inferior unit.

Prohibitions can be classified also as:

  (a) personal;
  (b) predial;
  (c) private; and
  (d) universal.

Where a bargain is struck between two parties binding one to a course of action in the interests of the other, there is always an element of the personal in the transaction—a covenantee–covenantor relationship, hand to hand. Persons (including *personae fictae*) are involved. But sometimes the relationship beween the parties is a special one in that each has a peculiar *modus standi* touching a particular parcel or area of land, as when an inferior land unit is carved out of a superior one. The purpose of the bargain is to establish the relationship between the parties but it is done by reference to the land itself. The primary element is the land and what is personal is secondary; whosoever steps into the shoes of one of the parties, therefore, stands in a special relationship to the land which was the subject of the original bargain. In this event where the bargain imposes a prohibition on one of the parties we can say of the prohibition that it is predial rather than personal.

At the same time, the prohibition which touches the land is one arising from an *ad hoc* bargain struck voluntarily and deliberately between the two parties; it is in this sense a private affair and the creation of a deliberately expressed agreement. Induced prohibitions on the contrary are implied by universal law from the relationship between the parties, and to the land and to each other. No specific action is taken by the parties to strike a bargain giving rise to the prohibition—the prohibition is incidental to another bargain creating a relationship which evokes an assumption at law. Hence the induced prohibitions are invariably universal and predial.

In sum, therefore, a general classification of prohibitions between the holders of inferior and superior land units can be:

A: express—(1, *a*) personal,
                          (2, *a*) private;
      —(1, *b*) predial,
                          (2, *b*) private;
                          (2, *c*) universal.
B: induced; predial; universal.

A few examples will help to clarify the distinctions. When in the early Middle Ages a derivative interest of a term certain was carved out of a fee, he who held the term and paid a render for it was called a fermor. The ancient Statute of Marlbridge (1267) stated that 'fermors during their terms shall not make waste'. Wherever the relationship of a fermor to the land existed, the law expressly imposed the prohibition against making waste of the land—an express, predial, universal prohibition (A: (1, *b*), (2, *c*)). The ancient statute is quite explicit ('shall not make waste'). Any act which destroyed or damaged the substance of or the title to the superior unit was waste; hence it was waste to plough a pasture (substance) and it was waste to sow a pasture (blurring evidence of title).[32] Whoever would plan the use of the land resources of the inferior unit had his hands tied by the doctrine of waste. Although express and explicit, the prohibition made no sense except in relationship to the land and was thus predial (1, *b*) and all fermors were subject to it, it was, thus, also universal (2, *c*).

It will be seen from the classification above that prohibitions of a personal kind are never other than private and are always express, never induced. Such universal obligations as, a man shall not derogate from this own grant,[33] are not personal but predial since the grant in the present context is of an interest in land and the creation of an inferior derivative land unit. The classification is, it should be remembered, concerned with property rights pertaining to the superior–inferior proprietary relationship. In the main, they will be those which touch the land, its use and misuse—that is predial. What is personal will in the nature of things be such as could not be imputed from the relationship of the parties to the land, hence personal in a marked sense and such as could not be universal without losing its personal character.

A covenanted obligation to repair demised premises is the positive counterpart of a covenant prohibiting neglect or dilapidation. It touches the land and yet is essentially a covenant between two clearly

---

[32] G. C. Cheshire, *The Modern Law of Real Property* (Butterworths, 10th Edn, London, 1967), pp. 186, 187.
[33] *ibid.*, p. 369.

identifiable parties and voluntarily entered into by them—indicated by the notation in the classification it is (A: (1, *b*), (2, *b*)). A similar prohibition, however, can be induced. Common law in England, in accepting the legal validity of a landlord and tenant relationship of an agricultural holding, will imply an obligation on the part of the tenant to farm the land in a husbandlike manner.[34] Unlike the universal obligation which the thirteenth-century statute imposed on fermors not to make waste, this obligation not to neglect cultivation is not expressed but implied from the existing relationship between the parties—it belongs to class B of induced prohibitions. Another example of this class is the induced obligation binding cultivators holding rights in Iranian villages, before the recent land reform. Cultivators were bound to cultivate the land of the inferior proprietary land units according to the customs of cropping and irrigation and in no other way.[35] The rationale of induced prohibitions is the need to safeguard the land resources of the superior proprietary land unit from the exploits of the holder of the inferior unit. The latter is bound, therefore, by the notions of the holder of the superior unit of what is damaging; ignorance could do harm to both parties, as happened in eighteenth-century England when tenants were prohibited from experimenting with the new crops of a pioneering agriculture.

Prohibitions when dishonoured can lead to a claim for recompense against the holder of the inferior unit at the time when the duration of the unit runs out. This counter-claim by the holder of the superior unit is analogous to the claim of the holder of the inferior unit for compensation for improvements. What was said earlier[36] about values and viewpoints is equally valid here. Both parties will take the contingencies of a counter-claim into account when planning the use of their resources. When, for example, money is dear, the holder of the inferior unit would probably deliberately neglect his repairs, creating a claim for dilapidations or damages to set against his own claim for compensation for improvements rather than spend money on repairs in the course of the duration of the inferior unit.

Express prohibitions which satisfy the category (A: (1, *a*), (2, *a*)), personal and private, must be such that they do not in any way relate to the relationship of the superior and inferior holders of the land. If they do so, they will take on something of a predial character. Essentially they are particular and peculiar to some

---

[34] See, for instance, J. Muir Watt, *op. cit.*, pp. 390–1.

[35] A. K. S. Lambton, *Landlord and Peasant in Persia* (Oxford University Press, 1953), pp. 172 ff.

[36] Above, p. 85.

private understanding between the parties and cannot have any universal relevance. An example of what is meant would be an agreement by the holder of an inferior unit to vote in a parliamentary election for a particular party. If breach of such an agreement were to lead to the termination of the inferior unit, the prohibition itself would be predial as touching the land and not personal, although private nonetheless.

At this point we face a contradiction. Prohibitions of a private kind whose breach puts in jeopardy the title to the inferior unit must be predial and not personal. The truly personal is so detached from all interests in the land that the prohibition itself could hardly be regarded as one of the rights in the bundle of property rights contributing to the abstract attributes of a proprietary land unit. As we are concerned only to classify prohibitions which concern the proprietary land unit, it would perhaps be logical to simplify the above classification in the general case to:

A: express and predial—
   i. private;
  ii. universal.
B. induced and predial—universal.

Setting Limits to Possible Motives. Motive is a subjective impulse. At the moment of origin it is hidden in the citadel of a man's desire, unassailable by others. So it may remain, a pointless fancy and the stuff of dreams. When the primary impulse moves to action and a man declares his hand, motive becomes patent. But it is just then, in the pursuit of action that motives suffer manipulation on the procrustean bed of circumstances. What is at first desired is modified and assimilated with what is possible.

The holder of a superior proprietary land unit cannot reach to the inner motives of the holder of an inferior unit. But the initiative is with the former. The holder of the superior unit is the creator of the inferior unit in the first place. Nothing obligatory impels him. And he who would take an inferior unit from the holder of the superior unit must be prepared to modify, if need be, his own motive to agree with the limits set by the attributes of the inferior unit as the creative hand of the holder of the superior unit has moulded them.

In the general case there are two ways in which the creative decisions of the holder of the superior unit can cause the holder of an inferior one to modify his motive or the pursuits associated with the achievement of them.

93

One way is negative and belongs to the prohibitions within the express predial and private category defined above. The holder of the inferior unit gets it on condition that the resources will not be used for specified purposes; or, turned the other way about, on the condition that he uses the resources only for stated purposes. Where the survival instinct is strong and is related to property in land, landowners are easily moved to make attempts to tie the hands of relatives to hold particular lands. Leases are offered or other forms of derivative interests and are made conditional upon the lessee or the holder residing in a named seat and maintaining it. On a more mundane front, derivative interests in shops or commercial premises are granted to holders binding them to use the resources of the inferior unit for a named trade, profession or commercial undertaking.

The alternative way is a positive one. The creation of the inferior unit is not an end in itself but a means to something ulterior. With the ulterior intention in mind, the holder of land resources carves out of his property rights a derivative unit, fashioned and equipped with attributes and resources suited to the end in view. The holder of the inferior unit has it to occupy and use for the set pursuit and for so long as he and the holder of the superior unit are bent upon it. Service tenancies, well known in the realm of land tenures, are simple examples of what is meant. Farmers, to use a typical illustration, provide houses for farm workers who occupy them as tenants as long as they remain in the employ of the farmers. A station-master often resides in a special house within the curtilage of the station, as a tenant holding an inferior proprietary land unit but only for as long as he is the station-master. The brewery trade in England has its tied houses occupied by tenants who ply the trade of retailers of the brewery's products.

There is nothing underhand or clandestine about such arrangements. Holders of the inferior proprietary land units are perfectly well aware of what is expected of them and of the limits set by the attributes of the units; they know about these things before they commit themselves to accepting title to the units. The ulterior motive of the holder of the superior unit is recognized and accepted. The holder of the inferior unit is not required to re-plan his resources to meet some unexpected predisposing turn of events.[37] His is a reciprocal relationship of a special kind with the holder of the superior land unit. Each benefits. The former by getting possession of the land resources he desires; and the latter by the receipt of consideration for the grant of the derivative unit and by the satis-

[37] Above, pp. 70–74

faction of knowing that the resources are being put to a purpose he wishes to see pursued and which in many cases is a special activity in close association with the use to which other land resources are put within the superior land unit—the station-master's house is the subject of a special tenancy and occupancy which plays an essential part in the use as a railway undertaking of the land resources of the superior land unit.

Determination of the Proprietary Character Form. Since proprietary character form is a critical feature of all proprietary land units, the holder of a superior land unit can exercise an immediate and considerable influence over the use made of the resources of the inferior unit he creates by his choice of a holder of the derivative unit.

A fiduciary owner by definition is bound by specific loyalties.[38] His motive is set by the measure to which he is faithful to them. A clear choice is before him—not primarily of this or that use of resources but of loyalty or disloyalty. When the holder of a superior land unit carves out of it an inferior unit and gives the derivative into the hands of a fiduciary holder he takes a decision which sets on a clear course the use of the resources of the unit derived from his superior rights. And he acts in a similar fashion when he agrees to the assignment of an inferior unit from the hands of a simple holder into the hands of a fiduciary one.

The fictitious proprietary character form is an artefact of law, a synthetic personality built up by a charter of incorporation or some other convention. The body corporate, the *persona ficta*, is begotten by an incorporating event, behind which is a deliberate intention; bodies corporate are not created *in vacuo*. The intention and the creative act would be pointless unless the communally conceived body were given executive powers equal to the achievement of the end in view. Like everything else about the fictitious *persona*, its powers of action have no natural genesis and the incorporate act must bestow them as a logical step in the creation process. The fictitious proprietary form, as with the fiduciary, has within its nature a specific end to achieve and the use of land resources in a proprietary land unit of that character will reflect the personality of the fictitious holder and the intention behind the act of incorporation or other creative act which brought the fictitious personality into being.

Imagine a limited company incorporated to run a school. Land is essential. The company may hold within the confines of a proprietary

[38] Above, p. 32.

land unit more land than it needs for the administration and teaching responsibilities but some at least of what it holds must be put to these purposes. Land resources in excess of administration and teaching requirements will be put to uses which reflect the innate character of the company and the intentions behind the act which incorporated it. The use of the resources will indeed serve schooling and the school—perhaps as an investment. If so, it would not be anything other than a school investment; that is one aimed at meeting the financial needs of the school *qua* school. Decisions taken about the ratio of capital to income would show this and might well contrast markedly with decisions which would have been taken if the land resources were held by a real person whose proprietary character form was simple. The use of all the land resources of the proprietary land unit held by the school company and not only those put to administrative and teaching uses is affected by the special proprietary character form of the company.

The holder of a superior proprietary land unit may not himself be responsible for an act of incorporation or for bringing into being a *persona ficta*. But if he grants an inferior land unit within his own superiority to such a body or permits the holder of an inferior unit to assign the unit to such a body, he, the holder of the superior unit, enters into a reciprocal relationship which sets the use of the resources of the inferior land unit on a specific course. Clearly, a landowner who grants a lease of land to the school company just mentioned will be benefiting the company by the grant of the land resources to it and himself, both from the financial consideration to be rendered for the property rights in the resources and also by having the land resources over which he holds his own property rights put to uses of which he obviously approves. Putting the resources into the hands of the company is tantamount on his part to committing them to a specific use and he does so by granting the inferior unit to a holder whose proprietary character form is consonant with that use.

Meeting the Predisposing Function of the Superior Unit. An inferior proprietary land unit carved out of a superior one is complete in all its attributes, abstract and physical. In the general case, we must assume that the holder of the unit would not have taken it if its attributes seemed likely to frustrate his plans for the use of its land resources. At the beginning there was agreement between the parties and the holder of the inferior land unit saw ways and means of establishing functional complementarity between the additions he intended to make to the resources and between assets of a chattel nature, items in the inventory of the consociate wealth of the unit, which would be brought on to and worked with the land resources. Implicit in this assumption are property rights among the bundle of rights contributing to the abstract attributes of the unit which would sanction the use of the land resources along the lines intended by the holder of the unit.

Because of the consensus between the holders of the superior and inferior, the superior unit cannot be said to exercise a predisposing function over the affairs and plans of the inferior unit. Predisposing functions originate in the unexpected as when the holder of one of a pair of land units in a particular relationship with each other[39] does something unexpected and unpredictable.

The unexpected, however, may not emanate from the 'other'; from, for example, what a holder of the superior unit does to upset the plans of the holder of an inferior unit. Circumstances change. New ideas arise. Motives alter and do so unexpectedly for the holder of a proprietary land unit, quite independently of what happens to the resources of other units in relationship with the unit held. And the unexpected calls for new plans, perhaps for new motives.

Faced with the unexpected from this or any other quarter the holder of an inferior proprietary land unit will invariably find that the new plans must take their cues from the attributes of the unit as these were fashioned by the holder of the superior proprietary land unit who devised them at the time when the inferior land unit was first carved out of the superior. The superior unit at this point can be said to exert a predisposing function over the inferior, although the unexpected turn of events did not originate with the superior unit.

The reciprocal relationship between the superior and the inferior units will be expressed at this point by the degree of freedom of action enjoyed by the holder of the inferior unit to redistribute, enlarge or alter the physical attributes of the unit – in particular the fixed assets and their land quotas – so as to create the maximum functional complementarity between each of them and other items of wealth used in conjunction with the inferior land unit; to create combinations with the highest coefficients of contribution to the achievement of motive, whether old or new.

In the general case, the control or lack of it exercised by the superior land unit over the freedom to re-plan the land resources of the inferior land unit will take one or another of the following forms:

[39] Below, pp. 99–123ff.

    i. absolute control with no freedom of decision-making for the holder of the inferior unit;

    ii. complete freedom of decision-making for the holder of the inferior unit;

    iii. freedom for the holder of the inferior unit dependent upon the *ad hoc* sanction granted by the holder of the superior unit, with or without compensation; or

    iv. authority in the hands of the holder of the inferior unit to demand the alteration by the holder of the superior unit of the physical attributes of the inferior.

The exercise of authority under (iv) above by the holder of the inferior unit could be a mixed blessing. The rearrangement of the physical attributes of the inferior unit by the holder of the superior might have both a beneficial and a detrimental effect on the holder of the inferior unit. For example, life tenants under the Settled Land Acts of English law[40] have power to cause the trustees of the settlement to pay for the costs of improvements and fixed equipment of a certain type for the benefit of the life tenant out of trust capital. Compliance with the request of a life tenant by the trustees would have an immediate consequence, presumably a beneficial one, for the affairs of the inferior proprietary land unit held by the tenant for life. It could be, however, that forcing the hand of the trustees at that particular time would cause them to realize investments at an unpropitious moment and thereby unduly to deplete the reserves of the trust and to diminish the chances of the trustees being able to meet similar requests in the future.

[40] R. E. Megarry and H. R. Wade, *op. cit.*, pp. 353–5.

Chapter VI

PREDISPOSING FUNCTION OF ANTECEDENTS

The holder of a proprietary land unit when making plans for the use of the land resources of the unit sometimes has his mind predisposed in a certain direction by decisions taken by others of which he has had no prior notice or knowledge and in which he has had no opportunity to acquiesce. We have already noted the circumstances in which decisions of this kind can exert a predisposing function.[1] Two proprietary land units are in a special relationship with each other and what is done in one of them affects the planning of the other. In these circumstances the predisposing function of the one over the other is always contingent upon the unexpected; what is done today was unpredictable yesterday. It is possible, however, for the outcome of decisions taken in the past to operate as a predisposing function upon the present; what was done yesterday tells upon the decisions of today. Antecedent decisions exert in their own peculiar way a predisposing function on the present. This form of predisposing function was not overlooked in the earlier reference to the concept. We distinguish it here from the other types of predisposing function because the antecedent decisions of the past can cover a far wider range of effectiveness than what is logically possible within the scope of the unexpected and the unpredictable decisions of the present. And the uniqueness of the predisposing function of antecedents warrants a more detailed presentation than we have given to the other types of predisposing function.

To clear the way ahead, we must be certain what is meant by antecedents. As already understood, the purchaser of a proprietary land unit presumably has full knowledge of what he is doing when he buys—*caveat emptor*, he acts on his own volition. The attributes and the combination of the resources of the unit are patent and known to him. Full cognizance prior to purchase makes of the act

[1] Above, pp. 72, 73.

of purchase an acquiescence of the attributes, character, make-up and potentialities of what is bought. The purchaser was a free agent to accept or reject what the vendor offered. The attributes of the purchased unit, although the outcome of past decisions taken before the act of purchase, do not exert a predisposing function over the present decision-making of the purchaser. They may gravely restrict the manoeuvrability within the purchased unit but an act of restriction of this sort is not what is meant by a predisposing function. Antecedents in the present context are not vendors and donors, parties to *inter vivos* transactions, whose prior decisions have shaped what they now sell or give away. Nor by antecedents do we mean the holders of superior proprietary land units whose action in the past was responsible for the form and attributes of a present inferior land unit.

The predisposing functions of antecedents, without exception, operate within a single proprietary land unit and not between land units as the other types do. An antecedent was the holder in the past of a proprietary land unit existent now, the title to which vests in the present holder by a process of law beyond his power to control decisively.

Inheritance is the most unambiguous form of this process. Inheritance is the process by which a successor at law succeeds to a proprietary title. Before his succession, the successor was an heir, one who stood in a particular blood or cognatic relationship with an antecessor—'only God can make an heir' the ancients used to say.[2] As successor he comes into his own through no action on his part. Common parlance often confuses the heir and the legatee. A legatee is a beneficiary consequent upon a testamentary disposition, and does not succeed as of right—someone must make a will in his favour. Nevertheless, legatees and beneficiaries under a will are for all practical purposes in the same position as heirs in that the title to what is vested in them by the process of law comes to them in the first instance through an act of disposition over which they have no decisive voice. Antecedents, therefore, are predecessors in a line of succeeding donors whose titles pass by testamentary dispositions or intestate devolution.

Incidence of the Predisposing Function of Antecedents
Unlike other forms of predisposing functions, that which is peculiar to decisions made by antecedents is contingent not so much upon the unexpected as upon the involuntary processes of law. The successor or legatee faces the full consequences of the function at the

[2] R. E. Megarry and H. R. Wade, *The Law of Real Property* (Stevens and Sons, London, 3rd Edn, 1966), p. 69.

moment the title to the proprietary land unit passes to him. He feels the weight of the function then upon his decisions. In the general case, the predisposing function of antecedents is likely to be less frequently felt by the holder of a proprietary land unit than the predisposing functions of unexpected decisions taken by the holders of other proprietary land units.[3] While in this respect the predisposing function of antecedents is less formidable than the other types, there is another side to its character which gives it a relatively greater weight. The range of its effectiveness can be very much wider because it can affect the attributes of a proprietary land unit and the combinations of its land resources in a way beyond the competence of decisions taken in other land units. Indeed the range of potential incidence is wide and in the general case covers:

   i. restraints on use;
  ii. imposition of charges;
 iii. creation of inferior units;
  iv. creation of collateral rights;
   v. limited and contingent descent;
  vi. proprietary character form; and
 vii. combinations of resources.

Restraints on Use. The holder of a proprietary land unit who wants to control the use to which the land resources of the unit will be put in the future has two alternative courses to follow. He can make a grant *inter vivos* between himself and a trustee or a body of trustees on the condition that the unit is held by the trustee(s) as a fiduciary holder on trust to fulfil in the future the wishes of himself, the grantor; or by legacy, to take effect on his death, he can leave the unit in trust for the fulfilment of similar wishes. Alternatively, the holder of the unit can convey it now or dispose of it by testamentary gift on the condition that he who takes will use the resources in a specified way and in the event of a cessation of the specified use there will be a gift over to someone else. Only the former course has any chance of success. Under the latter of the two alternatives, a holder of the unit could disregard the conditions restricting the use of the land resources with impunity, unless the one destined to acquire the title to the unit, he who waited *spes successionis*, was sufficiently vigilant to take action as occasion required it. Action taken to enforce a transfer of title would not in itself be a cast-iron defence of the original intentions of the primary donor. He who took at the first remove would need to be subjected to similar

3 Above, p. 74.

101

restrictions and conditions and this would mean a third watch-dog couched ready for action at the second remove. Moreover a change of title by definition[4] dispenses of the old unit and creates a new one and is an occasion when he who takes the unit is presumed to do so with full knowledge of and acquiescence in what has hitherto been done on the unit. The predisposing function of any antecedents does not survive beyond the transfer. Only by testamentary gift to trustees to use the unit as specified can a present holder impose restrictions on the use of the resources in a way which will exert a predisposing function over the future planning of the use of the resources, and do so in a manner which is within the realms of practical fulfilment.

Imposition of Charges. A holder of a proprietary land unit who is an antecedent of the present holder might have used the wealth of the land resources of the unit as security for payment of debts or as a source of annuities. The charges may have been imposed in his lifetime and continued thereafter or under the provisions of a will and be thus contingent upon his death. The means used by the antecedent holder to assure the continuation of the charges will affect the force and significance of any predisposing function they may impose. In the general case there are three forms of device. The entire unit may be put into the hands of a fiduciary holder for the express purpose of using the resources of the unit to meet the charges and financial obligations; in this event the antecedent holder will have caused the unit to pass out of the hands of heirs, and will in fact have broken the line of natural inheritance and terminated the duration of the unit held by him.[5] The predisposing function would then operate between two units, not side by side but in chronological juxtaposition.[6] Another device is the creation of an inferior unit to be held by the creditor or recipient of the benefit of the debt or charge until it is repaid or redeemed in some way. Both of these devices are dealt with in more general terms later on.[7] The other device requires what is virtually the creation of a form of property right in the recipient other than an inferior land unit carved out of the unit carrying the charge or other financial obligations. Exactly how such form is envisaged at law is a technical matter for the lawyers—under English land law, for example, it could take the form of a rent charge on the land of the burdened unit. However the law may see it, within the connotations of the present analysis it will have the effect of cutting down the bundle of rights in the proprietary land unit which passes from the antecedent holder to the present one.

Something must be said further about the predisposing function of

4 Above, p. 30.   5 Above, pp. 80–81.   6 Above, pp. 71–72.   7 Below, p. 104

antecedent debts as we shall not have another opportunity of discussing it. He who takes the proprietary land unit from the hand of the antecedent will willy-nilly in making plans for the future use of the land resources have to turn his mind to the implications of the debt or charges secured by the rights in the hands of the recipients. What he can and does do will be conditioned by the terms on which the financial obligations are imposed and in particular whether or not he, the new holder of the unit, can rid his title of them by paying them off at once in a lump sum. If he is permitted to do this, he may decide to proceed on those lines; in which event he will either have to realize part of the land resources of the unit and re-plan the remainder, or realize assets among the consociate wealth of the unit, or burden the land resources by a newly negotiated loan to service the paying off of the appropriated debt and charges. Alternatively the debt and charges handed down may be left where they are; in which case the gross income generated by the land resources of the unit and by the consociate wealth will have to bear the burden of meeting current payments of interest or annuity and thus reduce the net income and its power to provide for the future accumulation of capital. If he is clever, the new holder may be able to realign the combination of the land resources and consociate assets so as to generate an increase of income sufficient to meet the running demands of the debt and charges passed on to his hand by the antecedent in title. However it is done and whatever is done will be the consequence of the predisposing function of the decision of the antecedent exerting its influence over the planning of the resources of the unit.

Creation of Inferior Units. The holder of an inferior proprietary land unit who comes by the unit either as a legatee or by inheritance and succession is immediately aware of the predisposing function of an antecedent. At some stage in the past, the inferior unit will have come into the possession of the antecedent holder. Either he must have been the original holder and have negotiated the terms and conditions of the unit with the superior holder or have taken an assignment of the unit from one who had had it previously. In either event, the decision to take the unit set the course for the future and now requires the one who now holds the unit, by succession or by testamentary gift, to plan the land resources within the confines of an inferior unit. The antecedent's decisions are responsible for the type of unit, the form of its attributes and the combination of its land resources as at the time when the unit passes at death to the new holder.

Consider now the case of the holder of a superior land unit who

103

comes by it through inheritance or as a legacy. At some time in the past the antecedent holder must either have carved out of his unit the inferior unit now responsible for the superior–inferior relationship or he will have acquired the superior unit by purchase or other means complete with the inferior unit in existence. The holder who takes possession of the unit from the antecedent holder will be bound when planning the future use of the land resources to respect the privity created by the antecedent holder between the superior and the inferior unit and to this extent and in this way will experience the force of the predisposing function of the decisions of the antecedent holder. The requirements of law might cause the inferior unit created by the antecedent holder of the superior unit to end with the passing of the superior unit at death to a legatee. In this event, no predisposing function would operate unless the holder of the inferior unit defied the law and the new holder of the superior unit had to plan in consequence his immediate programme for the use of the resources and make allowance for delayed occupancy and litigation costs.

The impact of the predisposing function of an antecedent who had carved an inferior proprietary land unit out of his superior unit can be either short-lived or prolonged. In the general case, the terms on which the inferior unit is held will either permit the holder of the superior unit to terminate the inferior unit at his own instance and forthwith; or require him to recognize the presence of the inferior unit and to do so until the holder of the inferior unit acts so as to terminate it or the duration of the unit runs out by effluxion of time. The inferior unit, for example, may have been conceived by the antecedent holder of the superior unit merely to secure a loan from the holder of the inferior unit to the credit of the holder of the superior unit; the continued existence of the inferior unit would be conditional upon the outstanding loan. The new holder of the superior unit if he paid off the loan would terminate the inferior unit. While the funding operation would doubtless cause repercussions for some time and affect the asset structure of the new holder's fortune and bear upon his planning, the influence of it would be comparatively short-lived compared with the long-term impact on the planning of the resources of the superior unit by the creation of a lease for twenty-one years, held by a tenant expressly for farming purposes and who had fulfilled and intended in the future to fulfil the tenurial obligations.

Creation of Collateral Rights. A proprietary land unit may as a feature of its abstract attributes boast of collateral rights beyond the aggregate of the rights of property over the land of the unit and which are cardinal to its very being. Collateral rights are in the nature of things, appendages, and invariably arise to serve a distinct purpose and to equip the proprietary land unit in a discriminate way. Because collaterals are discriminate time works upon them to do what it does not and cannot do to the amalgam of rights which constitute property in the unit itself.

Consider one who is the present successor in an unbroken inheritance of ten generations upon whom title to a proprietary land unit has devolved. Presumably such a person would not wish to use the land resources of the unit in the same way as his sixteenth-century predecessors would have done. Within the general limitations set by the abstract attributes of the unit, he would by virtue of the rights of property over the land unit be free to use the resources to meet the needs of the twentieth century; the property rights are not discriminate and within limits can be invoked to sanction putting the resources to uses consonant as well with the sixteenth century's requirements as with those of the twentieth century. With the collateral rights of the unit he would not have a corresponding freedom. Each collateral right would have been granted and taken for a particular purpose germane to the needs of the time when it was established and which gives the right a distinctive unalterable functional character. The proprietary character of the right would not change with the changing years, and the time could well come when the purpose for which it was originally established is no longer congruent with the needs of the holder of the unit. Thus it comes about that collateral rights acquired by antecedent holders no longer serve a unit in a useful way; and if such rights were granted rather than taken by an antecedent holder to serve the needs of a contiguous proprietary land unit they can stultify the planning policies of the present day. Collaterals in a word become anachronistic, out of character with the requirements of the present hour, yet legally potent.

The predisposing function executed by such anachronisms can sometimes have strange effects. Take, for example, the manorial common rights of English agrarian history. Long ago these rights enabled the holders of proprietary land units to which they were appurtenant to pasture cattle and other beasts on neighbouring ground (the servient tenement) and to take timber, minerals and other resources from the land for the benefit of the unit they served. In numerous places today the rights are still legally valid but the need to exercise them has long passed. The proprietary land units subject to them cannot be developed in ways which would contravene

105

or conflict with the rights of common. So the land resources of the burdened proprietary land units lie undeveloped and all too frequently unused and surrendered to nature and the conquest of thicket and scrub so dense that the land is useless for even public recreation. Such can be the outcome of the predisposing function of decisions taken long ago to permit tenants of a manor to exercise rights of common over the land which at the time was a constituent feature of the physical attributes of the proprietary land unit of the lord of the manor.

Limited and Contingent Descent. The duration of an inferior proprietary land unit within the definition adopted for our analysis may be certain or uncertain. However it may terminate, the unit is by its very nature a derivative; that is to say its property rights are held from a superior source which is contemporary with the duration of the unit and is reciprocal to it. This point needs to be reiterated to distinguish an inferior proprietary land unit from one whose duration may or may not terminate on the happening of a specific event. A unit may, for example, be held on as near absolute terms as an ordered society can reasonably countenance save for the provision that if a specified event should take place the unit must be handed over to another. There is no superior–inferior relationship between the holder of the unit and the person who may eventually take it, should the contingency happen. Even an inheritance can pass from successor to successor until the happening of a certain event terminates the title and causes it to vest in another. Some time in the past, however, provision must have been made for contingent descent by one who in doing so could have broken an earlier unconditional inheritance.

Such hazards on the title to a proprietary land unit exercise a predisposing function over the planning of the use of the land resources of the unit when the provisions which introduce them were the decisions of an antecedent holder of the unit and the unit passes from him to the present holder as a legacy or succession. The holder of a proprietary land unit whose title to it might terminate on the happening of a specific event will be influenced in the planning of the use of his land resources by the extent to which his own hand and actions can control the critical happening. Where for example the title to the unit will remain intact for so long as the present holder is single, the destiny of the title is linked up immediately with the domestic affairs of the holder which are more or less within his discretion to control. The holder enjoys in this instance a high degree of autonomy, and can plan accordingly. The higher the degree of

106

uncertainty attending the critical event the more difficult it is for the holder of the unit to plan the use of the resources; as when his title remains intact unless and until his first born reaches the age of twenty-one. Sometimes interests in land depend upon unpredictable future events and the counterpart future interests that could arise should the contingency happen. The title-holder of the unit is then a beneficiary whose interests are the responsibility of a trustee or other fiduciary holder with appropriate property rights in the same physical land resources. He who stands to take over the title to the unit on the occurrence of the specified contingency has a proprietary land unit *in futuro* but for all practical purposes there would be little point for anyone so situated to plan the use of the land resources in expectancy.

Proprietary Character Form. The proprietary character form of a proprietary land unit can, as we have seen,[8] radically affect motive and the pursuits followed by the holder of the unit to achieve it: the fiduciary holder must be true to the faith held in him and the body corporate must not go beyond the powers of its constitution. Any action of an antecedent holder which sets the proprietary character form of a unit can exert a predisposing function of considerable moment over the affairs of the unit.

Let us remind ourselves that the predisposing function of antecedents only operates in the event of inheritance or the passage of a unit as a legacy to a beneficiary. Inheritance presupposes a blood relationship linking heir with heir. The body corporate cannot take by inheritance. An antecedent action therefore cannot establish a line of descent to fictitious holders. It is, however, within the realms of reasonable practicality for a unit to be put into the hands of a real person (simple proprietary character form) to be held by him for the benefit of another and thus in a fiduciary capacity; and to do so in such a manner that the heirs of the fiduciary holder take after him. Successors in title will in these circumstances find themselves, as death takes toll of their antecedents, holders of proprietary land units and committed to plan and manage the land resources to a predetermined end for the benefit of others.

Combination of Resources. One who inherits a proprietary land unit or possesses it through some other form of involuntary acquisition will, in the nature of things, when he comes to take stock and plan the future combinations of land resources, often find among the lay-outs of fixed equipment and other features of the inventory of

8 Above, p. 95.

107

resources resulting from the prior decisions of antecedents, departure points which are incongruous with his initial intentions. Circumstances, prospects, motives which made sense of the decisions of the antecessor at the time when he took the decisions have no parallel now; yet it is the past order of things and the decisions congruent with them which have left the physical resources of today distributed as the present holder finds them.

Infallible prescience is not an attribute of human consciousness. No one can blame an antecessor for taking steps far out of line with the best intentions of a successor who will come after him. The successor in his turn will make like decisions, as blameless or blameworthy. Could the Junker landowners of Lower Silesia who at the turn of the century set out farmsteads and estates to match the prevalent pattern of practice and tradition have foreseen the day some fifty years later when these very lay-outs would be the combinations of land and physical assets on which a Marxian-inspired peasantry would have to base plans for the disposition of compulsory collective farms (*kolkhoz*)? Even so, some holders of proprietary land units will never seriously attempt to look beyond their own established allotted span of life or occupancy to planning processes under successors, although they are not wholly incurious of the future, its implications and eventual demands. With others the future never seems to feature in their thinking at all. Decisions of these denizens of the ephemeral are of fortuitous consequence to those who come after them.

Yet so inept are we in judging the future and its needs that one who plans the combinations of his land resources today as if he were to be the master of the future generations can make as grave a misjudgement as the ephemerals whose prognostications reach no further than a few years. Imagine for a moment, the circumstances of a young man who has inherited an extensive stretch of woodlands. When the title vests in him the woodlands are immature. They were planted by an antecessor who at the time had two alternative views of the future: either he would live long enough to see the timber mature well and earn for the capital invested in the land, planting and other outlays a satisfactory rate of interest; or, should he die before the woodlands mature, the woodlands would be a means of relieving the estate at death of part of the burden of inheritance tax which but for the woodland plantings would encumber it. The successor sees things differently in the light of actual circumstances. He is a young man and hard-pressed to find liquid capital to finance his affairs. The woodlands if left to mature will call for running costs over many years and these would have to be met from an over-tight budget to finance an asset that yields no current income. Immature woodland is one of the most concrete of assets and not readily converted to liquidity. If the new holder realizes the wealth, he will have to face the risks of selling an immature investment on a market conditioned to transactions in mature standing timber; moreover the liquid receipts from such a sale would attract an immediate liability to inheritance tax which the woodland if left standing would not have borne. Furthermore, the income from the net realized wealth would be chargeable to income and surtax while the invisible income of trees growing silently into maturity would not be taxed in a corresponding way. An alternative to sale would be to raise a loan on the security of the maturing woodlands; the wisdom of this would depend upon the rate of interest on the loan and the income yielded from the capital raised by it—if the former were likely to be greater than the latter it would be foolish to proceed with the loan. One way of looking at the woodland resources which the new holder cannot adopt is to evaluate them as the antecedent holder did when he planted the trees. The new holder cannot place himself in the shoes of the antecessor as he, the present holder, has made no capital outlay of his own which he can use as an input, an essential factor in such a calculation.

This particular illustration is based on a supposition which is of no small moment to those concerned to understand the incidence of the predisposing functions of antecedents. Among the alternatives open to the new holder was the realization of the wealth of the woodlands through sale; an alternative which he would not have if he as successor or legatee were not permitted to realize the inheritance or legacy. History is witness to a prevalent desire among landowners in general to tie the course of the future devolution of land to a predetermined line of descent from which no generation in the years to come would be permitted to alienate it.[9] The point has previously[10] been made and will bear repetition here that restraint upon the disposal of assets passing by inheritance or bequest aggravates the force of the predisposing function of the decisions of the antecedent proprietor of the land who in the first instance inspired the restraint.

General Note

The present is prisoner of the past: this aphorism sums up all we have been trying to say about the notion of the predisposing functions of antecedents. Some of the primary truths of economic thought and

[9] D. R. Denman, *Origins of Ownership* (Allen and Unwin, London, 1959), p. 110.
[10] Above, p. 73.

social analysis are the common experience of the market place and street corner, and when presented as integral features of a systematic analysis and commented upon discursively appear to be no more than turgid statements of the obvious. Yet, paradoxically, it is the commonplace experiences of everyday taken for granted which, through familiarity, are overlooked and the significance of them never fully recognized, understood and heeded. So it might be with this introduction to the notion of the predisposing function of antecedent decisions. It is of the utmost importance in all period and process analysis to recognize and realize how far and deep the ramifications of present decisions can influence what can be done in the future. This is no less important to the present operators whose decisions are influenced by the ties of the past and whose plans for the future are harnessed to them, than it is for he who, as decision-maker at the present moment, can mortgage the future to his own intent.

Chapter VII

THE RECIPROCAL RELATIONSHIP
OF LATERALS

Laterals: Contiguous and Proximate

We have dealt in some detail with the ways in which the reciprocal relationship between superior and inferior proprietary land units affects the planning of the land resources within each and have touched upon how predisposing functions can arise as special consequences of that relationship. The time relationship between the decisions of yesterday and the decisions of today, between the units of yesterday and the units of today, has also been considered with special emphasis on the predisposing function exerted by antecedent decisions over the present pattern of resources. In introducing these ideas, mention was also made of the predisposing function that can arise as a consequence of the unexpected between units associated with each other in space. This particular form of the predisposing function, however, is one aspect of the general way in which the form and activity of one proprietary land unit can affect others contiguous with it or lying in near proximity to it. When one unit is spatially related to another in this way, we may refer to them both as laterals for the purpose of this analysis. It is necessary now to give some thought to the way in which the reciprocal relationship of laterals can affect the planning of land resources within each.

The morphological theory of capital envisages the formation of a capital structure of an economy made up of the several inventories of numerous combinations of assets, each combination comprising a capital order.[1] When capital is performing perfectly, the items of each capital order are in functional complementarity with each other and each capital order has a like functional relationship with other capital orders immediately associated with it. The capital structure is a honeycomb of capital orders in complementary relationship with each other. When functional complementarity is complete through-

---

[1] Above, p. 37.

111

out the capital structure equilibrium prevails. We can envisage equilibrium in this way and a universal functional complementarity because we are dealing with capital and capital which has a specific function to perform—the maximization of income or the profitability of investment. If the capital orders of two combinations of assets are in a state of disequilibrium because what is wanted for perfection in one is possessed by the other, and vice versa, there will be an exchange of assets and a movement all round towards universal perfection. The exchange will naturally take place because the assets are items of capital in the hands of the owners of them. Each item has a job to do—to perform as capital it should perform ideally in its own particular circumstances. There is no conflict of intent between the holders of each combination of assets. Each is after the same end and thus will willingly exchange with the other the discordant assets. The symphony and the symmetry of a capital structure as the morphological theory of capital sees it are possible because the component parts are all contributing to a single theme—the function of capital and the ownership of capital in an economy.

Plans for the use of land resources within a proprietary land unit take their cue from the motive which prompts the holder of the unit to have and to hold it. At this point the morphological theory of capital deserts us. We cannot argue for a universal structure of land resources replete in all its phases and parts with perfect functional complementarity, because one man's motive for holding a proprietary land unit may be entirely different from the motive which prompts his neighbour. There is no criterion common to both units by which the functional complementarity of land resources in each can be judged, and swops made in the interests of a universal equilibrium. It is of course always possible to dream up abstract notions like the welfare of the community and write fundamental equations to balance positive and negative contributions.[2] But to proceed in this way is to move away from the real world. What determines the pattern of land resources in a particular proprietary land unit is the motive prompting the holder of the unit, not the welfare of the community—an essentially abstract and hypothetical notion.

In every civilized society there is a proprietary structure of land. This is not by any measure analogous to the capital structure of the morphological theory of capital. There is no single theme to fashion a harmony between the several patterns of land resources within the honeycomb of the proprietary structure. Here and there the motives of different holders may be in sympathy with each other and one

[2] See, for instance, D. C. Shoup, *Advance Land Acquisition by Local Governments: A Cost-Benefit Analysis* (University of California, 1970).

may help the other by an adjustment of boundaries, or exchange or rearrangement of fixed equipment. More often than not, motives are in conflict, as when the ideals of freeholders who buy proprietary land units from residential motives are shattered by the motive and planning of the Minister of Transport whose nearby proprietary land unit carries an overhead motorway and creates hell for the residential holders of the contiguous proprietary land units.[3]

A frequent source of conflict between proprietary land units is the disregard which a proprietary structure has for the natural lie of land resources. Nature's equilibria are not consulted. Springs, the very life-source of a prairie may lie wholly within the boundaries of a single proprietary land unit and under the control of the owner of the unit who may use his control to deny the surrounding lands the water which nature would otherwise have given them.[4] Clearly the attributes and planning of land resources in one proprietary land unit can have a radical influence over what can be done on contiguous and nearby units. Units in spatial relationship with each other experience the force of predisposing functions when the holder of one unit makes an unexpected and unpredictable move which cannot be disregarded by the others. A contiguous or nearby unit can exert a predisposing function over the other not as a consequence of a change of plan for its own land resources, but because circumstances have unexpectedly changed and provoked changes in the other unit.[5] Reciprocal relationships between these units, these laterals,[6] give rise not only to predisposing functions but also to mutual influences which affect the planning of resources within the units and which do not emanate from the unexpected; they are obvious, or should have been so, to each holder on the occasion of his voluntary acquisition of the unit.

We proceeded previously[7] to attempt to analyse the incidence of the influences between units in special relationship with each other without separating those influences which exert predisposing functions from those that do not. We shall do the same now. There is a distinction, however, which we shall need to make in the interests of clarity. We shall classify the laterals as 'contiguous' and 'proximate'; the former category to include units which are truly contiguous with each other and the second category to include those which are nearby each other but not contiguous. We shall further

---

[3] See, for instance, D. Jay, 'The cost of urban motoring', *Town and Country Planning*, Vol. 38, No. 2, February, 1970.

[4] W. Calef, *Private Grazing and Public Lands* (University of Chicago Press, 1960), p. 66.

[5] Above, p. 74.   [6] Above, p. 111.   [7] Above, p. Ch. V.

advance the analysis by seeing how the relationship of laterals affects the physical attributes of proprietary land units on the one hand and the abstract attributes on the other.

Physical Attributes and Contiguous Units

The physical attributes of a proprietary land unit can, in the general case, influence those of a proprietary land unit contiguous with it by their bearing upon:

   i. common services;
  ii. conflicting aims; and
 iii. complementary benefits.

Common Services. The substance and structures of certain land resources, especially the soil itself, are by virtue of the contiguity of two or more proprietary land units sometimes shared between the units. The way in which the land resources are used on one unit immediately affects what can be done on the others. Obvious examples apart from the continuum of the virgin soil itself, are access roads, arterial watercourses, drains and dividing walls. A watercourse which gravitates through two proprietary land units, if over-exploited by the holder of the higher of the two will lead to a shortage in the lower, and cause the holder of the latter to re-plan the use of his land resources and perhaps even change his motive for holding the unit. Some types of land resource need to be maintained by the holder of one unit to the benefit of others; as, for example, when an arterial drain serves two units and he whose unit is on the lower ground must keep the drain in good order so as to prevent flooding on the higher unit. Structures standing athwart a common boundary so that, as with a party wall, one portion belonging to one of the units is essential to the support of the other portion pertaining to the contiguous unit provide another example. Sharing land resources in this way may be facilitated by provisions in the law which permit the holder of one unit to claim as of right the maintenance or proper use of the shared resource by the holder of the contiguous unit—as when the holder of a lower unit has a legal claim to the continuous flow of a certain volume of water along a watercourse from a higher and contiguous unit. These rights put the relationship we are dealing with on a different footing. The one holder may not be entirely dependent upon the activities of his neighbour in respect of the common land resource; fate and action are in his own hands to a large extent. The rights are themselves a feature of the abstract attributes of the unit benefiting from them,

114

and are only mentioned here to make the distinction between the circumstances wherein each holder of a contiguous unit is entirely at the mercy of his neighbours—and the use or misuse they make of shared resources—and circumstances in which the law intervenes to give one of the parties special rights either of access to, or control over, the portion of the shared resource in the adjoining unit.

Conflicting Aims. The shared services of a land resource which has a special function to perform, like a watercourse, may be a cause of conflict between two or more proprietary land units. The conflicts arise in a general way between two or more contiguous proprietary land units from the clash of motives and development use patterns. The only common continuum is the land itself, split between the contiguous units. Conflict, the obverse of complementarity, ensues when the land resources on one unit adversely affect what is or would be done on the other.

Conflict reduces or prevents complementarity between the total land resources of contiguous units. Underground rock is the natural complement of the subsoil and surface soil in that it is essential to their support and proper functioning. A proprietary land unit in underground minerals will be horizontally contiguous with the proprietary land unit in the subsoil and surface immediately above it. If the holder of the subterranean land unit cuts shafts and mineral galleries through the supporting rock his actions could let down the surface of the land and cause a total conflict between the land uses of the contiguous units. Inevitably, the holder of the superficial proprietary land unit must take cognizance of what his neighbour is doing and re-plan the use of the disrupted land resources. It is important to note at this point that the adverse effect moves in only one way—from the lower unit to the superficial one. An example of the same principle but from a very different angle can be found off the shores of Annacis Island in the Fraser River as it flows through Vancouver. The island has been developed as a single proprietary land unit with an industrial development use pattern. The river authority has a proprietary land unit in the river bed and waters and this latter is contiguous with the boundary of the Annasis unit along the north-eastern shore-line. In the early days of development, the island benefited by extensive wharfage on to the river along the north-eastern shore. Later the river authority, in order to accelerate the rate of flow of the river and prevent silting, erected a boom off the north-eastern shore of the island but well out in the stream of the river. The boom serves the purpose in the mind of the river authority, the holder of the proprietary land unit containing the river and its bed. But the boom has completely sterilized the wharfage of the north eastern-shore of the island, and caused the holders of the island unit to re-plan radically the use of their resources to provide new means of disposal of goods.

Complementary Benefits. Conflicts are divisive; what is of benefit to one proprietary land unit is harmful to the contiguous neighbours. In contrast, what is done with the land resources of a particular proprietary land unit may benefit not only the holder of the unit on which the development takes place but the potentialities of the land resources of the contiguous units. In other words the attributes of a proprietary land unit and the features of its land resources may be complementary in function with those of the contiguous units. Conflict, as we have just seen, is a one-way process: the advantage gained by one unit results in a reciprocal disadvantage in the other. Complementarity moves two ways, back and forth: the action or development is simultaneously of benefit to the unit on which it takes place and to the contiguous unit.

Complementary benefit may be realized by the recipient unit without any action or deliberate response on the part of the holder of it. A subterranean proprietary land unit used for mining, when developed by cutting galleries in the rock and leaving sufficient undisturbed rock above them to provide a ceiling against the downward pressure of the rock and soil above, provides a complementary benefit to the superficial unit. In this instance the benefit is immediately realized without the holder of the superficial unit doing anything specific; the ceilings which support the galleries in the lower unit support also the subsoil and surface for the upper unit. Another special feature about a complementary development of this kind is that, while after the construction of the ceilings in the lower unit there follows a complementary benefit shared by both units, the upper unit has in fact enjoyed no net gain—the support of the subterranean ceilings is no different from the previous support of the entire rock mass. An example of a complementary net gain where the benefit was realized without any need for action on the part of the recipient would be provided if it could be shown that the boom in the Fraser river, in the story told above, kept the silting sands off the north-eastern shore of the island and secured the protection of the wharves; the holders of the island unit would benefit without having to do anything themselves to secure the benefit. The net gain in this instance would be invisible, since it is only if action had not been taken and the wharves had become silted up that the benefit of a boom in the river would have become apparent. In both of these cases the benefit gained by the passive recipient was a realized benefit, and in consequence the holder of the benefiting unit need not re-plan the use of his land resources in order to reap the advantage to his unit of the developments on the contiguous unit. The complementary benefit can be such that the recipient unit gains an advantage, the full worth of which can only be realized if the holder of the unit reaps its potential by re-planning the use of the land resources of the recipient unit. The daring and far-seeing householder who takes the freehold of a derelict house at a knock-out price in a down-town 'twilight' area, and renovates it with taste and panache, can enhance not only the market value of his own proprietary land unit but the value of the neighbouring residences.[8] The full benefit of the new tone given to the neighbouring units will not be realized until the holders of them recognize the new potentialities and renovate the houses in keeping with the lead given by the pioneer. There is, nonetheless, an element of realized benefit in what the recipient units enjoy even in these circumstances, for those who have them can sell them and reap the value of the new potentialities instead of themselves doing the re-planning and renovating. What would have happened in such an event would have been a change of motive on the part of the holder of the recipient unit as a consequence of the development of the contiguous unit—a residential motive would have given place to something like an entrepreneurial one.

Abstract Attributes and Contiguous Units

The rights and obligations, which for the purpose of our analysis are the fabric of the abstract attributes of a proprietary land unit, set up a reciprocal give-and-take between contiguous units. What we are concerned with now are the reciprocities which arise because of contiguity, and we assume that but for the contiguous boundaries of the respective units they would not arise. The number and nature of them vary with the concepts, theories and principles peculiar to specific juridical and land tenure systems. As before, our interest is with the general order of things and in this particular case to identify the common categories, if any, of the reciprocities which must issue from the pragmatic fact of contiguity. None can avoid the simplest general form of reciprocity which demands the mutual respect by the holders of two contiguous proprietary land units of each other's boundaries. Because X respects the boundary of his neighbour Y's unit, X is subject to an obligation, and Y benefits from an implied

[8] D. R. Denman, *Public appropriation of Unearned Land Values*, Occasional Paper No. 4 (Faculty of Commerce and Administration, University of British Columbia, 1969), p. 12.

right to demand of X the recognition of the boundary when he, X, is planning the use of the land resources of his unit. Apparent in this example of the general form is the even more fundamental principle that between contiguous units, for every obligation binding one of them in favour of the other is a corresponding and reciprocal right or benefit pertaining to that other. A positive right in favour of one has its negative counterpart in the other.

Property rights which stem from the fact of contiguity and add to the bundle of rights which constitute the abstract attributes of a proprietary land unit can in the general case be classified as:

   i. particular rights—
     (a) express; and
     (b) implied;
  ii. general rights, implied.

Particular rights have specificity, have been created to serve a particular purpose and actually or by implication are the outcome of an agreement or covenant between the holders of the respective contiguous units. What is agreed to can by the same token be disallowed. Express particular rights are by definition the subject of a formal and deliberate agreement to which the parties can adhere or from which they may agree to depart. The same flexibility does not pertain to the implied particular rights as the implication is usually incidental to a relationship which in this context is contiguity. Contiguity is the key to our thinking here. We are not concerned with all and every form of express particular right which adds to the sum of a bundle of rights. Our focus of attention is solely on express, particular rights which owe their form, creation and function to contiguity between two or more proprietary land units. A right of access, for example, to X's proprietary land unit over Y's unit could not possibly have been established in favour of X unless the proprietary land units of X and Y were contiguous. Express particular rights will tend to have a wider range of diversity than implied particular rights. But because they are wittingly conceived and agreed to between the parties to serve some particular need of the favoured proprietary land unit at the time of their creation, they can with the passage of the years become anachronistic[9] until the point is reached when what was once a benefit is now a burden, or at best a useless appendage. The right, for example, to a continuous flow of water along a defined watercourse to supply water to a proprietary land unit, used at the time when the right was negotiated as a dairy-farm

[9] D. R. Denman, R. A. Roberts and C. J. F. Smith, *Commons and Village Greens* (Leonard Hill, London, 1967), p. 206.

on condition that the holder of the favoured unit reciprocated by keeping the watercourse clean, will become a burden when the mains of a water company supply the fields. The holder of the favoured unit would have to do sums to show whether it would benefit him more to install piped water and maintain the watercourse in accordance with the agreement, or keep the old supply and the risks of pollution and scarcity and the higher costs of cattle management which go with it. If the entire development pattern of the favoured unit changed from dairy-farming to corn growing and arable farming, the right to the water with its attendant obligation to maintain the watercourse would be an unmitigated burden.

Particular implied rights between contiguous units owe their origin to the way in which the law interprets the incidents of contiguity. If, for example, a wall or fence stands as much on the land of one proprietary land unit as upon the land of another, contiguous with it, it is reasonable to assume in the absence of litigation between the parties that the holder of one unit accepts an obligation to give support to the wall or fence to the benefit of his neighbour, and vice versa. The law may imply mutual obligation either on the ground that it is necessary in order to make sense of the position of the wall standing across the boundary of two separate units; or on the ground that as neither party has challenged the action of the other in putting part of the wall on the other's land, each has tacitly acquiesced in the use of his land in this way and to the mutual rights of support. Many less obvious rights, such as the right of access across the land of a contiguous proprietary land unit may be implied on the grounds of long user. Natural rights are a principle of some legal systems. These are related to natural phenomena shared by contiguous units—as when a river flows across the lands of two units and water from the upper reaches waters the lower unit. The law may recognize a natural right peculiar to the lower unit, to have an undiminished flow of water on to its land from the upper reaches on the contiguous unit. One should, however, guard against the error of assuming that the obvious and the desirable are invariably evidence of implied rights. There is, for example, no implied right under English law in favour of the owner of a freehold proprietary land unit giving him a claim to an open view over the land of a contiguous proprietary land unit.

General rights and obligations are those which do not arise from *ad hoc* agreements, express or implied, but are the privilege or burden of all citizens or of all the members of class within the community—such as landowners. Much will be said of these rights and obligations later on when we shall treat of them comprehensively in relation to

119

the decision-making process within proprietary land units. They are mentioned here for the sake of completeness, for where two or more proprietary land units are contiguous with each other the very contiguity gives a special significance to the run of the rights and obligations between the contiguous units. The common law maxim *'sic utere tuo ut alienum non laedas'*,[10] is, for example, impartial in its general incidence but as between two holders of contiguous proprietary land units becomes specific in a manner which reflects the special relationship between the units and sets up reciprocities of first consequence to the planning of the use of the land resources of the units. If one holder, following the maxim, is to dispose of his land resources so as not to harm his neighbour's interests, he must above all else respect his boundaries[11] and not disturb his neighbour's peace by entering upon his land without leave. Such incidence of the general obligation and right would operate counter-wise to the establishment of mutual respect and quiet enjoyment. Where the rule prevails, what is harmful and what is not, to a neighbouring contiguous proprietary land unit would be questions of fact and not of law. The use of his land resources in the conduct of a particular pursuit by the holder of a proprietary land unit may, one morning, be the cause of an unexpected and successful injunction against him at the instance of his neighbour on the ground that the plan being pursued was detrimental to the use of his contiguous unit. The unexpected and successful action on the part of the neighbour and the enforcement of the defendant to rearrange the plans for the use of his own proprietary land unit, would be an example of the operation of a predisposing function exerted as a consequence of contiguity by the plans for the use of the resources of the unit of the successful litigant over the plans for the use of the resources of the unit of the unsuccessful defendant.

Attributes and Proximate Units

We say two proprietary land units are proximate when geographically they are near enough to one another to set up a field of mutual influence, and yet are not contiguous. Because of proximity, each unit is in a lateral relationship with the other.

The physical attributes of a proprietary land unit in proximate relationship with another unit can influence the use of the land resources of the second unit in the same way, in the general case, as the physical attributes of a unit influence the use of the land resources

[10] P. H. Winfield, *The Law of Tort*, Ed. J. A. Jolowicz and T. Ellis Lewis (Sweet and Maxwell, 7th Edn, London, 1963), p. 395.

[11] Above, p. 52.

of another contiguous with it. The principles of conflicting aims and complementary benefits described above apply to the reciprocities between proximate units as they do to the reciprocities between contiguous units. There is, however, in the general case an important exception. Between two proximate units there can be no common services as these have been defined when classifying the three general ways in which the physical attributes of contiguous units interact upon the use of the land resources of each unit. A watercourse may run through a line of contiguous proprietary land units A, B, C, D, arranged in such a way that A is contiguous with B, B with C, C with D, and D with C. In these locational circumstances, A would be proximate to C and D; B to D; D to B and A; and C to A. The watercourse would flow from D through C and B to A. There would be a common service given by the watercourse to all four units. We could not say, however, that this was a common service shared by A and C, for example, by virtue of their proximate positions. It is common to A and C because A is contiguous with B and B with C; the common status of the service of the watercourse is the consequence of a series of contiguous units, and illustrate the general principle that common services are a feature only of contiguity.

The abstract attributes of two or more proximate proprietary land units are affected by rights and obligations acting reciprocally between the units and classifiable in the same way as the rights which in the general case may modulate the abstract attributes of contiguous units. There are, however, one or two important qualifications of a general order. The particular lateral rights which run between two proximate proprietary land units are more likely to be express than implied. So many of the rights implied between contiguous units are the consequence of the physical affinities of contiguity, affinities which from the nature of things do not exist between two proximate units. Local enactments can provide for rights and obligations between two proximate units, but the usual genesis of these is long user which the law recognizes as grounds for assuming the existence of a usuage, custom or prescriptive right or obligation. Because the proprietary land units are relatively close together some kind of traffic has passed between them over long years, and links have been forged to which the law gives its protection. Villagers holding plots and farmsteads in the Black Forest frequently have the right, associated with the plot, of cutting timber in the nearby natural woodlands according to a well established custom of shifting swards (*allemande*). To the abstract attributes of the proprietary land unit held as a small farm and dwelling are added the lateral rights of systematic timber-cutting in the woodland. The woodland

121

itself would be a dominant feature of the development use pattern of a proprietary land unit held either by a local landowner or by the whole village communally. It is the proximate positioning of the units which have given rise to the taking of wood from the one unit to serve the needs of the plot for fuel and timber over the generations. The proximity of two proprietary land units can also give special point to the application of general rights between two units. The nearer together they are the greater is the influence for good or ill that one exerts over the other. The common law maxim '*sic utere tuo ut alienum no laedas*' will be of no consequence to the holder of a proprietary land unit in Cornwall with regard to what is done by the holder of a unit in Dumfriesshire, 400 miles away.

Note on the Land Cradle

We have been looking at the way a proprietary land unit related to another in time or space or by derivation, can influence the planning of the land resources of the other; how an unexpected turn of events in one unit can predispose the planning of the use of land resources in the other; and how more general reciprocities, foreseeable and consequential to the relationships are voluntarily accepted. Our attention has been on the proprietary land unit, the central theme of our analysis. We have not been and will not be concerned with the use of other forms of wealth. But it is incumbent upon us to note in passing that the attributes of a proprietary land unit can have a decisive influence upon the inventory and function of chattel assets used in association with the land resources of the unit.

Every physical thing makes some demand upon the land. Chattels, *choses mobiles*, cannot exist by themselves, independent of and indifferent to the land, its use and supply. Each several effect, item or article must stand somewhere on land—ships need anchorage and an aircraft its hanger or parking crib. All things in short, lie in a land cradle. The cradle and the provision it makes for accommodating chattel assets depend upon, in any particular case, the attributes of the proprietary land units which honeycomb all land. Recognition of the relationship between an array of assets and the proprietary land unit in which they lie is of the utmost importance to a full understanding of the functional distribution of wealth in a society, but it is only incidental to our main analysis and we can but give it a passing glance.

When the holder of a proprietary land unit furnishes the land with assets he will do so so as to harmonize as neatly as possible the functions of the land resources of the unit and the chattel assets.

122

The land resources are by nature relatively less mobile. Consequently their pattern will tend to anticipate what the inventory of the chattel assets shall be. The holder of a freehold proprietary land unit who puts his land resources to dairy-farming must needs look to the make up and distribution of the land resources of the unit in deciding the size of his dairy herd, especially in climates where cattle have to be in-wintered. The shape of the land cradle is the prima facie determinant of any inventory of chattels selected for a set purpose.

The aim will be functional complementarity between the land resources and the chattels. The influence of the attributes of a proprietary land unit will not be unduly felt where a choice of chattels can be made to function harmoniously with the land resources so as to achieve the fulfilment of the motive of the holder of the proprietary land unit. Choice will be made to achieve the greatest joint contribution between chattels and land resources towards satisfying the motive. While harmony and functional complementarity may prevail, it is not the same thing as achieving full satisfaction. The holder of a residential proprietary land unit may find he has enough space on the land surface to park a car but insufficient consociate wealth to finance both a car and the erection of a garage over the space. Doubtless he will procure the car – as he has space to park it – and achieve as much residential user satisfaction as he can in this way. There is thus functional complementarity between the land used for parking and the car, but not so as fully to achieve the motive of the holder of the proprietary land unit. In these circumstances it should be noted that the size of the parking space available, that is the particular shape and size of a feature of the land resources, would determine what the maximum size of the car could be to be parked on the land and used in association with the proprietary land unit to achieve the residential motive of the holder of it. Where two or more proprietary land units share the same land and the holder of one unit has a dominant authority over the others, as with a superior and inferior relationship, the risks of disharmony are greater between the land resources of the proprietary land unit which gives rights of occupancy and the assortment of assets used by the occupier, than they would be where only one proprietary land unit accounted for the use and occupancy of the land.

Chapter VIII

THE LAW OF PROPRIETARY MAGNITUDES AND UNIVERSAL PROVISIONS

Before we introduce a new aspect of our theme, let us take a quick glance back over the road we have come. Behind all we have said, is the simple notion that the use of land is decided by those who own it; we have avoided the word ownership because it has more than one meaning for lawyers. We have kept to the general idea of proprietary rights and have identified the proprietary land unit as the area of land and resources to which a man's proprietary rights pertain to give him the power of positive decision-making. The use of land and resources is planned within each unit. Ideally, land and the fixed assets upon it should complement each other in the fulfilment of a plan, the objective of which depends upon the motive of the holder of the property rights. Proprietary land units are formed in different ways. These have standard forms and one unit is influenced by what happens on others.

So far then, we have directed attention upon the individual units themselves and their relationships with one another. Now we must turn away from the particular to see how public provisions affect all proprietary land units universally. The provisions of universal law embrace both the positive powers of doing and encouraging doing and the negative restraints. We shall deal with the two together. But before doing so in a general way, we must divert our attention to see how innate human limitations must be taken into account by the politics which distribute powers of positive planning and execution over land.

The Seat and Range of Powers of Positive Action

Individuals and Communities. Care has been taken so far to refer to the *holder* of a proprietary land unit and not to the *owner* of it. As explained at the beginning, this was done deliberately to avoid the

124

ambiguities that so easily arise over the use of the words owner and ownership. Ownership of land is more prone to confusion than is the ownership of chattels. What matters in the practical world is the answer to the question of who has the power of decision-making and action over the use of land resources. Ownership to the lay mind is the seat of power over land and wealth. It looked like it to the Western world of the eighteenth and nineteenth centuries, to Marx and the radical left, when the scale on which wealth was held was within the competence of an individual person to hold and manage. Technological advance has forced a collectivism upon us which has confused the issue. The joint stock companies of modern industry, of the technostructure, are the root cause of a radical change of power. Directors and executives hold the reins of control and not the corporalities, the owners of the companies' assets in the eyes of the law, whose wishes and will are but weakly manifest once a year at formal meetings of shareholders.

We see more clearly today than ever before that it is the incidence and seat of power over land and resources which is crucial to the use of them. The keener vision should cause us to be wary of the specious statements and policies about the use and ownership of land, especially polemics advocating land nationalization. When we speak of using land this way or that, our reference in reality is to land and property powers, and our speech and thought are shallow if we debate the use of land without conscious awareness of the incidence of property rights over it.

To see land always as the subject of property rights over it, rights which in themselves convey the power of decision-making and action, reveals for us more precisely the inescapable difference between individually and communally held land. There is no further question to ask when, in response to the question of who decides how to use this land and those resources, how to alienate them or to assimilate them with others, the reply is—this man, for it is he who has the property rights over them. No problem exists because he who holds the property rights is a real person, a human being who possesses the innate faculty to make decisions and to act upon them. But if in response to the question, the answer is – this company of men, that loose association of folk, the community, the people, for it is by them that property rights are held and exercised – intelligent curiosity is not satisfied. How can an amorphous mass of men, or even two persons for that matter, so fuse the individual identity of each person or each member of the group or community, so as to fashion a unitary consciousness, competent and capable of taking decisions and acting upon them such as are required to give expression to the

125

use of property rights? This is the problem which stretched the minds of medieval jurists struggling to bring to birth the notion of the body corporate[1]—this, indeed, is the paradox of democracy.

Whether we like it or not, there is no common voice. Mass man, whether in clubs, councils or soviets, has no means of taking or making decisions. Majority opinion, even unanimous opinion, of the constituent members of the group or community is not the common voice, the will of the community as an entity in and by itself, self-conscious, unitary. Once a group of men take counsel together to decide upon actions, each man in his turn separately weighs the issues as if he were at the moment of his cogitation in sovereign command. According to his temperament his decisions may further his own ends solely, or the ends of other men. He may speak of a preference for this cause as an alternative to that cause, as the former is in his opinion better for the many. His preferential judgement, however, is no less personal on that account. He did not come to it by listening to some mystic voice of the community within himself. In expressing the alternative, he is giving his ideas as to what the majority of the other members of the group or community are likely to decide if each one were intent upon his own personal interest. To this extent he is altruistic. All decisions are, in the last resort, personal, of individual persons and concerning individual persons. A community cannot make decisions, for it is not among the self-conscious, volitional decision-making orders of creation.

Decision-making is in the last analysis and as a consequence of the created order of humanity and human society, a society of the I-thou, of the mine and thine, an expression of the personal. Because we cannot escape this divine order conditioning our intercourse and social communication, the law has had to devise ways for making into one a loose association of men. In the Western world it has created a fiction whereby many persons become one person. Decisions can only be taken by a single will. The holder of property rights must have personality, must be a person—real or fictitious.[2] There can be no communication between a person and an it. *Cor ad cor loquitor*. Where a loose association of men have by legal ficton a bodiliness, are incorporate, the constituent members of the body will arrange for each person as a person to give his decisions on the use of property rights over land which the law sees as held by the *persona ficta*.

[1] F. W. Maitland, *Township and Borough* (Cambridge University Press, 1964), Ch. 11.
[2] Above, pp. 31–33.

The Law of Proprietary Magnitudes. Decision is the prerogative solely of individual personal consciousness and human will. But the will to do and the ability to do are not the same things. Human faculties are limited in the scope and range of their inherent potentialities. A man may, in the eyes of the law, hold property rights over vast stretches of land and resources, yet the exercise of them personally and effectively could be far beyond his and any other human ability. He must delegate his powers and distribute them into hands able to use them. There is a relationship universally valid between the extent of the powers of property in land, the range of the physical domain to which they pertain and the intensity of human activity pursued in the exercise of the powers. In other words, autocrats cannot wield all the powers all the time. They must delegate, or society as we know it could not exist. If delegation is inadequate inefficiency follows. Delegation may mean the formal assignment of the ownership of land and resources to other hands, or no more than a grant of authority to make and execute management plans for land and resources. Where, constitutionally, autocracy does not obtain, the principle is nonetheless valid among the lesser autonomies. We are not concerned here with the niceties of distinction between ownership and management. For the purposes of our analysis what are held and what distributed are property rights, the powers of positive decision-making over land and land resources.

Human incapacity imposes limits on the intensity of power any one person can effectively wield over a given area of land for specific purposes. Inability to use the whole range of property rights is not a morbid incompetence but an innate limitation of human ingenuity.[3] The head of a family firm may at law have near absolute powers of property over the land, plant, assets and other resources of the firm but he himself is quite incapable of using these powers continually and comprehensively. To do so is far beyond his mental and physical abilities and beyond those of any other single person. The head of the firm must delegate, in part, to others in a way which leaves in his own hands just such powers of direction and decision-making as can be easily and conveniently handled by him. Nowhere is this general relationship more clearly manifest than where the law in theory vests plenary powers of property in the state. By a constitutional process, delegation at the first remove takes place and actual or analogous powers of property (in our terminology always actual powers of property) are vested in a Minister of State or commissioner. He may be responsible for agriculture but he cannot himself farm

[3] D. R. Denman, 'Towards A Modern Theory of Property', *Land And People* (L. Hill, London, 1967), p. 93.

127

all the land all the time. Subsequent delegation ensues to commissioners, chairmen of committees and farm managers down a staircase of sub-delegations.

Intensity of human activity varies with the type of land use. The greater the degree of intensity the more exacting will be the tasks of positive planning, and in the interests of efficiency the smaller should be the size of the proprietary land unit whose abstract attributes are geared to the pursuits of human activity at that intensity. One man, for example, could efficiently take all the decisions required fully to manage 200 acres of sheepwalk in his occupation; not so with 200 acres in the heart of a modern city. No one man could himself use fully every house, shop, office and factory. He who holds property rights at law in the city similar in number and range to those held by he who is responsible for the sheepwalk, must in the city share the rights in some way, either by delegating them to managers of hotels, businesses or shops or by assigning them through the creation of derivative interests in the land.

This relationship between the powers of positive planning over land and land resources, the intensity of human activity and the size of the physical domain is universal throughout all civilized communities and can be stated axiomatically as a law to proprietary magnitudes. Within the terms of our analysis, the law maintains that the physical size of a proprietary land unit most conducive of competent, effective positive planning is a function of the intensity to human activity over the land of the unit implicit in the rights of property pertaining to the unit. The relationship can be symbolically expressed as:

$$O_s = f(i)$$

In the equation O_s is the optimum size of the proprietary land unit and (i) an index of the intensity of human activity to the degree permitted and implied by the rights of property which in association with the land resources comprise the unit. More simply, we can say that the optimum physical size of a proprietary land unit changes inversely with the intensity of human activity on the land of the unit within the sanction of its rights of property.[4]

The symbol (i) must not be taken as an index of the concentration of population per unit of land area. Its magnitude is a measure of the intensity of human activity in a typical sense; some types of activity are more intense in the demands they make upon the application of human energies than others are. Suppose, for example, we

[4] D. R. Denman, 'Capitalism and Property', *The Case for Capitalism* (Michael Joseph, London, 1967), p. 12.

128

were concerned with the optimum size of a proprietary land unit for residential purposes. Should the population increase over a given area of land, the average size of proprietary land units used for domestic purposes would decrease, but the optimum size would not be affected and would remain constant. Expansion in the number of residents heightens concentration but it does not magnify the coefficient of intensity of the typical human activity—in this instance, the occupation of a proprietary land unit for domestic and residential purposes. When, for some reason, the actual size of a proprietary land unit is less than the optimum, the optimum size itself is not affected. To change the illustration, consider the difference in the degree of human intensity of activity between extensive livestock husbandry and horticulture. In the notation used above, horticultural activity would be symbolized by (i), whose magnitude would be higher than the magnitude of (i) for extensive livestock husbandry and for horticulture the value of O_s would be correspondingly less than it would be for extensive livestock husbandry. The change in the index of intensity follows a change in the type of activity. Official statistics for England and Wales for 1969 show the number of agricultural holdings between $\frac{1}{4}$ acre and 20 acres as 31 per cent for the nation at large. In areas where horticulture and market gardening were widely practised, as for example in Holland (Lincs.), the corresponding percentage was over 50. Because of the greater intensity of human activity in these areas, the numerical percentage of the relatively smaller-sized proprietary land units given to horticultural enterprize increased.

The holder of a proprietary land unit faced with the prospect of shouldering responsibility for an activity on the land of his unit too intense to satisfy the equation $O_s = f/i$) will usually retain the unit and alter its abstract attributes and reduce the executive and administrative activity (i) by distributing some of the rights of property and creating inferior units out of the original unit. The multifarious human activities which normally go on over twenty acres in the heart of a modern city would be far too many and too intense, for a single holder of a proprietary land unit to control and manage. Under English land law, the administrative task would be brought within workable dimensions by the freeholder granting leases and permitting subleases to occupants of derivative proprietary land units, while holding to himself the freehold reversionary interest in the twenty acres contingent upon the many leases. In this way the property rights of his unit would be reduced and brought within the competence of his managerial ability; in other words, (i) would be diminished to the point where the twenty acres of reversionary free-

I

hold satisfied the optimum size O_s. Similar arrangements under the civil codes of the Continent would not be regarded as creating a hierarchy of ownerships each commensurate with the managerial demands of the human activity to which the proprietary land unit is subject. There could and would, however, be analagous derivative arrangements which within the terminology of our analysis would amount to a redistribution of property rights and the carving of inferior units out of a superior one.

The value of (i) for a superior proprietary land unit can be so slight that the human activity and related powers of property within the proprietary land unit have little or no practical significance. A classical example is today the reduction to a mere legal convention of the paramount seignory vested in the English Crown over every acre of English soil, from which in legal theory all fee simple estates are derived. In the terms of our equation, (i) is so attenuated that the magnitude of O_s extends without difficulty to the entire domain of the nation.

Collective Proprietorship and the Law of Proprietary Magnitudes. Decision-making, as we saw just now, is invariably and by the nature of things an expression of personal will and consciousness. It is so, even where the decision purports to be an expression of a collective will. Communes, co-operatives and committees are no more than the sum of their members and they have no wisdom higher than the wisdom of the most intelligent voice among them. In the last analysis, the decisions of a committee are personal and limited therefore by the innate incapacities of human knowledge and ingenuity. Today is the day of mass man and the collective idea. All too readily attitudes are taken and policies pursued on an implied, half conscious notion that the collective mind of a committee is wiser, more competent, better informed than human wisdom itself—as if a committee had powers of revelation not vouchsafed to individual humans. But it is not so. Rather the reverse is true. If the powers of property are always wielded democratically and at every point, so that each constituent member of a committee or group has his say, time at best is lost where swiftness of decision-making is the criterion of efficiency. The more complex the operations, the more time-consuming and cumbersome can the execution of them by collective thought and action become. To turn again to our equation, we can say that where a body corporate or committee holds a proprietary land unit, for any given human activity on the land of the unit, if all decisions involved in it are to be taken by the committee, (i) will assume a greater magnitude with a corresponding effect on O_s,

130

because the very collective discourse leading up to a decision intensifies the human activity of whatever type it may be with which the collective or committee are concerned. Further, the increase in intensification is a function of the number (n) of articulate voices used in the collective decision-making procedures, so that the greater the magnitude of (n) the greater the intensity of activity (i).

A proprietary land unit in the hands of a collective will take on a fictitious proprietary character form. Adjustments in the interests of efficient planning and use of the land resources of the unit can be made in one of a number of alternative ways:

i. By reducing the size of the unit so as to provide an optimum O_s according to the given type of human activity pursued by the concerted will of each member of the collective.

ii. By delegating property powers from the full committee and giving them into the hands of groups where (n) is equal in each case, and the intensity of activity is reduced for the original committee by the creation of derivative proprietary land units with fictitious proprietary character form. In that event the size remains the same, but the value of (i) is diminished. The original committee now holds a superior proprietary land unit to the point where the constant size of the unit is O_s for the reduced number of property rights now to be exercised. Likewise for the new derivative units, the size will be coincident with that of the superior unit and the intensity of activity reflected in the delegated powers will be such that the size equals O_s for the purposes of the delegated functions.

iii. By reducing the number of articulate participating members (n) of the holding committee while keeping the size of the unit constant until the number is so reduced that the size of the unit was O_s for the new value of (i).

iv. By increasing the number of articulate members of the committee (n) and delegating powers of property from the augmented committee into the hands of an individual person so that the size of the unit was O_s for the purposes of the committee now expanded and functioning as the holder of a superior proprietary land unit; and the size of the unit was also O_s for the derivative unit now in the hands of the individual person. The intensity of human activity of the dimension (i) will then be reflected in the range of the property rights delegated to the derivative unit by the augmented committee as holders of the superior unit.

This particular feature of our analysis demonstrates that where at

131

law a group, committee or collective of some kind (the state) is the fictitious holder of a proprietary land unit, inefficiency of planning and management can result from failure to delegate powers of decision-making from the committee to lesser groups or individual persons, so that the responsibilities of the committee as a committee add up to an intensity of activity too great for the competence of the committee within the given size of the proprietary land unit.

Those who have studied and experienced the operation of centrally planned economies bear witness to rigidities and an inflexibility resisting adjustments of policy to meet changes in consumer demand.[5] The cause of the maladjustment is probably in many cases as much the consequence of failure to delegate planning and management responsibilities from a central board or council as it is of the inherent complexity of making overall national production plans. Recent experiences in Poland bear out the possibility. The relentless working of the law of proprietary magnitudes had frustrated the aims of the central planners. Reluctance in the past to make full and effective delegations of rights had led to inefficiency in the conduct of commercial undertakings. Now, autonomy is encouraged by leasing shops and business houses, where before the commercial concerns had been administered from a central executive department of government. In the language of our analysis, the holders of a supreme fictitious proprietary land unit in the name of the state had subsequently carved derivative proprietary land units out of it thereby relieving the central authority of responsibilities beyond its combined competence to shoulder, and creating smaller autonomies fashioned to the limits of human ability exercised by small groups and individual persons. The outcome in Poland has been a patent improvement in economic efficiency. An improvement brought about only by vesting property rights in individual lessees and giving them freedom of decision-making to match their natural abilities.

If the law of proprietary magnitudes was better understood, we would have less woolly thinking about land nationalization and the state purchase of land as an adjunct of land use planning. Advocates of land nationalization and state purchase of land as one of the factors of production are confused in their thinking by failing to see that we cannot in reality think of land and the use of land without at the same time taking into our reckoning the property rights in land. The state is the greatest collective of all, for which (n) in our notation is the number of all citizens within the body politic. All the people cannot take all the decisions all the time. Delegation is

---

[5] Sir Paul Chambers' contribution to *Economics, Business and Government* (Institute of Economic Affairs, 1966).

essential; but to whom? If Ministers of state hold property powers over the land *in nomine populi*, the power of decision-making is personalized, as it is when an individual citizen holds rights of private property. Ministers of state are but human. No one man can supervise all the planning and use of land moment by moment throughout a nation—the totality of the national estate would be far too extensive for it to satisfy O_s where the human activity responsible for (i) was every action taken over every acre every moment. The Minister for lands, agriculture or whatever his designation might be, must himself delegate to satisfy the law of proprietary magnitudes. But again the question comes—to whom? and how? If he creates inferior derivative proprietary land units, as he must, these will either be held as property, as with leases under the land law of England, and hence will constitute private property in the land—the very anathema of the land nationalization devotee—or they will be constituted of property rights which in terms of power will run closely parallel with what is meant by the private property of a lessee. The law of proprietary magnitudes cannot be circumvented or only circumvented at the expense of economic efficiency and social order. The planner who thinks he has the answer to the problems of positive planning through the use of state purchase, has not begun to confront the realities which the law of proprietary magnitudes will impel him to face—having acquired the land and created a proprietary land unit in it, the questions arise by whom shall it be held and how will the manner of the holding of it affect the use and planning of the land resources in the future.[6]

A practical lesson has recently been read us in the application of the law of proprietary magnitudes by the sorry history of the setting up of a Land Commission in Britain under the provisions of the Land Commission Act 1967. The market price of interests in building land was soaring. Promises were made to control the price of building land and appear to have been prompted by the ill-digested notion, following some earlier theorizing,[7] that by buying land through a state agency the price could be controlled. That land has no part to play in an economy except as it is administered within the sanction of property rights does not seem to have been realized in the heady days of political polemics and facile promises. The sober facts later experienced were that either a state commission would have to hold the proprietary land units after acquisition and develop all the building land themselves—an activity of such intensity as to have

6 D. R. Denman, *Land Use and the Constitution of Property: An Inaugural Lecture* (Cambridge University Press, 1969), p. 18.

7 Labour Party Publication, *Signposts For the Sixties* (1961), pp. 19–23.

been beyond the capacity of a small body of men over so wide ranging an expanse of land, an extent far too great for it to be an optimum magnitude for so intense an activity under the hand of a collective; or, the commission would have had to delegate authority to sub-commissions to develop the land carefully calculated so that the delegated property rights were in each case within the competence of the sub-commission to handle; or, the primary commission would have to sell interests on the land market in a way which would satisfy the current demand and the competence of individual builders and companies. Both of the first two alternatives would have deprived the building industry of its essential stock-in-trade and done nothing to reduce the price of houses which is the consequence of the house market and not of the land market.[8] The third alternative would have done nothing to steady or lessen the price of land, as the disposal of the interests in it would be at prices which took their lead from the same demand as was already there before the commission had acquired the land. If as some supposed was possible, the commission bought land at sub-market price compulsorily and undersold it on the market, there would have had to be set up a complicated and invidious machinery of selection of the privileged buyers and control of all future transactions. The intensity of operations would thus have been greatly increased, and the management of the land resources of the proprietary land units in the hand of the commission to achieve the motive for which they were held by the commission would have been such as to require substantial delegations of power away from the commission itself; and a new genus of decision-makers would control the supply of land to the market, with no effect upon house prices but with all that the radicals seem most to object to in the incidence of property power in the hands of a few.

The law of proprietary magnitudes stands on an unshakable fact—the limits to human capability. Advocates of land nationalization and the state acquisition of land for the development of specific sectors of an economy should realize that the crucial question raised by such advocacy is always one of rights and powers over land. The simple truth of $O_s = f(i)$ requires us to ask in what manner and to what extent shall the paramount holder of rights in land *in nomine populi* delegate power, as power must be delegated, into the hands of private citizens and institutions. When a state board holding title over land in absolute power delegates part of the power into the hands of holders of inferior proprietary land units derived

[8] D. R. Denman, 'The Land Commission in Profile and Perspective', *National Provincial Bank Review*, No. 78, May, 1967, p. 9.

from the paramount unit which becomes a superior one in relationship, the power of positive planning over the land resources will in large measure be foregone over intermittent periods. The sum of the positive planning power remaining in the hand of the state board will depend upon the duration of the proprietary land units. Only if and when duration is finite will the power of positive planning revert to the board and will do so as and when the inferior units terminate. While they inure, the power of the state board is positive only in respect of the planning of the use of such revenues as may accrue from the creation of the inferior units and by exercising power of entry upon the land as may have been reserved to it for undertaking specific developments. Otherwise the board's power over the use and planning of the land resources is negative, requiring the holders of the inferior units to seek the permission of the board for developments contemplated by them. In this respect the negative powers of the board over the affairs of the inferior proprietary land units resemble, in the effect they have upon the abstract attributes and property powers of the inferior units, the public restraints and sanctions which impose prohibitions on the planning and use of land resources within proprietary land units and to which we must now turn our attention.

Universal Provisions

The rights of property over the land resources of a proprietary land unit are the creation of law, and the law, in this sense, can be said to exert a universal influence over all proprietary land units. But the law has a private and a public face. What I can do with my own in relation to my neighbour is sanctioned by the law of persons. We have already seen how what one holder of a proprietary land unit can, and is permitted to do, affects in sundry ways what his neighbours can do and are likely to do with their own proprietary land units. These reciprocities lie within the sanctions of private law or the law of persons. It is the public face of the law which we must now look at, at the way in which the law conditions the abstract attributes and use of land resources within proprietary land units in a universal way, irrespective of what private or personal relationships may or may not exist between neighbour and neighbour.

We referred earlier to the cardinal divide between positive powers of executive action over land and the powers of restraint. The universal provisions we are now concerned to look at, by their very nature belong to the negative side of the great divide. Because of the law of proprietary magnitudes, positive powers of decision-making

135

must be distributed among persons and institutions as holders of proprietary land units. Public, universal law cannot say to each and every citizen that he has absolute power to use the land and its resources. Positive power is distributed power. But in the political chronology of societies, once the distribution of the positive powers of property in land is accomplished, public law can impose restraints and prohibitions which affect all holders of proprietary land units— simple, fiduciary and fictitious, personal and institutional, private and public. Universal provisions can also possess a quasi-positive character in that by universally valid law the holders of proprietary land units everywhere or within a class or region can be encouraged to act in a certain way towards their land and its resources; encouraged, but not compelled, for the end of compulsion is a redistribution of the powers of positive decision-making. The use of land in a particular way can only be enforced against the will of the present holder of the property rights in the land by removing him and transferring (redistribution) the rights to another.[9]

A Classification. Universal provisions within the framework of law which affect the structure and character of proprietary land units and the use of land resources in the units, can, in the general case, be classified as a step in systematic analysis. The classification scheme suggested is set out in Figure 1 and explained and commented upon in the following paragraphs.

Modes of Influence: Indirect. The primary classification is into direct and indirect modes of influence. Indirect modes of influence are very familiar to the post-war generations of the western world since World War II. In the context of our present analysis they would not be aimed at the use of land and land resources in a pointed and specific way. The cause of the influence could be so remote from land affairs as to evince in itself no obvious connection between its aims and the use of land. Within this subclass come the numerous aspects of financial and fiscal policies directly pointed in a general way at curbing investment or controlling expenditure. An indirect influence may, however, be aimed directly at some aspect of land use, tenure or development but in such a way as to avoid formulating express directives or prohibitions, and which leaves the decision and the choice of action entirely open to the holder of the proprietary land unit. The indirect influence can act either as a deliberate encouragement of a particular line of action or as a discouragement.

---

[9] D. R. Denman, *Land Use and the Constitution of Property*, An Inaugural Lecture (Cambridge University Press, 1969), p. 18.

Since encouragement and discouragement are in a relationship of polarity, an argument could be sustained for only one category—a policy which encourages a hoped-for line is effectively a discouragement of the alternatives. This, perhaps, is taking sophistry too far, and for the purpose of classification and clarity, indirect modes of influence will be further sub-classified as shown on the chart, into

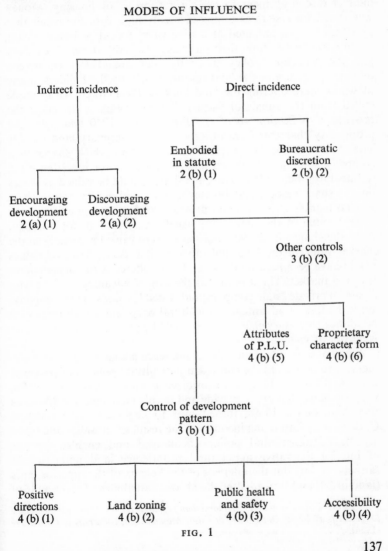

FIG. 1

those which encourage (2 [a] [1]) and those which discourage (2 [a] [2]).

To illustrate the sub-categories by a few examples: take the effect of recent monetary policy (1970) in Britain on the use of proprietary land units held by building firms from an entrepreneurial motive to develop the resources for housing. The monetary policy acted as an indirect discouragement to use the resources for housing. Money was short, interest rates unprecedentedly high with the result that production costs mounted at a time when would-be house buyers could not afford to fund their purchases. Effective demand fell away and the monetary policy indirectly, but nonetheless effectively, influenced the use of the land resources held by the builders, many of whom were offering the land back to the market. An example culled from the annals of fiscal policy in Britain is the effect the provisions of Section 46 of the Finance Act 1940 had upon the proprietary character form of agricultural proprietary land units.[10] The change in the law altered the manner in which shares in a company holding agricultural land were valued for inheritance tax (estate duty). Before the change the shares would be valued as shares on the share market and because almost without exception there was no market quotation and profits were low or non-existent, the market value of the shares was usually very low, if not nominal. After the change in the law, the shares were valued according to the market value of the land and other capital assets, as those values would have been realized if the land were offered with possession on the land market. The upshot was the loss of advantage to one who created a private estate company and vested his lands in the company. With the loss of advantage, agricultural proprietary land units of a fictitious proprietary character form held by private estate companies went out of vogue.

A patent example of an indirect influence acting as an encouragement, is to be seen in the consistent agricultural policies of post-war Britain. British farming was subsidized in such a way that but for support, acres that are now wide and deeply cultivated would be, as they were in the 1930s, turned over to neglected cattle ranches. Continuously improving incomes as the result of subsidies and other aspects of agricultural policy encouraged and enabled holders of inferior derivative agricultural proprietary land units (tenant farmers) to buy out the interests of the holders of the superior units (landlords), and thus to alter the abstract attributes of thousands of

---

[10] *Estate Duty Anomalies: Memorandum prepared for the Economic Secretary to the Treasury by the Department of Estate Management, University of Cambridge* (1954), p. 7.

units and the proprietary land pattern of rural England. One is reminded of the indirect, but more pointed policy, pursued at the turn of the century in Ireland. Land reform was in the air. Tenant farmers were eager to buy out the landlords. The government of those days was opposed to coercion and introduced sundry measures which acted indirectly to encourage the landlords to make the change and invest the holders of inferior proprietary land units with freehold interests. Policy varied, from immediate cash payments through the Government Land Commission to Government stocks exchanged for the landlords' interests at the going value of the land and not at the par value of the stocks. Thus the indirect encouragement was sometimes more effective than at other times. When in the early years, land stock at par value was offered as consideration of sale, transactions dried up: the encouragement had, because of the plight of the stocks on the Stock Exchange, become a discouragement.

Modes of Influence: Direct. Universal laws which exert a direct influence on the formation of proprietary land units and on the use of resources within them are themselves the immediate vehicles of policies designed to control the use of land resources by prohibition or directive. Nothing ostensibly obscures the intentions of the legislature. Nonetheless, basically there are two principal ways of legislating and hence, as a second remove, direct modes of influence can be subdivided into two inclusive categories. Provision may be made by embodying regulations in the text of a statute, written code or statutory regulation; or, by authorizing bureaucrats to give *ad hoc* decisions of a prohibitive or impellent nature within their personal discretion. Thus, we have two sub-classes of modes of influence: direct influence by provisions embodied in a statute (2 [*b*] [1], and by decisions given within the sanction of bureaucratic discretion 2 [*b*] [2]). The purposes for which, in the general case, direct modes of influence are pursued give rise to further sub-classes, and the illustrations given later to exemplify the subclasses will at the same time indicate the differences between the law as it is embodied wholly in a statute or written text, and as it is administered by bureaucratic discretion. To help us at this stage, we should compare the basic principles behind town planning policies and legislation in the United States and in Britain. States in America each have their own zoning ordinances and as a general rule the use of land is controlled by delineating use zones and density zones on land use maps prepared under the sanction of state laws and ordinances. Holders of proprietary land units know they have to plan the use of their resources within the prohibitory requirements of the zones as

139

interpreted by the written laws. The direct mode of influence is the patent law, open for all to see who would wish to do so. Admittedly, the full implications of the law cannot be understood from the texts alone, and the citizen must consult the plans of the planners and the text of the law; but having done so, he knows where he stands. In Britain, since the radical change in the town and country planning policies in 1947, the holders of proprietary land units cannot know where they stand under the law, except to know that they must not proceed with the development of their land resources without permission from the planning authority. They cannot go to the written text of the law and know whether or not what they intend to do will comply with, or breach, the law of the land. Such critical and essential knowledge will only be obtained when, within his discretion, a planning officer (or a planning committee) has decided whether or not to give permission for the holder of the proprietary land unit to proceed with his designs. Judged by the principles which condition the constitution of political and social liberty, the form of direct control of land use now practised in Britain is a running breach of the rule of law. The rule of law requires of a polity and constitution that the citizen should know where he stands under the law at any moment and that he should not be the victim of the exercise of arbitrary power and caprice.[11] Dealing with general examples, it is interesting to note how far policy in Britain has moved away from the rule of law and the days when the development of land resources was controlled by minute, express provisions embodied in a public statute, such as the London Building Acts of the eighteenth century—a more straightforward example of the embodiment of provisions in a statute, 2 [b] [1]).

Direct Influence over Development Use Patterns. In either one of the two ways just described, the law may make provision for directly influencing the decision-making by holders of proprietary land units over their units. We can take the classification of the modes of influence into deeper categories by separating off the provisions which influence and control the actual uses to which a holder of a unit puts his resources from those which impinge upon and affect the abstract attributes of the unit: thus, we have two further sub-categories (3 [b] [1] and 3 [b] [2]). We shall turn our attention for the moment to the former.

The purposes for which a legislature may impose direct controls over the development use pattern of proprietary land units are mani-

[11] D. R. Denman, 'The Professions and the Constitution of Liberty', *Chartered Surveyor*, Vol. 101, No. 12, June 1969, p. 604.

fold. They will depend upon the geographical, topographical and physical features of the country, its economic circumstances, national policies and aspirations, social traditions and much else: too wide, we may suppose, to attempt an acceptable further sub-classification into functional categories. Human societies and settlements, however, have common traits and needs, and it is possible to suggest some further standardization. It will be seen from the chart that the following are suggested:

4 (b) (1): positive directions;
4 (b) (2): land zoning;
4 (b) (3): public health and safety;
4 (b) (4): accessibility.

Positive Directions. By positive direction is meant the exercise of authoritarian demands by a central or local government department directing the holders of proprietary land units to use their resources in a prescribed manner. Thus by the provisions of the law governing the execution of the land reform in modern Iran, holders of proprietary land units who had land in hand under a *melk* title and wished to keep it were obliged to cultivate it by modern mechanical methods. From English experience we may cite, by way of examples, the provisions of the Public Health Acts which require all holders of proprietary land units developed for housing to see that the houses are provided with sanitary appliances of prescribed standards. And in wartime Britain the Minister of Agriculture through his accredited agents, the War Agricultural Executive Committees, was empowered to direct the holders of agricultural proprietary land units in possession to plant the land to a specified cropping pattern. Positive direction is not a contradiction of the general proposition that positive planning power is solely the prerogative of the holder of property rights in the land. Ultimately, the only way an authority issuing a direction can ensure its execution against a recalcitrant landowner is to step into the landowner's shoes or put someone else in them more in sympathy with what is wanted than is the present owner. A right of entry to perform the task is but a special way of acquiring property powers over the land of a type and duration suited to the task in hand.

Land Zoning. Because land use zoning was used above as an illustration to distinguish direct influence by provisions embodied in a written law text (2 [b] [1]) from decisions given within the sanction of bureaucratic discretion (2 [b] [2]), we should not lose sight of the fact that these final subclasses of the classification scheme are open to both types of provision. The rules of the game in Britain, while putting the final authority in the word of a bureaucratic officer or committee, nonetheless require the authority to prepare zoning maps as guides and criteria against which to make their *ad hoc* judgements of application for planning permission. Land use zoning is a sophisticated approach to the reconciliation of competing demands for land resources on a national or regional scale. It aims at sorting out priorities and is not in any exclusive way concerned with a particular use of land and resources for, say, public health or safety. It is separated from such specificities in these subclasses. Because of its catholicity, it has a relevance to even the early, primitive stages of all systems of land use planning.

Public Health and Safety. Historically the control of the use of land resources in the interests of public health and safety takes precedence, in the Western world at all events, over the comprehensive, generalized attempts to reconcile competing demands for land which have become refined as land use planning. With an eye to public health and safety, governments have imposed controls, by statute, bye-laws and other formal regulatory means, upon the development of land by prescribing the way in which buildings may be erected, streets and squares laid out and lit, and sewage disposed of. The control is invariably specific and judged against what is required to secure public health and safety, with no reference to priorities for the use of land and the merits of amenity and conservation. Although we live in an age of sophisticated land use planning under government control, these more particularized concerns of public health and safety must still be objectives, and primary ones, in any programme of universal provisions for the use of land resources.

Accessibility. As a feature of the development use pattern of proprietary land units, accessibility takes on a special and narrow meaning. In modern urban societies, with dwellings, factories and commercial accommodation crowded and hunched over congested communication routes, the use of the land resources of proprietary land units giving access upon public streets and thoroughfares needs to be watched. And, for similar reasons, the use of land resources to provide roads and other means of communication and access needs to be related specifically to known criteria to ensure right widths, alignments and engineering.

Direct Influence upon Other Attributes of the Proprietary Land Unit and the Proprietary Character Form. Legislative texts themselves and the exercise of discretionary powers by bureaucrats can directly influence the powers and activities of the holders of proprietary land units by imposing control over the abstract attributes and proprietary character form of the units. Here, then, we have two further sub-classes and these on the the chart are shown as (4[b][5]—controls over the abstract attributes of a proprietary land unit; and 4[b][6])—controls over the proprietary character form of units.

Variations on a common theme exemplify the way in which universal law can control and mould the abstract attributes of proprietary land units in the different provisions found in the legislation of many countries limiting the maximum size of proprietary land units. Danish law restricts the area of farm land over which a private person may exercise property rights which by Danish legal theory amount to ownership of the land. The maximum is determined by reference to value based upon an ancient fiscal assessment of the land. In Poland the land law has similar examples limiting the size of peasant holdings. Agrarian law governing the structure and tenure of collective farms in eastern Europe frequently permits individual members of a collective to hold their own proprietary land unit up to a specified size. Land reform legislation abounds in examples; as under the first phase of the land reform policy in Iran when landowners were permitted to retain a *shesh dang* village and no larger proprietary land unit.

Even more frequent and more varied are the provisions which control the proprietary character form of proprietary land units. In many countries of the world controls of various kinds determine what categories of persons may or may not hold proprietary land units. Sometimes the control is an outright prohibition; as in postwar West Germany where land could not be bought for farming except by purchasers who possessed credentials and qualifications of a standard type accrediting them as qualified agriculturists. Swiss law limits the holding of land by aliens. In Sweden the holder of an agricultural proprietary land unit is not permitted to sell his unit wholly or in part without the permission of the Lantbruksnämnd.[12] Similar restraints until recently were imposed over the sale of land under the jurisdiction of Rural Development Boards in England.[13] Where controls of the kind operate, they influence both the bundle of property rights of the proprietary land unit and its proprietary character form. The property rights are cut down because the holder of the proprietary land unit cannot exercise an unconditional right

12 D. R. Denman, *Rural Land Systems*, International Federation of Surveyors, Commission 4 (London, 1968), p. 13.
13 See S (49), Agriculture Act, 1967.

of disposal over his resources. The proprietary character form is
affected because the authorities may preclude corporations, charities
and other potential purchasers of a distinctive proprietary character
form from buying proprietary land units from the present holders.
In many developing countries, for example, there is an aversion to
companies holding land whose registered offices are extra-territorial.

Chapter IX

CONSOCIATE WEALTH

Its Definition

From time to time, as we have expounded our analysis to the present point, we have had occasion to mention consociate wealth. At sundry places it was necessary to see the proprietary land unit against the background and in association with other forms of wealth. Consociate wealth has a special relevance to the proprietary land unit as a unit of decision-making because a full understanding of the influences and forces which move a holder of a proprietary land unit to plan and use his land resources one way and not another way cannot be gained, unless the part played by consociate wealth is realized and acknowledged. It is requisite, therefore, at this stage to define consociate wealth and consider its function in relation to the proprietary land unit and in the general scheme of our analysis.

One of the fundamental liberties associated with property rights is the freedom to assimilate[1] the thing held or owned with other possessions, to use one thing with another thing in a common bond of title. The power to assimilate the wealth of a proprietary land unit and other wealth held by the holder of the unit has been demonstrated as a factor of practical consequence to the management of the land resources of the unit.[2] Consociate wealth is the term used in and coined for the purposes of our analysis to denote the wealth which in the hands of he who holds a proprietary land unit is capable of assimilation with the wealth of the unit. The power of assimilation is dependent upon a common title to ownership or the rights of property. It is not excluded by niceties of the lawyer's phraseology such as draw distinctions between property in estates and interests in land and the outright ownership of things. What is critical is the incidence of the power: it should lie in each case in the hands of the same holder, whether individual person or institu-

---

[1] Above, p. 55.   [2] *ibid.*

tion. A man may hold some wealth unconditionally as an individual, real person[3] (simple proprietary character form) and other wealth in a fiduciary capacity; although in either case he is the same being, what he holds unconditionally and as an individual person cannot be freely assimilated with the wealth he holds as trustee or fiduciary holder; the two forms of wealth are not consociate with each other.

Consociate wealth, then, consists of the total resources of a holder of a proprietary land unit other than the wealth in the unit itself with which the external wealth is consociate. He who holds other wealth besides a particular proprietary land unit enjoys through the common title a medium of affinity which enables us to think of the resources external to the proprietary land unit as being associated with it.

A person may hold more than one proprietary land unit in a common title. In these circumstance, each proprietary land unit is consociate with each and every one of the others. Consociate wealth is a relative term: according to how we look at it, a particular proprietary land unit may be either the centre of association with which another proprietary land unit is consociate, or be itself an item of the consociate wealth of that other unit. The relationship can be expressed in symbols. Where A is a proprietary land unit and C external resources consociate with it, we can write:

$$A\!\!\!-\!\!\!\!\!\begin{array}{c}\\ \llcorner C\end{array}$$

Where a person holds two proprietary land units, A and B, with similar proprietary character forms and an inventory of chattels and other wealth r, we can write of A:

$$A\!\!\!-\!\!\!\!\!\begin{array}{c}\\ \llcorner B\\ \llcorner r\end{array}$$

and of B:

$$B\!\!\!-\!\!\!\!\!\begin{array}{c}\\ \llcorner A\\ \llcorner r\end{array}$$

Adventitious Wealth

It will be apparent from the little progress we have made so far that stress has been laid on the similarity of proprietary character forms.

[3] Above, p. 31.

External wealth is not consociate with a proprietary land unit unless the holder of the one is simultaneously the embodiment of the same proprietary character form as the holder of the other. The holder of a proprietary land unit may be secured in the title to it as a real person, thereby giving the unit a simple proprietary character form; and at the same time hold another proprietary land unit or other wealth as a trustee, that is to say in a fiduciary capacity. The person himself is a common link between the wealth he holds as a proprietary land unit and the wealth he holds as trustee. But it cannot be said of the latter that it is consociate with the proprietary land unit for, despite the common link, the proprietary character form of the trust wealth is not the same as the proprietary character form of the proprietary land unit. Nevertheless, acknowledging the common link, we can speak of the wealth held in a fiduciary capacity by the holder of the proprietary land unit as adventitious wealth of the unit. Adventitious wealth can exist only where a person or persons hold title to proprietary land units and other wealth either under differing proprietary character forms or similar character forms with different identities. A man, for example, may hold a proprietary land unit having, through him, a simple proprietary character form and be chairman of a family company which holds another proprietary land unit. One unit is not consociate with the other because one is held by a real person and has a simple proprietary character form, while the other is held by a fictitious person, a company. There is a link, however, in that the chairman of the company is the holder of the proprietary land unit in his own name. The simple unit is a form of adventitious wealth with the unit held by the company; and the latter is adventitious wealth with the unit held by the chairman in his own right. Now, if the holder of the unit with the simple proprietary character form were to form another company and assign that unit to the company of which he becomes chairman, the proprietary character form of one unit is similar to the proprietary character form of the other. Even so, one unit does not thereby become the consociate wealth of the other and vice versa. The two units cannot be consociate with each other, since the holder of one, although the embodiment of a similar proprietary character form, is not the holder of the other. The proprietary character forms are similar but the identities of the embodiment of their proprietary character forms are different. There is, however, the common link through the chairman of each being one and the same real person and this is sufficient to make each unit an item of the adventitious wealth of the other. The link has a practical significance where the voice of the chairman prevails

147

LAND USE

over the counsels of the directors of the respective companies, What is done with the resources of one unit could be materially affected by what is done on the other and with the consociate wealth of the other which would be owned by the holder of the other. The common interest of the chairman in the affairs and wealth of the two companies is ground for supposing that the wealth of the one could well back up the fortune of the other.

Before we move on to more particular considerations and attempts to define standard forms of consociate and adventitious wealth, there is something more to be said of the relationships of which 'consociate' and 'adventitious' are qualifying adjectives. The terms are terms of association. A proprietary land unit and its consociate wealth contribute to the fortune of one and the same person or institution. Both are held in the same hands. Consociate denotes a particular functional relationship between the proprietary land unit and wealth external to it. Adventitious wealth displays a similar functional character but in a lower key. Care should be taken lest we fall into the error of referring to the adventitious wealth of the landowner. Unlike consociate wealth, adventitious wealth is not held by he who holds the proprietary land unit to which it is adventitious. There is a functional similarity, a criterion which makes of consociate wealth and adventitious wealth a single species whose varieties have no meaning apart from their relationship to the proprietary land unit. Consociate and adventitious wealth can, therefore, never be other than consociate with, and adventitious to, a proprietary land unit. They should not be referred to as the consociate wealth and adventitious wealth of a proprietary land unit.

Demarcation Lines

Demarcation lines setting a proprietary land unit apart from the wealth consociate with it can be drawn with some assurance in most cases. Distinction between the scattered and the many[4] is a factor to be reckoned with when we have to decide whether a parcel of land is a portion of a scattered proprietary land unit or a separate unit consociate with the other. Items not physically attached to the soil of a proprietary land unit present no problem. Difficulty is encountered and the demarcation lines become less certain where there is physical attachment. A wooden hut erected on the allotment of a freeholder illustrates the equivocality. The freeholder will think of the hut as one among the other things he owns—the motor cycle and the garden tools. His attitude puts the hut with the items

[4] Above, p. 28.

148

of wealth consociate with the proprietary land unit, although if the allotment were sold and nothing was said about the hut in the conveyance, it would at common law pass to the purchaser as part and parcel of the land resources of the proprietary land unit. In the general case, it is preferable to follow the lawyers here and draw the demarcation line between the resources of a proprietary land unit and the wealth consociate with it by including among the land resources all things that would at law pass as land in a conveyance of land. This general statement requires a particular qualification and calls for a special explanation.

A Particular Qualification. There comes a moment for land used for primary production when the product upon it is ready for marketing, to be severed from the placenta of the land as a commodity exchangeable for cash. Although still physically one with the land, and at law in most circumstances part of the land, the marketable commodity should for the purposes of the present analysis be counted as an item of consociate wealth and excluded from the land resources of the proprietary land unit. Growing crops and minerals will be land resources while, through condition or position, they cannot be separately marketed off the land as commodities. Immature timber trees are thus one with the land resources of a proprietary land unit, while a stand of mature timber is wealth consociate with the unit. Sandstone running back from the line which behind a quarry face sets the limit to what is immediately marketable will be counted with the land resources of a proprietary land unit, and the stone at the margin, along the marketable quarry face, will be wealth consociate with the unit.

A Special Explanation. Whatever is attached to the soil by the holder of an inferior proprietary land unit may be regarded at law as an integral part of, and inseparable from, the land resources of the superior unit out of which the inferior is carved. Such fixtures and attachments made by the holder of the inferior unit would also become integral parts of the land resources of the inferior unit, similar in all respects to the fixed equipment provided on the land by the holder of the superior unit. Complications arise because inferior units are usually limited in duration. A day will come when the time span remaining to the holder of the inferior unit is too short for the unit and its resources to be marketable on the land market, and for the holder to be able to recoup in some measure the cost of what he has put into the land. When the end comes and the life span of the unit runs out, the assets attached to the soil by the holder of the inferior unit merge with the land resources which

149

at that moment pass into the occupation of he who was the holder of the recently existing superior land unit. There is no difference where compensation is payable by the holder of the superior proprietary land unit, except that the right to ultimate compensation as one of the property rights of the inferior proprietary land unit, adds value to the unit and increases its worth as security for a loan which if raised would provide as cash wealth consociate with the inferior unit. When the inferior unit runs out, the right to compensation is simultaneously transformed into a title to claim a kind of para-consociate wealth. Compensation money never becomes truly consociate wealth since the moment it is payable is the point in time when the inferior unit terminates and there is no entity with which the compensation money can be consociate.

Significance of Consociate Wealth

So far we have been definitional. Definitions are important but they do not tell us why we should bother to survey the external realms of wealth beyond the land resources of a proprietary land unit and which we have called consociate and adventitious wealth. In the general case, there are five answers to this question, and we shall consider them briefly under the following captions:

   i. manœuvrability;
  ii. size and abstract attributes of a proprietary land unit;
 iii. static or immobile relationship;
 iv. the national land use pattern; and
  v. Government control over the proprietary land unit.

Manœuvrability. Of first and obvious importance is the influence consociate wealth has upon the manœuvrability of resources within a proprietary land unit. We have seen[5] how manœuvrability is a function of the cost of removal and of other factors. Mere knowledge of the cost of removal is no help to one who wishes to remove a building in the course of re-planning the use of land resources. Unless finance is available to meet the cost, nothing can or will be done. But finance, however raised, is a form of consociate wealth. And when removal is to make way for replacement consociate wealth is doubly significant. Adding to the land mass of a proprietary land unit or to the bundle of rights of a unit would be impossible without consociate wealth in the form either of other land or cash. Failure of the early land reforms in Ireland in the 1870s was due to

---

[5] Above, p. 46.

the false assumption that the holders of inferior proprietary land units (the tenants) whom the reforms were intended to emancipate possessed consociate wealth sufficient to finance down payments for the purchase of the interests of the landlords.

Size and Abstract Attributes. It is axiomatic that in the absence of consociate wealth the removal, replacement or addition of land resources within the proprietary land unit will reduce the size of the unit or the range of the bundle of property rights, and thus in some way alter the abstract attributes of the unit. The holder of a proprietary land unit with no other wealth consociate with it cannot meet the costs of any readjustment of the land resources of the unit unless he sells part of the land, carves an inferior unit out of what he has in consideration of cash, or raises a mortgage or other form of loan on the security of the land resources. Each one of these expedients in its own way cuts down the range of the property rights of the unit, either spatially by cutting back the size of the unit, or by the assignment of rights to the holder of an inferior unit or to one who has a charge upon the wealth of the land resources. To demonstrate the force of the axiom, the holder of the proprietary land unit has been assumed to have a unit with no consociate wealth whatever. Even so, he will get nowhere without creating it, albeit only for a moment in the course of the transactions. The consideration received from the sale, the creation of the inferior unit or the loan although used to finance the desired adjustment of land resources will, until committed to that purpose in the hands of the holder of the unit, be wealth consociate with the unit. The control of consociate wealth by Government could have an immediate effect, therefore, upon the use and planning of land resources.

Static or Immobile Relationship. The two previous answers to the question about consociate wealth make the case for recognizing and considering it by pointing to its functions in relation to the dynamics of mutation within the proprietary land unit. In these circumstances, consociate wealth is interchanged with land resources or with property rights over land.

Consociate wealth may be just as needful, however, in certain circumstances for maintaining a relatively static condition of a proprietary land unit. In the general case, this can happen where:

(*a*) the present use of land resources and the form of the proprietary land unit are wholly dependent upon the availability of consociate wealth; and

151

(*b*) consociate wealth stimulates action to preserve the proprietary land unit.

The first of the two contingencies is met with in circumstances where the land resources of the proprietary land unit are insufficient or used in such a way as to be self-supporting. Without the aid of income generated by the investment, or use of wealth consociate with the proprietary land unit, the holder of the unit would not be able to retain it. Take the case of the owners of estates in rural Britain in the immediate post-war years. Early in the 1950s building licences were removed as a control measure and landowners were confronted as a general rule with enormous back-logs of disrepair and foregone improvements. Costs had risen steeply while rental income from the land had barely moved above pre-war levels.[6] Yearly repair bills more than swallowed up rental revenues.[7] Rural estates accumulated deficits. In these circumstances they could not possibly survive as cradles of leasehold farms at easy-going rents, unless the landowners possessed with their estates consociate wealth sufficient to meet the yearly short falls and provide a livelihood for the landowner into the bargain. The supreme importance of consociate wealth to the fortunes of the proprietary land units was underscored at the time by a particular provision in the income tax law. Where the rental revenue of an agricultural proprietary land unit was inadequate to meet the yearly repair bill, the adverse balance of cost could be set off against income from other sources in assessing the landowner to income tax.[8] Income from consociate wealth thus provided a means of financing out of untaxed income repairs to the equipment of the agricultural estates which the revenues from them could not touch. The right to set off the excess expenditure against other income was of no consequence to the holder of a proprietary land unit devoid of consociate wealth.

An example of the second possible contingency will be found in the attempts made to preserve a proprietary land unit and the pattern of its land resources against the ravages of inheritance taxation. Title to the unit changes hands, from those of the present holder vulnerable to death duty to one of the immortals[9] to be held in trust and for the preservation of the existence of the unit. Although the proprietary character form of the unit undergoes change, it does so somewhat paradoxically, in the interests of the

[6] D. R. Denman, *Estate Incomes* (University of Cambridge, Department of Estate Management, 1955), p. 23.

[7] D. R. Denman and V. F. Stewart, *Farm Rents* (Allen and Unwin, London, 1959), pp. 171–2.

[8] D. R. Denman, *Estate Incomes, op. cit.*, p. 5. [9] Above, p. 32.

status quo so far as the use and disposition of the land resources goes and the incidence of the monetary benefits, if any. The point for us to note here is the critical role played by consociate wealth. With few exceptions, it is the presence of consociate wealth, in other land and assets, swelling the total fortune of the holder of the proprietary land unit, which prompts him to make over the unit to trustees. The sheer magnitude of the consociate wealth is the touchstone. Trusts can be formed to handle relatively small proprietary land units and modest fortunes – a surburban villa and a life insurance to match – but to do so would be pointless and exceedingly uneconomic if the only end was to avoid an Exchequer demand for death duty, as the duty would be relatively so small as to make the incurrence of the cost of the trust a nonsense. The value of the consociate wealth is the critical factor.

National Land Use Pattern. The immediate bearing consociate wealth has upon the use of land resources within a proprietary land unit points to the significance of consociate wealth in national distributions of land resources and national patterns of land use. A government could radically affect the way in which land resources are used by controlling the amount and the form of consociate wealth permitted to be held. Let us take an extreme: suppose the hypothetical condition in which government had successfully banned all forms of consociate wealth. In such a wonderland, the size of proprietary land units would never change, except by the introduction of communal holdings or by the free gift of contiguous units. The land use pattern of the nation would remain locked within, and wholly dependent upon, a more or less static structure of proprietary land units. There would also be an immediate and nation-wide sale of proprietary land units which at the time of the control edict would have been consociate with other units. Something on these lines recently happened in Iran where in the process of land reform no landowner was permitted to hold more than one village and had to dispose of all villages which were consociate with the one retained.

Under the hypothetical conditions of our wonderland, a landowner who wanted a change would have to choose one of the following alternatives:

    i. to exchange his own proprietary land unit for another whole unit;

    ii. sell his proprietary land unit outright;

iii. accept the gift of a proprietary land unit which could be immediately absorbed into his existing one;

iv. enter into a co-operative or communal arrangement with holders of other proprietary land units to form one larger unit from two or more contributory ones.

The holder of the proprietary land unit would not be permitted to sell off parts of it so as to create a smaller unit because the proceeds from the sale would form a pool of wealth consociate with the smaller unit so created. The proprietary land unit received by way of gift would have to be entire and more or less contiguous. If it were not so, the gift would create landed wealth consociate with the proprietary land unit of the donee. What was given would need to be an entire unit. If part were given, there would be a moment for the donor when what he was parting with would appear as wealth consociate with what he had retained.

Government Control over the Proprietary Land Unit. To the control of land use and resources through the control of the holding of consociate wealth there is a reverse counterpart—the control of the use of consociate wealth through government interference with the type of proprietary land unit. Land reform in India provides an interesting example. Government set its face against the inferior proprietary land unit in rural societies.[10] Letting land for farming was proscribed. Before reform extensive superior proprietary land units existed as *zamindari*, owned by men of wealth and substance who by and large avoided all direct contact with the land and its cultivation. Under reform a landowner could hold a proprietary land unit of any size provided the holder cultivated land resources of the unit properly. The upshot was for the landowners to take in hand as much land as they could and as quickly as possible, to deprive the cultivators of their inferior holdings, and to put to immediately effective use the wealth which prior to land reform was consociate with the superior proprietary land units by investing it in fertilizers, stock and equipment for the cultivation of the land. Thus, by controlling the type of proprietary land unit permitted, the government found a means by which much private wealth consociate with the holdings of the *zamindars* was committed to the advance of agriculture.

[10] See, for instance A. N. Jha, 'Agrarian Reform in the State of Uttar Pradesh, India', *Land Tenure*, Ed. K. H. Parsons, R. J. Penn, P. M. Raup (University of Wisconsin Press, 1956), pp. 146 ff.

Categories of Consociate Wealth

An analysis of the structure and land use planning of proprietary land units would clearly be inadequate if we were to leave consociate wealth out of the picture. It must be included and we must now look a little closer at its features.

Consociate wealth in certain circumstances reflects perfectly the classical concepts of capital. There are occasions, many occasions, when we must follow the accountants and take consociate wealth into our reckoning as if it were a lump of plasticine having size and consistency but no diversity. As we have seen when dealing with land and land resources this concept of homogeneity obscures the functional role of the items of wealth.

Now the functional is critical in the relationship between consociate wealth and the proprietary land unit. So we must leave the accountants to their plasticine and look at consociate wealth as an array of items linked together in a functional way. We must see the items for what they are and what they do. Each particular combination of consociate assets is unique. That, we must accept, but while a hundred items may display as many different forms and a thousand different features, it is possible for each item to perform a similar function with its companions and we can put the hundred into one functional category. By this functional approach it is possible to classify very broadly the types of consociate wealth in the general case.

The following scedule based on general functional performance is proposed:

    i. immediately convertible;
   ii. mediately convertible;
  iii. contingent;
   iv. emergent;
    v. static;
   iv. militating;
  vii. independent;
 viii. multi-form;
   ix. mutually exclusive forms.

Immediately Convertible (*i*). One way of looking at consociate wealth is to regard its convertibility. That is to say, the way in which an item of consociate wealth is exchangeable for land resources of a proprietary land unit with which the wealth is consociate. Convertibility in this sense should be distinguished from liquidity. Liquidity usually, and certainly the Keynesian connotation,[11] means cash savings held as such and not committed to investment in the pursuit of interest or an equivalent reward. Money, of all forms of consociate wealth, can be converted to land resources by using it immediately to finance improvements or purchase equipment. Because it is liquid money is immediately convertible but this is not the whole story. Although all money is immediately convertible consociate wealth, all immediately convertible consociate wealth is not money. We can say consociate wealth is immediately convertible when it can be transformed into, or exchanged for, land resources, without having recourse to an agency which will first of all convert the consociate wealth into money ready for a subsequent transformation, before commital to the land resources of a proprietary land unit.

Let us suppose the holder of a proprietary land unit which we shall call the primary land unit A (represented by PL_A) has a gravel quarry which for managerial reasons is a separate proprietary land unit B (represented by PL_B). The gravel at the quarry face (G) is not part of the land resources of the proprietary land unit B but belongs to the wealth consociate with B. Reverting to our previous notation we can write $B \rceil G$ for the proprietary land unit B and the consociate wealth (G). The gravel at the quarry face (G), however, is immediately convertible as it can be used by the holder of B for making roads and other improvements to the land resources of B. Now B, as a secondary land unit with the consociate wealth (G) is consociate with the primary proprietary land unit A; and we may express the proprietary syndrome as:

$$PL_A \rceil \atop \qquad \rfloor PL_B \rceil \atop \qquad\qquad \rfloor G$$

But the gravel at the quarry face could be used as immediately convertible consociate wealth for improvements to the land resources of A, in which case we write the relationship as:

$$PL_A \rceil \atop \qquad =\rfloor PL_B \atop \qquad\quad \rfloor G$$

As a further refinement of our notation we can use the suffix (i) to indicate that we are handling immediately convertible consociate wealth. Our examples then become:

---

[11] J. M. Keynes, *The General Theory of Employment, Interest and Money* (London, 1936), Ch. 13.

i. where the gravel at the quarry face is regarded as consociate wealth only with the proprietary land unit B:

$$PL_A \text{—} \\ \quad L_{PL_B} \text{—} \\ \qquad L_{Gi}$$

ii. where the gravel at the quarry face is regarded as consociate wealth only of proprietary land unit A:

$$PL_A \text{—} \\ \quad |= PL_B \\ \quad L_{Gi}$$

iii. where the gravel at the quarry face is regarded as consociate wealth with proprietary land units A and B.

$$PL_A \text{—} \\ \quad |= | PL_B \text{—} \\ \qquad L_{Gi}$$

Mediately Convertible (*m*). Consociate wealth is mediately convertible when the services of an intermediary are required before the wealth can be transferred to, or used upon, the proprietary land unit with which it is consociate. Normally, the intermediate agency is a market of some kind. The consociate wealth is converted into money by sale and the proceeds invested as improvements and additions to the land resources of the proprietary land unit. Markets, however, are not the only available forms of intermediate agency. A government authority, for example, may have a right to veto the sale of consociate wealth and permission to sell will be a prerequisite to the first stage of conversion. Examples are found in recent French legislation which introduced a mild form of land reform. The law requires holders of proprietary land units who wish to dispose of them to offer them first to the *Sociétés d'aménagement foncier et d'établissement rural* (SAFER). This right of pre-emption in the SAFER means that holders who hold two proprietary land units, of which one is consociate with the other, cannot dispose of the former without offering it first to the SAFER. The SAFER then is an intermediary and the proprietary land unit which the holder wishes to dispose of is only mediately convertible consociate wealth. Similar restraints may introduce third parties into the picture. The third parties have powers of sanction, to restrain the holder of a proprietary land unit from using consociate wealth in specific forms for immediate invest-

157

ment in the land resources of the unit; the common law, for example, restrains a tenant for life under a strict settlement from cutting mature timber for the benefit of his life tenancy, and the holder of the life tenancy cannot use consociate wealth in the timber without first obtaining permission of the trustees of the settlement.

Another standard form of intermediary and one which is not uncommon is technical processing. The holder of a proprietary land unit in oil-bearing land may use oil for developing the resources of his unit but is precluded from using the oil from his own unit immediately because it has to be processed externally and brought back to the unit before it can be used for land improvements.

The categories we have just mentioned, namely immediately convertible and mediately, are mutually exclusive in so far as an item of consociate wealth which is mediately convertible cannot be at the same time immediately convertible. Nevertheless, a particular item of wealth may be immediately convertible up to the point where the demand for it is satisfied. From then on it may be mediately convertible. For example, the gravel at the quarry face in the example just given,[12] may be used for making roads and thus be immediately convertible. It will be so used until the roads are made. Thereafter, the remaining gravel may be sold and the money used for other types of improvement to the land resources of the proprietary land unit. In these circumstances the gravel at the quarry face becomes mediately convertible consociate wealth. Using in our notation the suffix (m) to denote mediately convertible wealth we may write of the above dual situation the following expression:

$$PL_A{\rightharpoondown} \atop {=} \Big| \; PL_B{\rightharpoondown} \atop {\underline{\qquad\qquad}} \Big\rfloor \; Gi, \; Gm$$

We should not write:

$$PL_A{\rightharpoondown} \atop {=} \Big| \; PL_B{\rightharpoondown} \atop {\underline{\qquad\qquad}} \Big\rfloor \; Gi, \; m$$

Since in this expression, Gi, m is a contradiction: immediately convertible wealth and mediately convertible wealth being mutually exclusive.[13]

---

[12] Above, p. 156.   [13] Below, p. 164.

Nor should we write:

$$PL_A \begin{bmatrix} \left((PL_B \begin{bmatrix} \\ \end{bmatrix} Gi, Gm \right) m \\ \end{bmatrix}$$

because this indicates that the consociate wealth (G) is, initially, immediately convertible and afterwards, mediately convertible with respect to both PL_A and PL_B, and in these circumstances, cannot be sold or disposed of in a package with the unit PL_B.

Contingent (k). Some types of wealth are anticipated and do not emerge in tangible form until the happening of a particular event. The right to the future enjoyment of them is a present right and the holder of a proprietary land unit may take advantage of the right and plan the use of his land resources in the expectation of possessing what he has a right to in the future. Consociate wealth of this kind can be referred to as contingent, denoted in our notation by the suffix (k).

We should be careful to distinguish contingent consociate wealth from a certain kind of proprietary land unit, the title to which is contingent upon a satisfied event. A landowner who will be vested of an estate in the event of his reaching the age of 21 may be said to hold a proprietary land unit whose property rights give him power of possession and action after a certain event; or it may be argued that he has no proprietary land unit, and cannot have, until the contingency transpires. He either now possesses a proprietary land unit or he does not hold one at all—it all depends on how we look at things.

Contingent consociate wealth as we would define it here is wealth to which the holder of a proprietary land unit will be entitled and be in a position to enjoy, precisely because he holds title to the proprietary land unit with which the contingent wealth is consociate. Two examples may help to clarify what is meant. We have already mentioned the condition in which growing crops which yesterday were part of the land resources of a proprietary land unit are today ripe for harvest and are thus consociate wealth. This is one form in which contingent consociate wealth is found. Until harvest the holder of the proprietary land unit can but look forward to the day when he realizes consociate wealth, today locked up in the growing grain. He has contingent consociate wealth. The holder of a superior proprietary land unit may also possess a present right to contingent consociate wealth. Not infrequently, the holder of an inferior

159

proprietary land unit will have agreed to pay compensation to the holder of the superior unit at the termination of the inferior unit, for damage caused to the land resources of the superior unit by the holder of the inferior. The holder of the superior unit plans his resources in the light and expectation of the compensation payment which, however, is not realizable until the inferior unit expires.

Emergent (*e*). The counterpart of the superior owner's claim to compensation for disrepair and deterioration is the claim of the holder of an inferior unit to compensation for contributions and investments made by him so as to enhance the value of the land resources to the holder of the superior unit. The tenant or holder of the inferior unit has a present claim to wealth, tangible in the future. While he is in possession of the inferior unit he enjoys the contributions and improvements he has made—they are present land resources for him. His claim for compensation for what remains in them of value when the inferior unit terminates is similar to the claim of the holder of the superior unit to compensation for disrepair; similar but not identical. The inferior holder's claim is unlike the claim of the superior holder because at the moment when the former materializes the claimant will have no proprietary land unit with which it would be consociate—the claim arises at the moment when the inferior unit ends. Nonetheless, the right to claim at the end of the inferior term draws a distinction between the land resources of the inferior unit over which the holder has no claim or interest at the end, and those in respect of which a benefit remains to him when the inferior unit terminates. The shorter the term of the inferior unit, the more pronounced will the consociate wealth become. It emerges, as it were, like a rock in an ebbing tide, gathering bulk as with the passage of time the inferior unit drains away. It is emergent and yet only consociate as long as the inferior proprietary unit exists.

Static (*s*). Consociate wealth in the categories so far described has a dynamism about it—it is convertible, contingent, emergent. There is also a static form of consociate wealth. We come across it whenever wealth is inalienable, especially land. An owner who is prohibited from selling, leasing or mortgaging his wealth may use the income from it to improve the land resources of a proprietary land unit, but he cannot turn the capital into land resources, unless, in the rare event, it is goods of a kind he can use in an immediate way to improve the land of the proprietary land unit. Although prohibition may be qualified and alienability made dependent upon

160

the sanction of another person or institution, it makes no difference to the form of consociate wealth. Until permission to sell or lease is given, the wealth is inalienable and in that sense static. Consociate wealth which cannot readily be converted to money at any particular moment, because of a dead market is not static in the sense in which we use the term. Inalienability is seldom found among non-derivative proprietary land units and tends to be countenanced by law among the derivative, inferior proprietary land units. For consociate wealth to be static, the inalienability must be non-selective, as with the alimentary life rent of Scots law. What is alienable to some persons and not to others cannot be static, however stringent the prohibitions against disposal to the barred purchasers might be. If an item of consociate wealth is disposable no matter how narrow the limits of eligible alienation may be, it is in some measure convertible and, as consociate wealth, will be seen to function as convertible wealth and should not be classified as static.

Militating and Independent (*t*) and (*d*). A holder of a proprietary land unit may dispose of wealth consociate with the unit and invest the proceeds in the land resources of the unit so as to achieve a beneficial objective, only to find the primary advantage gained by his disposition has precipitated a secondary reaction. The secondary reaction might militate against the benefit gained, or enhance it. Imagine a factory owner who is tenant of the land on which his factory is to be erected and freeholder of a country residence with magnificent views and open vistas. The inferior proprietary land unit he holds in the factory site would be consociate with the residential proprietary land unit. He proposes to erect the factory on the leasehold site which unfortunately is in full view of the dwelling and will mar the outlook. Yet, without the income from the factory, the owner of the freehold would not be able to afford to run the country house and maintain the structure and grounds. To build the factory means putting consociate wealth to a use of critical and primary consequence to the achievement of the motive which prompts the factory owner to have the residential proprietary land unit. But the primary advantage of a source of revenue for the upkeep of the freehold proprietary land unit is militated against by the loss of amenity, the secondary consequence of having used consociate wealth to develop the inferior proprietary land unit. Consociate wealth which behaves in this way should be distinguished from wealth whose benefit to the proprietary land unit with which it is consociate is free of secondary effects, and in that sense is independent. Consociate wealth whose primary function is influenced

L   161 for better or worse by a secondary reaction can be classified as militating consociate wealth (t); and consociate wealth whose function is free of secondary effects, as independent consociate wealth (d).

Multi-form. Consociate wealth can perform two or more functions simultaneously. A particular asset such as the inferior proprietary land unit occupied by the factory in the above example can fit into two categories—mediately convertible (m) and militating (t). The limits of multiplicity are set by mutual exclusiveness which we shall refer to later.

The number of dual and multiple roles which can be played simultaneously by items of consociate wealth is limited. A dual function frequently exhibited by consociate assets is to be mediately convertible and also either militating or independent. The holder of the inferior proprietary land unit just mentioned on which the factory stands has in the inferior unit a form of wealth consociate with the residential proprietary land unit and which is mediately convertible, as the leasehold factory can be sold, and militating in that it generates a benefit favourable to the holding of the residential proprietary land unit and a bane at the same time. If by taking advantage of the mediately convertibility the factory were sold, the substitute consociate wealth (cash from the sale) would have different but also dual functions, as it would be immediately convertible (i) and independent (d).

Contingent consociate wealth can never be mediately convertible since, by definition, it is not saleable apart from the land resources with which it is integrated. Once the contingency happens, the wealth takes another form and usually becomes mediately convertible. Nevertheless, if in relation to a particular proprietary land unit (PL_A), the proprietary land unit (PL_B) with which wealth H is contingently consociate (k), is itself consociate with the proprietary land unit (PL_A), then it and the contingent consociate wealth are together mediately convertible (m). Using our notation, we can write:

$$PL_A \llcorner \left(PL_B \llcorner Hk \right)_m$$

It should be noted that it is a contradiction to write:

$$PL_A \llcorner \left(PL_B \llcorner Hk.m \right)$$

since the symbols indicate that H is both contingent and mediately convertible, which is impossible. And so it is with emergent consociate wealth (e). We can happily write:

$$PL_A \lceil \left(PL_B \lceil_{He} \right)_m$$

But not:

$$PL_A \lceil \left(PL_B \lceil_{He.\,m} \right)$$

It is certain that PL_B would be either militating (t) or independent (d) in its relationship with (PL_A) and according to the circumstances, we could write:

either—

$$PL_A \lceil \left(PL_B \lceil_{He} \right)_{m.\,t}$$

or—

$$PL_A \lceil \left(PL_B \lceil_{He} \right)_{m.\,d}$$

Imagine the factory site in the previous illustration sublet and a dilapidations claim giving contingent consociate wealth Dk to the head-lessee, the holder of the freehold proprietary land unit on which the residence stands. The holder of the residential proprietary land unit (PL_A) suffers and benefits from the inferior unit (PL_B) but is in the position to sell and assign the head-lease at any time. We then have:

$$PL_A \lceil \left(PL_B \lceil_{Dk} \right)_{m.\,t}$$

From the viewpoint of the holder of the inferior proprietary land unit the proprietary syndrome is:

$$PL_B \lceil \begin{matrix} Dk \\ PL_A \end{matrix}_{m.d}$$

163

on the assumption that the holder of the inferior proprietary land unit (PL_B) can dispose of the proprietary land unit (PL_A) which does not in itself militate favourably or adversely in respect of the inferior unit (PL_B) with which it is consociate.

Growing crops could in certain circumstances be both contingent and emergent consociate wealth. This can happen on an inferior proprietary land unit with an uncertain duration and where the holder of the inferior unit has the right to claim compensation for the growing crops at the end of the duration of the unit. If the duration of the inferior unit was certain, the claim would produce contingent consociate wealth if harvest were to take place before the end of the duration, and emergent consociate wealth if the harvest were to come later. Where the end is uncertain, we can but assign a dual role to the wealth represented by the claim and the right to the harvest.

Static consociate wealth will take a dual form, either militating (t) or independent (d). Inalienability does not prevent the inalienable asset being used in a manner which is either beneficial or harmful to the proprietary land unit with which it is consociate.

Mutually Exclusive. The function of consociate wealth is relative. The residence in the example used before is independent (d) consociate wealth because in relation to the inferior proprietary land unit (PL_B) it is neither beneficial nor detrimental unless it can be shown that the efficient working of the factory is dependent upon the leaseholder having a nearby residence to live in; in which event the freehold residential proprietary land unit would take on a militating character. Change takes place over time. What was independent consociate wealth yesterday can be militating consociate wealth today. But at any one moment certain classes of consociate

TABLE VI: *Forms of Consociate Wealth in Mutually Exclusive Pairs*

I	Immediately convertible		IV	Militating
	Mediately convertible			Independent
II	Immediately convertible		V	Immediately convertible
	Static			Contingent
III	Mediately convertible		VI	Immediately convertible
	Static			Emergent

164

wealth may play two or more roles while others are mutually exclusive. Mutual exclusiveness is inherent in the nature of the functions. Table VI arranges the classes of consociate wealth in mutually exclusive pairs.

Adventitious Wealth. Categories

With one or two exceptions, all that has been said above about the categories of consociate wealth applies to adventitious wealth. Adventitious wealth can never be contingent or emergent as these two forms of wealth can only materialize when there is a consociate relationship between them and the proprietary land unit. We must, therefore, omit from the categories of adventitious wealth these two categories. There are, however, two to add—deliberate adventitious wealth and accidental adventitious wealth. Deliberate adventitious wealth is formed when what was consociate wealth is deliberately made adventitious by the holder of it; or, when what could become consociate wealth remains adventitious at the instance of the holder of it. A landowner may, for example, deliberately incorporate the adult members of his family into a family company for the purpose of conveying to the company a proprietary land unit now owned by himself. After the transfer, and supposing he holds the controlling shares in the family company, the wealth he holds personally becomes the adventitious wealth to the proprietary land unit held by the company. At the same time, the erstwhile owner of the proprietary land unit has the power to wind up the company and have the proprietary land unit vested in himself; in which event the personal wealth that was adventitious to the proprietary land unit held by the family company becomes consociate with the unit now back in the hands of its former owner. Accidental adventitious wealth does not become such by deliberate action. As the term implies, it is created not by design but by historical accident. A man, for example, who holds a controlling interest in a company owning a proprietary land unit inherits wealth. The inherited wealth becomes, through no design on the part of the holder of it, adventitious wealth to the proprietary land unit in the hands of the company.

Chapter X

CURRENT REWARDS AND RATIOS

The premise from which our analysis sets out is the critical role of motive in determining the planning of the land resources of a proprietary land unit. At any one moment in time, the lay-out and land use pattern of the land resources of a unit cannot be understood until we have ascertained what in the past has motivated the decisions of he who has held the power of decision-making and execution over the land resources and brought his plans to the present pass. We have steered our thinking away from attitudes to wealth which must quantify it in money terms and evaluate it *en masse* as so many units of money's work. Our approach has been to comprehend the functional and this is a logical step from and to an analysis based on motive. Land and assets fixed to it in such a way that at law they are regarded as an integral feature of land are seen as a combination of land resources in relationship to combinations of other forms of wealth, each item in the inventory performing a function more or less in harmony with the functions of others towards the fulfilment of motive.

We have said very little up to now about how we should look at things in relation to the passage of time. Mention has been made of the periodicity within which old plans give way to new.[1] But what of the period in which a particular combination of resources remains constant, and represents the best that in the circumstances can be achieved towards the fulfilment of motive? What is the relationship between the assets in the combination, and the moment by moment contribution they make to the achievement of motive? Can it be measured and told? The question commends itself because when wealth in the form and function of capital is evaluated in money terms, the achievement of the capital wealth in the generation of income is measured in money terms also, over given periods of time—income per day, percentage yield per annum and so on. Is it possible to think of current rewards to the use of the land resources

[1] Above, p. 39.

of a proprietary land unit over time periods? As a final step in our analysis, we shall consider the answer to this question in the general case.

Only as a special case is the motive of a holder of a proprietary land unit entrepreneurial, concerned, that is, to maximize a net money income from the use of land resources. Where this is so, achievement can be measured in money terms. Sometimes, and not infrequently, the land resources are held as factors of production contributing with assets and labour to a joint enterprise. A monetary revenue separate from the money output derived from other factors is neither sought nor estimated. Again, motive may not be entrepreneurial nor specifically productive in an economic sense; the current reward is in fact non-monetary and often defies all attempts to evaluate it in money terms. And combinations of all three of the above possibilities must also be reckoned with.

Clearly, we have two categories of current reward from the holding of a proprietary land unit: rewards that are monetary and those that are not. We propose to look at each of the two types of current reward, to discuss their characteristics in the general case, and to touch in passing upon the effect the attributes of a proprietary land unit might have upon them.

Money Flow and Rent

The classical division of the social output of all productive effort into wages as the current reward to labour, interest to capital and rent to land provides us with a convenient set of labels. In the real world it is almost impossible to draw demarcation lines dividing one type of reward from the other, largely because both of what are classically regarded as labour and capital cannot operate without some kind of purchase on the land, and what might arbitrarily be taken as the dole of labour from the social pool in fact owes something to the land for the use labour has made of it. Be that as it may; rent is a useful label which we intend to use in a generic sense for the monetary revenue from the land resources of a proprietary land unit. Equipped, with this ticket, let us see what it may denote in the general case; what meanings rent can and does have in the real world where men hold land to their comfort.

To the classical theorists who followed in the train of Ricardo, such as Von Thünen, rent was a residuum,[2] a surplus to the rewards of labour and capital. Later, the more modern approach of Jevons and

[2] J. H. von Thunen, *Der isolierte Staat*, trans. C. M. Wartenberg, Ed. Peter Hall (Pergamon Press, 1966), p. 147.

Walras[3] saw it as being equal to the value of the marginal service rendered by land to the production process. Theories more recent still have refined the concept of rent by introducing the notion of opportunity costs.[4] All these theories presuppose a kind of biopsy, whereby land in the virgin sense can be dissected from other wealth, and its rental processes and rewards examined. All very well for theory: but in the real world where land as the classical economists saw it is as lost to human experience as the age of innocence, we must see rent as an actual or potential cash flow receivable as reward for the use of land resources in the sense that we have used the term for the purpose of this analysis.

As an actual cash flow, it is attendant upon the existence of an inferior-superior proprietary land unit relationship. Cash flows in the form of payment from the holder of the inferior land unit to the holder of the superior, as consideration for the use of the land resources of the inferior land unit. Because of the reciprocal relationship between the two units, the rent payment is a revenue to the holder of the superior proprietary land unit and an outgoing to the holder of the inferior unit; we shall meet it again in its role as a debit when we are dealing with outflows.[5]

We are dealing with a concept and not a universally accepted term of speech. Payments made by the holders of inferior proprietary land units to the holders of superior ones may have many demoninations—renders, tributes, farm and so on, even in the English language, to say nothing of the words used in the living and dead languages of men to denote the same idea. Variations in terminology do not prevent us from getting behind them to discover the general characteristics of the rent payment. The payment may be the outcome of voluntary and free agreement between the parties to an inferior-superior relationship; or it may be imposed upon the holder of the inferior unit by law and custom, or in some more imperialistic manner by the holder of the superior land unit—the renders of various kinds paid by villein tenants to the lords of manors in medieval days were determined by local custom. Payments, also, may not in the strict sense be rendered in cash. In many parts of the ancient and modern world renders made by the holders of inferior proprietary land units to the holders of suprior ones are made in kind—the actual produce of the harvest or the products

[3] W. S. Jevons, *Theory of Political Economy* (Macmillan and Co., 1871), p. 205 *et passim*.
[4] J. A. Schumpeter, *History of Economic Analysis* (Oxford University Press, 1954), p. 938.
[5] Below, p. 172.

from the livestock are divided between the holders of the respective units or the rent is yielded to the holder of the superior unit in the form of a labour service by the holder of the inferior unit.[6] We can look upon these services and renders in kind as the equivalents of a flow of cash payments. Where custom and tradition have their say, the renders might have no or little economic significance, being tokens of a social relationship and not payments for an economic benefit. Although we should classify them among the monetary current rewards, we should accept that the motive that prompts the taking of them is not commercial, but political or social.

Whether we are handling cash or kind, dealing in commerce or acknowledging status, in the real world and in the general case, rent will take one of the following forms:

  i. what is actually paid or rendered;
  ii. what should be paid or rendered at law; or
  iii. what could be paid or rendered.

It is possible and indeed not unusual, that an actual rent sum is equal to what is legally required and what in any event would be rendered. The distinctions just made are far from being merely academic. If the holder of a proprietary land unit has a commercial motive or is concerned in some way with the receipt of rent payments, what he actually receives is of primary consequence to him. Under a formal agreement or by some other process at law, there may be due to him rent payments far in excess of what he in fact receives; and sometimes, in the face of universal statutory rent restriction, receipts, ostensibly for another purpose, may exceed what is legally required. Litigation may be too costly, too cumbersome or socially undesirable for the holder of the superior unit to proceed to exact the law's just dues from the holder of the inferior. In the great depression and farming doldrums of the 1890s in England, the landlords remitted rents wholesale,[7] and what on paper, in the terms of a counterpart lease, might look a handsome rent and represent a sound investment yield was something the landlord never, or seldom, asked for or received.

Actual rent paid, coincident, let us suppose, with what is at law required might be far below what the holder of the superior land unit could receive if he were to offer the inferior proprietary land

6 This proprietary relationship is of the Dependent Derivative Type. See D. R. Denman *Proprietary Patterns and Land Use*, The World Land Use Survey, Occasional Paper No. 9 (Geographical Publications Ltd, 1970), p. 33.

7 *Report of the Departmental Committee of the Board of Agriculture on Tenant Farmers and Sales of Estates* (1912), Cd. 6030.

169

unit on the market; in other words, the rent payable could be less
than the market value, in rental terms, of the inferior land unit.
The overt evidence of the rent audit could grossly misrepresent the
true rental value of the land resources of the superior land unit.
In particular cases, many different explanations could be given—
reluctance on the part of the landlord to disturb his tenant, a long
binding lease keeping the inferior unit off the market, a premium
taken by the holder of the superior unit from the holder of the
inferior unit on entry, and so on. Immediately after World War II,
rents of farms in Britain were below the rents which the landlords
could have obtained if they had taken their tenants to arbitration;
they accepted the sub-market rents because they did not wish to
engage their tenants in public dispute.[8]

A situation may arise which could cause some confusion in
analysis. In many parts of the world, the holder of a proprietary
land unit may depasture his cattle on the lands of a neighbour, or
he may take from the land natural resources, such as stone and wood.
For the privilege, the beneficiary pays his neighbour a consideration
which may well be termed rent. What is the true nature in the terms
of our analysis of the transaction and the payment? At first sight,
it looks as if the neighbour has sold to the recipient of the benefit
an item of wealth which is immediately consociate with his, the
neighbour's proprietary land unit. This, indeed, could be the explanation but for the relationship of contiguity or proximity. The actual
state of affairs would depend upon the nature of the legal right
invoked by the grazier or beneficiary under the arrangement. If he
depastured his cattle in the exercise of a property right collateral
with the property rights over his own proprietary land unit, we
should look upon the payment made to the neighbour as rent in
consideration, not for growing grass, but for the derived right carved
out of the rights which the neighbour has over his own proprietary
land unit. The application of the principles of our analysis would
require this explanation in almost every case. The position with an
itinerant grazier would be different; it could be said that a bargain
had been struck to sell him the grass as an item of the wealth consociate with the proprietary land unit to which the grazing land
belongs.

Rent as a potential cash flow (using the term in the comprehensive sense of the above paragraphs) is the form the reward takes
for the holder of a proprietary land unit who is in occupation of
the land, working or exploiting it in some way. Potential rent is the
higher of two figures: what the present holder can earn from the

[8] D. R. Denman, *Estate Capital* (Allen and Unwin, London, 1957), p. 100.

land resources; and what somebody else would be willing to pay for the occupancy and use of them.

The holder of the proprietary land unit who aims at generating a money income from his land cannot look to the land resources alone. He must either employ himself or others to work the resources, and it is difficult to envisage his being able to do anything without chattel assets of some kind—machinery, plant, livestock, equipment. As his aim is a money income, he will doubtless compare what income his labour and other inputs could earn if put to alternative uses. The alternative marginal rewards would reflect the opportunity costs to him of pursuing the intended plans with the labour and capital assets employed. It would be rational to assume that the opportunity cost would be less than what by his estimates he would earn or in fact does earn. He must, therefore, apportion in some way part of the gross social earnings from all his wealth devoted to and consociate with the proprietary land unit, to the use of the chattel assets and labour. We are back to the idea of a residuum: for the rental worth of the land resources to the holder of the proprietary land unit would be the residue of the social revenue after making apportionments to the chattels and to labour.

It is at this point that the other figure for potential rent comes into the picture. What is left as a current reward to the land resources may be considerably less than the figure the market would be prepared to render by way of rent payment for the use of the land resources. If it is above the residual figure, it is this market figure which is the true measure of the potential rent. It is in short, what the holder of the unit could get if he were to offer an inferior land unit on the market in exchange for a current rent. Potential rent in these circumstances is always an estimate. The amount of rent payable will patently depend upon what is offered, and it is just this kind of decision which is difficult to make and which affects so radically the aggreate of the potential rent. The holder of the proprietary land unit may have to decide in which ways the division of the land resources and distribution of the property rights should be made so as to maximize rental rewards. Gross income will not be the best guide; a complicated division of land and rights could result in costly and complex management and heighten the risk of income not being sustained at the estimated level. No general pattern can be laid down. What is important for this analysis is to realize that potential rent is not simply the rent the market would offer for an inferior land unit coincident in boundaries with the boundaries of the superior unit, and conditional upon the observance of one set of property rights giving form to the abstract attributes

171

of the inferior land unit in respect of which the rent would be payable.

Money Flow and Outgoings

The holder of a proprietary land unit who is looking to the unit for a monetary income will have to offset sundry outgoings from actual or potential rental revenue. In the future text, rental revenue will denote the gross figure actually or potentially receivable as rent and rental income as the net figure after deducting the appropriate outgoings. An outflow of money payments does not necessarily imply the counter benefit of an actual or potential rental revenue. No matter the motive and the current reward, land resources suffer an actual or potential outflow or wastage. Current outflow is thus a characteristic of all proprietary land units, and for the purpose of our analysis we are concerned with the pattern in the general case. There are the following standard categories into which all types of outflow from the land resources of a proprietary land unit can be fitted.

   i. payments to holders of superior land units;
   ii. payments to holders of contiguous and proximate land units for lateral rights;
   iii. maintenance costs;
   iv. amortization;
   v. financial obligations peculiar to the proprietary land unit as such;
   vi. local levies; and
   vii. fiscal dues.

Payments and outgoings in the above categories are in the main obvious enough and do not call for further explanation. As we have already noted, the rental payments peculiar to inferior proprietary land units are the primary source of revenue to the superior unit from which the charged inferior is derived. Payments for lateral rights are similarly consequences of reciprocal relationships. Maintenance costs do call for some comment. Actual records of payments on repairs and maintenance are invariably but part of the burden, and should never be taken as evidence of total ouflow. Outflow like revenue inflow must be related to a passage of time; a flowing is a flowing in time. A flow may be steady over a week but erratic over a year. The period within which the flow is measured is all important. If it stretches backwards into the past only, actual maintenance costs are a more reliable guide to total outgoings than

172

they are when the period extends to the future. In inflationary economies, maintenance costs over future periods can but take their cue from past actual costs, but they should be adjusted to make allowance for upward movements in price (and the reverse adjustment in times of deflation). However nicely adjusted actual maintenance costs may be, the aggregates in themselves can be most misleading as indices of the outflow from land resources due to disrepair, wastage and neglect. There can all too frequently be a patent outflow of disrepair, decay and neglect where the repairs done and costed do not keep pace with what is needed to maintain the resources in sound condition. The patent evidence from the actual costs must have added to it estimates for making good the latent outflows. Even when the closest attention and care are paid to the upkeep of resources, the changes of time outpace what is possible. Resources are whittled away by an accelerating wear and tear and their effectiveness is overtaken by obsolescence. These latent outflows can only be offset by charging the current revenues of the proprietary land unit with periodic contributions to amortization funds, designed to be built up against the day when the cost of a complete replacement has to be met. It should be noted that amortization funds would be included among the items of wealth consociate with the proprietary land unit and earmarked as a reserve. Charges and running debts of various kinds are only appropriate deductions from revenue as items in calculations of outflow when they have by law or from some other cause a definite affinity with the proprietary land unit, such as interest payments of a mortgage secured against the land wealth of the unit. And so it should be with local taxes and fiscal dues; only those whose incidence falls on the land resources as such of the proprietary land unit should be taken into account.

Money Flow and Discounts

The holder of a proprietary land unit whose motive it is to obtain a sustained income flow from the use of his land resources may ask no more questions than are required to tell him how particular plans and combinations of his resources contribute to the achievement of his desire. He is content with the evidence of the income from the resources, much in the same way as a man will normally regard the stipend he earns. He does not bother his head with calculations to show what the present value of his current earning capacity is in terms of its future promise. That he has an income from the land, that he can increase it one way and reduce it another is usually as

173

far as the financial interest of the holder of the proprietary land unit goes. We can leave him happily juggling with his resources for a moment and turn our attention to a different kind of person who wants to know how to maximize the income flow from his land resources because he looks upon them as a financial investment, and would compare their performance as such with alternative investments open to him.

We find our investor sitting with the accountants playing with their plasticine notions of income. His income is a jointless flow of money, a homogeneous stream, not an articulated necklace of mineral royalties, shop rents, farm residues and wayleaves. Pounds and pence flow as a river through time: so much money in a week, in a month, in a year. And it is this amount and the rate of its flow which he would wish to compare with similar flows. Simple records of the amounts and the rate at which they were generated would not tell him very much. He would want to see these figures against calculations of what he has invested. A fast and full flowing stream from a relatively small effort is a much more impressive sight than the same performance from an effort three times as big. If we are to follow up the motives behind one who holds his proprietary land unit as an income generator and investment we must interpret his actions and their outcome in money terms. At once we are among shifting sands. Evaluation of the land resources within a particular proprietary land unit, even if we are reducing all our values to money terms, raises far-reaching questions of procedure and value concepts. It is not the purpose nor the place of the present text to dive in among the eddies of this whirlpool of ideas. Some notion of what is involved is obtained when we realize that the relationship between the capital invested and the income flow can be presented in at least the following seven ways:

    i. original capital cost and present income;
    ii. current capital cost and present income;
    iii. current value of capital and present income;
    iv. original capital cost and past income;
    v. original capital value and past income;
    vi. current capital value and the external rate of interest;
    vii. current capital value and the internal rate of interest.

The last two of these seven possibilities are, perhaps, the most satisfactory way of presenting the evaluations the holder-investor is after and we shall spare a few moments to take a look at them.

Our holder of a proprietary land unit is an investor among other investors. Like other investors, his judgments are speculative.

174

Furnished with the figures we have given him of estimated income from his land resources over the long future, he will try and judge the risks and the hazards likely to be faced in the future, and compare these with those which would have to be encountered were he to invest his wealth elsewhere. Future income will be foreseen as coming to him over regular periods—years rather than fortnights. He will, in theory, take what he expects to receive each year, and year by year, and discount it back to the present moment at a rate per cent which in his opinion reflects his judgement of the hazards attending the anticipated income receipts. The rate per cent at which the future receipts are discounted will be chosen by his knowledge of the money and investment markets generally, the bank rate and other evidence of the going rate of interest. He will in short, look over his shoulder for the rate of interest. It will be external. The sum of the present values of each of the anticipated receipts will represent for him the capital value of his proprietary land unit and its land resources as an investment yielding a return at the chosen rate of discount. If his calculations and forecasts are correct, the income as it is received each year will equal the present value plus interest at the chosen external rate compounded at yearly intervals (if a year is the interval chosen) from the present time to the time of receipt. This general formula for the valuation of invested capital is orthodox procedure in the land investment markets of the West. There are modifications of it, to allow for incomes limited in time and subject to other contingencies. Expressed as a mathematical formula, the valuation principle in the general case is:

$$V = \sum_{y=n}^{y=o} i(1+k)^{-y}$$

Where V = value of the proprietary land unit and land resources given to the generation of a monetary income for investment purposes.

k = external rate of interest.

y = number of years from investment to receipt of income.

i = income for the year, y years from investment.

n = number of years over which income will be received.

Income for the first year of investment does not suffer discount since $y = 0$ and $(1 + k) = 1$. Values based on the external rate of interest presuppose the receipt of a constant income year by year, an assumption which becomes more and more problematical as the period of investment lengthens. Uncertainty is taken care of to some extent in the choice of the appropriate rate of interest. But this is a tactic which prepares against eventualities; it does not remove them. Seldom in a long run will an investor actually receive the anticipated income, true in amount, at the time foreseen. If he is a landlord, his tenants and their tenancies will change, maintenance costs will rise and fall, management becomes more complex and costly, governments intervene and the unforeseeable will cause him to change plans. It will be seen as the years pass that the valuation he made at the chosen rate of interest was the best possible at the time but events have played havoc with the expectations.

Instead of handling expected receipts and discounting them backwards to arrive at present values, it is possible to calculate the rate of interest internally generated as it were, using actual or anticipated expenditures and receipts. Dealing with actualities, one takes the costs of construction and acquisition of the land resources at the outset, the periodic expenditures since then together with the actual receipts, and the market value of the resources at the time of the valuation. From these known facts, the rate of interest can be calculated which will equate the results when the receipts and expenditures are discounted backwards to the time of the original outlay with the amount originally invested. Added to the actual periodic receipts is the difference between the original outlay and the value of the resources at the time of the valuation, and this additional sum is in its turn discounted backwards. This device for the internal rate of interest can be used to make comparison of investments by applying it in principle to estimated future expenditures, periodic receipts and final values, using the forecast figures as if they were in fact actual. A mathematical formula for calculating the internal rate of interest is:

$$V_o = \sum_{y=n}^{y=o} t(1+v)^{-y} + (V_o - V_n)(1+v)^{-n} - \sum_{y=n}^{y=o} a(1+v)^{-y}$$

Where V_o = original sum invested;

V_n = value of resources at time of valuation;

v = internal rate of interest;

y = number of years from date of investment to year of receipt or of income or incurrence of expenditure;

t = revenue for the period (year), y periods from investment;

a = expenditure for the period (year), y periods from investment;

n = number of years from investment to date of valuation.

It is possible to choose an external rate of interest and discount everything backwards to the date of the original investment, arriving at a calculated figure which can be compared with the actual original investment in order to demonstrate whether for the rate of interest chosen a gain or a loss has been made over the original outlay. The formula is:

$$P = \left[\sum_{y=n}^{y=o} t(1+k)^{-y} + (V_o - V_n)(1+k)^{-n} - \sum_{y=n}^{y=o} a(1+k)^{-y} \right] - V_o$$

Where the notation is the same as for the internal rate of interest, and

P = the gain or loss; and
k = the external rate of interest.

Non-monetary Rewards

By a non-monetary reward we mean the current fulfilment, or reaching towards fulfilment, of plans dictated by motives other than to generate money income, by creating inferior units from a superior one for consideration in money or renders in kind or service, or the use of the proprietary land unit for production or commercial purposes. We must not fall into the temptation of trying to evaluate in monetary terms or equivalents current non-monetary rewards. The simple fact that the holder of the unit is not seeking to exploit its resources for monetary gain indicates a motive whose achievement may be difficult if not impossible to relate to monetary quantification. Absurdities abound when the devotees of cost-benefit analysis are blind to the realities of subjective values and desires whose satisfactions are immured too deeply in the soul of man for the measurements of the market place to reach them.

We can play along with opportunity costs and values up to a point but probably to no purpose other than to satisfy an academic craving for objectivity and mensuration. Holders of proprietary land units who are not deliberately turning their resources to monetary ends are not likely to be interested or impressed by arguments about opportunity costs. There is, nonetheless, a certain logic in thinking of the resources in hand to the holder of the proprietary land unit as having a potential rental revenue equal to what the market would give in rent for the resources if leases were granted in them; or, by the same token, we could argue for the evaluation of the current reward in terms of the residuum of income which would be reaped if the resources were put into a production enterprise, and which in the circumstances has been foregone. These monetary measurements are opportunity costs to the holder of the

M

proprietary land unit of following the motive which at present inspires him.

The logic of the opportunity costs approach, however, does not take us far. It is a way of looking at the situation but one which fails to reach down to its fundamental realities. Only he who follows the requirements of a non-monetary motive knows what the value of his achievement is to himself, and in the last analysis, it is he and he alone who has the right to judge—to judge for him as some of our cost-benefit devotees are all too ready to do is presumption. Non-monetary rewards lack objectivity and it is this that makes them so irritating to the quantifiers. The true significance and value of the rewards is personal to the pursuer of them. The holder of a proprietary land unit whose current reward is the subjective attraction of residential occupation foregoes the rental revenue he could reap if he were to lease the place. The foregone rent is no true index of value of the current reward to him in money terms. Obviously, he would be prepared to offer more rent than the market will give: but how much more? None can tell. To approach the problem from the other angle and ask what rent would he have to pay to lease a residence which would give him the same reward as the place he now holds, takes us up the same blind alley. For one thing the substitute satisfaction would be as subjective and elusive as the present enjoyment to one who would try and size it up; moreover, to get such a substitute, he would only have to bid the market a fractional margin above the rent at which he could let his present residence, and none could say whether the declared margin represented the true difference between what he would give and what he has offered. All we can say of such a holder is that to enjoy what he now enjoys, he has turned his back on the income he would have received if the wealth now sunk in the proprietary land unit had been put to another advantage, or the land itself had been put to another use—whichever is the greater of the two represents the highest cost to him of his present enjoyment but not its benefit.

Assessments of values along the line of opportunity costs always leave open the question of why the postulated substitution is not in fact made. Logically, the answer must be that what is now held is preferred above the substitute and must therefore be of greater value to the current possessor than the substitute would be. In the illustration of the holder of the residential proprietary land unit just given, we could only have an inkling of what the present enjoyment, the current reward, meant to the holder in money value if we could indulge in some fancy blackmail and ask what sum he would pay to buy off the exercise of compulsory acquisition powers. A holder might put the question to himself, especially if compulsory purchase were threatened: he would certainly in the normal course of events keep the answer to himself. In all circumstances like this, we should accept the facts of life as they are and not try and measure immensurable values by ill-fitting yardsticks. A non-monetary reward is a non-monetary reward: it should be seen and accepted as such and allowed to shine in its own intrinsic light. All we can say is that the holder of a particular proprietary land unit uses his resources in such and such a manner at the instance of a declared motive. We can assess what it costs to him to do so. But the costs are no measure of the reward—and it is the pursuit of the reward which determines the land use.

Monetary rewards are received as income flows over periods of time; the longer the period, the greater the accumulated sum. Non-monetary rewards are not in the nature of things cumulative. They are not received as a continuous flow of a particular benefit over time; and this is a fundamental reason why it is illogical to try and equate the value of the current non-monetary reward to an income flow foregone. The intrinsic virtue of the non-monetary reward is experienced moment by moment, as a total impact. He who holds a proprietary land unit for residential and amenity enjoyment, experiences his reward totally and only in the present moment. Residential enjoyment does not build itself up in a cumulative fashion, so that at any given moment one enjoys greater residential benefit than ever before. It is false to assume that as the present is always successor to the past, the further away the past the longer the time over which the present is able to apprehend residential enjoyment, and that the degree of such enjoyment today must surpass the degree of yesterday's enjoyment. Periodic time, a span of days or weeks, might, however, be necessary for the full impact of a total experience. A camping weekend can only be experienced as a weekend, as an event over and related to a given time span. But this is only to say that the time allocation associated with the particular enjoyment and experience was of a certain duration; the whole experience would be a once and for all affair—a weekend; there would be nothing resembling the flow of a continuous benefit.

We might suppose that an exception would be found where the motive for holding a proprietary land unit was a sense of posterity and inheritance, of sitting in the seat of a long line of ancestors, the guardsman for the future of what they had in the past safeguarded for the present. But even this commitment to the genius of time is no exception to the discontinuity of non-monetary rewards. The present reward is not the accumulation of similar rewards over the past; the holder of today does not enjoy the sense of posterity more than he did yesterday simply because he had enjoyed yesterday's experience. The enjoyment of today owes everything to the yesterdays, not because similar enjoyment was experienced yesterday but because the yesterdays are for today the evidence and the measure of a past which is the cause and the subject of the enjoyment in the present moment.

Where current reward is continuous over time, it is possible to calculate for a given period a ratio between the amount of the reward, or output, and the value or cost of the total resources employed in the exercise—hence the orthodox yield rates of the investment markets. Measurement of the moment by moment non-monetary rewards cannot be made in a similar fashion. Because there is no flow, there is no rate of output. The holder of a proprietary land unit following a non-monetary motive may, however, well be able to assess for himself how far his achievement has reached. The degree of his achievement will be a function of the total inventory of the land resources available and of the way in which each item is used in relation to the others. Sometimes, it is possible to evaluate the land resources by summing the costs of the provision of them or, as we have seen, by employing opportunity costs techniques. By such devices, the total cost or value of the resources could be related to the holder's estimate of the degree of achievement reached. Total costs could in the normal case be reduced to unit costs per unit of land area. Comparisons could then be made between alternative plans by comparing the ratios between unit costs and the degree of achievement.

Consider, by way of a concrete example, a holder of a proprietary land unit consisting of a freehold building plot, costing in the market £1,000. The holder intends to build a house for his own occupation. He has to decide between two alternative lay-outs which will use the same quantity of bricks and materials at a cost of £3,000 and a third alternative whose lay-out will follow one of the others but by using a different type of brick and house design costing £4,000. No one lay-out and design measures up to the ideals of the holder of the proprietary land unit. His assessment of the degrees of achievement gives 70 per cent to the house whose construction and land will cost £5,000 and 65 per cent and 60 per cent respectively to each of the others. The ratios of costs to degrees of achievement are thus: 5/7, 4/6·5 and 4/6 respectively. Reduced to money's worth the sequence beccomes: first the house giving 65 per cent achievement; then the one giving 60 per cent and finally the £5,000 house giving 70 per cent.

180

Monetary and Non-monetary Conflict

Earlier on, when introducing the centrality of motive in our analysis, the point was made that two or more pursuits could be followed within the confines of a proprietary land unit under the dominance of the one motive. Not infrequently, the holder of a proprietary land unit will wish to use his resources to generate a money income while at the same time satisfying a non-monetary desire. The motive is to follow two or more pursuits and is not in itself a double motive. Nevertheless, the two pursuits may reach a point where they are in conflict and the holder of the proprietary land unit will have to decide which shall dominate the other.

Harmony will prevail wherever the input of resources which achieves the highest marginal output of income per unit of input corresponds with the amount and combination of the resources which gives the greatest degree of non-monetary achievement. The position is illustrated graphically in Figure 2. Contributions to land resources are measured along the x axis and marginal returns in the form of money income up the y axis. A vertical scale of degrees of achievement of the non-monetary pursuit is erected opposite the y axis at the other end of the diagram, and against this spot readings are taken indicative of the degree of non-monetary achievement resulting from a certain combination of land resources which will also have a corresponding reference on the x axis—spot readings are shown as X. Let it be imagined that combinations of land resources A, B, C, D and E are alternative choices open to the holder of the proprietary land unit. In the circumstances depicted in Figure 2 (1) the combination of resources C gives the highest marginal output of income flow and the highest degree of achievement possible to all alternatives. Harmony reigns.

The position represented by Figure 2 (2) obtains when the highest marginal output of income flow answers to an input of OB and the combination of resources which gives the greatest degree of achievement of the non-monetary pursuit is at C as before. The holder of the unit will have to decide which of the two alternatives he will choose. If he is mercenarily minded, he will doubtless note that the best of one of the two worlds, that is the highest marginal output of income flow, can be gained by a lesser commitment of resources. Not infrequently, in such circumstances, the non-monetary pursuit dominates and the holder willingly forfeits income to achieve it.

In Figure 2 (3) the highest marginal output of income flow is obtained by an input of OD land resources while the best achievement of the non-monetary pursuit is, as before, to be gained by the

181

combination of resources C. In these circumstances, the monetary pursuit loses the advantage of a relatively lower resources input. The odds will be in favour of the non-monetary pursuit; although it is open to the holder of the proprietary land unit to decide to provide more resources than are required to achieve the best possible non-monetary results and go for the highest marginal output of income.

A situation could come about in which, by arranging combinations of resources to achieve non-monetary results, the range of the degrees of non-monetary satisfaction in no circumstances coincided with the range of the marginal outputs of income. The position is depicted in Figure 2 (4). The marginal output curve shows the highest output for an input of OC resources and combination C provides the best result possible for the non-monetary pursuit; but

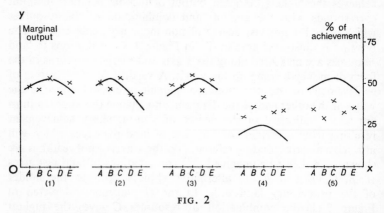

FIG. 2

with this difference compared with the situation of Figure 2 (1), that the peak of the marginal output curve is way below the level of non-monetary result which is the reward for the use of combination C. In Figure 2 (5) the reverse position is shown. The pursuit of a money income will, with all possible combinations of resources, depress the results of the non-monetary pursuit so that for no combination of resources will the ranges of degree of achievement and marginal incomes coincide. An input of OC resources gives the highest income output and achieves the best of the non-monetary alternatives but the apogees are far apart. The position depicted in Figure 2 (5) is the obverse to that depicted in Figure 2 (4). Both figures represent circumstances where the conflict between the two pursuits is open and the choice of dominance relatively clear-cut. The figures could be redrawn with the scale to the right representing the ratio of cost to achievement and the points in the diagrams

182

indicative of the non-monetary achievements would indicate, by reference to the scale, not the percentage of contribution towards achievement made by the respective combinations of land resources, but the cost per 1 per cent unit of achievement.

Attributes and Current Rewards

In the course of the foregoing observations on current rewards, incidental mention has been made of particular attributes of the proprietary land unit. Rent, for example, as the basis of revenue from land resources could not be considered without reference to the proprietary relationships of inferior and superior proprietary land units whose reciprocities know both the burden and the benefit of rent payments. The attributes of a proprietary land unit in the general case exert some bearing upon the current rewards provided by the unit, monetary as well as non-monetary. The odd incidental references made so far have left this aspect of the subject somewhat untidy, and so we intend to tie up a few loose ends quickly with the help of some brief general remarks.

The size of a proprietary land unit can have a direct bearing upon the non-monetary rewards. Sheer bulk of land mass and structures can be as deleterious as an insufficient supply. With income flow, however, size usually means a *pro tanto* increase or decrease in the total output; but there is some evidence to suggest that rental revenue and outgoings per superficial unit can, and do in certain circumstances, move in inverse ratio to the size of the proprietary land unit.[9]

Lateral rights are sometimes the cause of conflict between two pursuits, especially when one is monetary and the other is not. A residential motive could, for instance, welcome a way through the woods over a neighbour's land as a major contribution to the fulfilment of a residential motive, but the cost of acquisition and maintenance could well cut roads of a different kind into the current resources of the proprietary land unit. In general, the benefit of a right often means a corresponding financial burden, and the burden of allowing a servitude over one's land brings a corresponding financial reward.

We have touched upon the essential part played by time in the calculation of income flow and hence, by implication, of the importance of duration to the evaluation of the revenues and income of a proprietary land unit. Other things being equal, the longer the duration, the greater the period of income accumulation and hence

9 D. R. Denman, *Estate Capital* (Allen and Unwin, London, 1957), p. 133.

of the power of a proprietary land unit to accumulate wealth from income; but as a counter to this, duration if lengthy means change and uncertainty, both undesirables in the eyes of one seeking a sound investment for his land resources.

Proprietary character form influences current rewards and does so in different ways. Because of the proprietary character form of a unit, the revenues may be affected by contributions, tax reliefs and charges. In recent years investment companies holding proprietary land units in the course of their trade in Britain have been exceptionally badly hit by the incidence of corporation tax and betterment levy—their plight was the direct consequence of the proprietary character form of the proprietary land units held by them and the commercial pursuits which occasioned their incorporation. A particular type of land use may be in character in a special way with the proprietary character form of a unit, and the current reward issuing from the land use would take its colouring from it. An agricultural development corporation is not likely to use its land resources for a steel mill and the agricultural user will bring in its wake income generated mainly from agricultural developments. Sometimes a policy is followed not because it is in keeping with, and essential to, the fulfilment of the purpose for which the fictitious or fiduciary holder of a land unit was conceived but because, taking its cue from the proprietary character form, the policy has a special appeal. Because of their fiduciary character and special tax position in Britain, charities find it to their advantage to direct their land resources away from silviculture and the planting of timber; it pays them better to devote their resources to other land uses. Fiduciary arrangements can often have a direct bearing upon the generation and disposition of income, as those with fiduciary responsibilities (trustees) are bound to follow specific priorities in the discharge of their duties as financial administrators.

Chapter XI

A SIDELIGHT ON COST-BENEFIT

Alongside the theory of relativity, the quantum theory of the physical fundamentals and other twentieth-century shifts in thought from positions of accepted orthodoxy, should be put the new way of looking at economic phenomena. In sheer desperation to find a solution to the unemployment sickness of America, groping steps towards the new light were taken by the Roosevelt administration when framing the formularies for the New Deal with its commitment to relatively large-scale public expenditure. But the prophet who made the message live, first as an acceptable diagnosis of the prevailing economic malaise and then as a cure, was John Maynard Keynes. Salvation, he said, is not to be had in savings alone; but in savings taken up as investment, savings sown as seed corn to multiply into harvest.

If private investors had neither the means nor the wit to invest for expansion, the government should take the initiative. Keynes was not advocating state ownership of the means of production, he was calling for a blood-transfusion—someone had to put new life into the stagnant economies. He made his case by turning the focus of attention upon the total anatomy of a national economy, upon the aggregates of labour, capital and spending power. If the New Deal administrators wanted a rational justification for their public spending, Keynes had provided it for them. His way of thinking gradually permeated the economic schools and influenced the outlook of administrators. New habits were formed, habits which today have become so ingrained as to affect thought, speech and action. One whole side of economics is now given to the study of national and community concepts—the national income, national gross and net product, national growth rate, national input, national output and so on.

The classical and neo-classical economists always kept much nearer to reality and human values in their theorizing and model imagery than do those who juggle with the concepts of national

185

aggregates. The classical economists seldom departed from the face-to-face encounter of the market place and the individual transaction. Real people confronted real people. And yet, economic theorizing and practical application are both pursued by the human mind resident and incorporate in a human person. We find in the result that those who deal in aggregates use the language of human encounter. A person who enters into a market transaction or is party to some other deal, is conscious of that which transpires to his own advantage or disadvantage, and he can express his personal awareness of benefit or disease. When those who deal in national or other forms of social aggregates wish to justify their thoughts, actions and policies on moral grounds they perforce borrow the speech of real persons and personify society or the community. On every side today, one hears politicians advocating policies 'for the good of the community' as if the community had a bodiliness and in its personalized form and needs stood over against the good of individual real persons, an articulate 'person' with mind and welfare known to the spokesmen whose agents they are. While it is perfectly reasonable and indeed requisite that politicians and policy-makers should pursue actions which in their judgement should improve the national income, it blurs social moral judgement to set the community as a person apart from real people. The national income should be thought of morally in its relationship to each and every individual citizen. The personal encounter which is the only ground of a moral human encounter is not, then, evaded.

Those who make personalized-community judgements appropriate to themselves a wisdom none can possess. No man can tell truly what is of benefit or gain to another, let alone to a multitude of folk, unless that other reveals to the interlocutor the subjective assessments of value peculiar to himself. Revelation in terms of monetary values is made by the declarations of the market. The kind of value judgement, however, which turns on the good or ill 'of the community' by its very nature, usually arises in connection with developments which do not involve market transactions. And even if public property were sold on the market, the sale price would only reveal the subjective judgement of he who is responsible for executing the transaction, his notion of the usefulness and hence of the value of what was sold for fulfilling the function for which it had been held. The price would reveal nothing of the value 'to the community'—it could never do so, for the community has neither heart nor mind to make such judgements.

The habit of looking at investment and resource use policy from the viewpoint of the community has engendered sophisticated techniques of cost-benefit analysis for measuring what have come to be called social benefits and costs, to distinguish them from individual benefits and costs. Because social costs and benefits are not market costs and prices, the determination of them rests upon the personalized-community approach and in the last analysis is the subjective assessment of the social accountant or analyst of what is of benefit or cost 'to the community'. Inevitably no two results are likely to be the same.

The purpose of this chapter is not to decry cost-benefit analysis. It is to suggest that more perspicacious judgements and assessments of the results of public and other forms of investment and land use can be made and costs and benefits brought closer to real responses by seeing the allocation of land and resources as set within a proprietary-structure framework.

All aggregate figures are made up of digits. National propensity to consume and invest are meaningless abstractions without some knowledge of the wills and the ways of the individual citizens. Stripped to its fundamentals, the use of land and all other resources is not ultimately a matter of planning but of motives and power, of intent and doing. And only those who have the power to use resources and do in fact use them, experience true benefits and incur real costs. It is imprecise and vague to say that the preservation of a purple-headed mountain, because it enhances natural beauty, is in the interests of the community. The preservation of the mountain is of benefit to those who appreciate its peculiar form of beauty (and let it be noted, mountains to some people are ever dark and foreboding) and have the right to enter upon land in the vicinity of the mountain, whether the king's highway or a private lawn, from which the mountain in its beauty is visible. To these people and to these alone is there a benefit in the form of the opportunity to behold natural beauty. No man can tell what the benefit of the mountain is to these people, unless he first finds out who they are and they subsequently reveal their thoughts to him. Apart from such action and revelation, any assessment of benefit he may make is entirely peculiar to himself, albeit it is reasonable from his viewpoint of the community.

Proprietary land use analysis is of immediate relevance to cost-benefit analysis because in any actual or proposed land use pattern it identifies the points where motives can be discerned and true benefits and actual costs made known. Admittedly, the costs and benefits would not be assessed from the viewpoint to the personalized community: but, this is just the point—judgements from that viewpoint cannot but be other than false insights, for the viewpoint of

187

the community is always a chimera of the imagination of he who has the arrogance to presume to take it. Before explaining further what is meant, we must take a glance at orthodox cost-benefit analysis.

Cost-benefit Analysis

The germinal intellectual concept of costs and benefits was pioneered in the middle of the nineteenth century by J. Dupuit. In a classic paper,[1] written as long ago as 1844, he emphasized the distinction between a firm's utility and public utility. Briefly, he pointed out that in general it is not untrue to say that the profit motive is the dominant motive of the firm as seen in economic analysis. Consequently, utility in relation to the firm is fairly easy to specify. The firm's utility is its monetary profit, and maximization of profit implies maximization of utility. On the other hand, there is no simple way of defining the desirable and the deleterious effects of economic activity on the public, as a whole. There arises, therefore, a major conceptual problem, to define utility in relation to public undertakings. And, paradoxically, it is only when the utility of a specific scheme has been defined that it becomes possible to enumerate what the costs and benefits are likely to be within the framework of broad policy.

Dupuit drew attention to the notion of consumers' surplus, which he interpreted, in quantitative terms, as a measure of the difference between the maximum amount that consumers would be willing to pay for a given quantity of a commodity rather than to forego it, and the cost of the same quantity of that commodity at its competitive market price. He suggested that the true measure of benefits to the public, of enterprises such as the building of roads and bridges was not simply the revenue generated as a direct consequence of their construction, but rather the public's willingness to pay for them. In other words he viewed total benefits as the sum of actual payments together with the consumers' surplus.

In this century, the first systematic attempts at applying cost-benefit analysis to public investment came into prominence in the United States, especially in the field of water-resource developments. During the 1930s, the time of the New Deal, as a result of the continued increase of public investment activity, the idea developed that social justification should properly be given weight in the choice of projects and their evaluation. The Flood Control Act of 1936[2]

[1] J. Dupuit, 'De la Mesure de L'Utilité des Travaux Publics', first published in *Annales Des Ponts et Chaussées*, Sér. 2, No. 8, 1844. English translation in *International Economic Papers*, No. 2. (Macmillan, 1952).
[2] 49 Stat. 1570.

restricted federal participation in flood control schemes to projects in which 'the benefits to whomsoever they may accrue are in excess of the estimated costs'. The Act did not, however, specify the criteria for the measurement of costs and benefits. The various agencies concerned developed their own criteria, favourable to their own policies and programmes. Disagreements quickly arose about the choice of criteria and the methods used in evaluations. In 1950, an inter-agency committee made certain recommendations regarding the uniformity of standards and criteria,[3] but these recommendations failed to obtain official sanction. In 1952, the Bureau of the Budget, which is responsible for receiving all proposals from agencies before transmission to Congress, introduced its own set of criteria by which it would henceforth evaluate proposals submitted to it by the agencies. These criteria were detailed in a memorandum[4] and remained the basis of appraisal during the next decade.

Early in 1961, the Bureau of the Budget commissioned a panel of consultants to review these criteria and standards and to make fresh recommendations. These were duly submitted in June, 1961.[5] The Bureau of the Budget, however, under severe criticism of the restrictive nature of the standards they had adopted during the previous ten years, felt it politic to disavow the report for the time being. A new inter-agency committee was then appointed and its recommendations were finally approved in 1962 as the general basis of appraisal in respect of water-resource investments.[6]

Since then, interest in cost-benefit analysis has grown rapidly among economists, and a variety of techniques have been evolved in attempts at the identification and measurement of costs and benefits in such diverse fields as urban renewal, recreation, health, education, transport, research, development and defence.[7] In

[3] United States Government, Federal Inter-Agency River Basin Committee, Sub Committee on Benefits and Costs, *Proposed Practices for Economic Analyses of River Basin Projects* (*Green Book*) (Washington, May 1950; revised, May 1958).

[4] United States Government. Bureau of the Budget. *Budget Circular A–47* (Washington, 1952).

[5] United States Government, Panel of Consultants to the Bureau of the Budget, *Standards and Criteria for Formulating and Evaluating Federal Water Resources Development* (*Consultants' Report*) (Washington, 1961).

[6] United States Government, *Policies, Standards and Procedures in the Formulation, Evaluation, and Review of Plans for Use and Development of Water and Related Land Resources*, Senate Document No. 97, 87th Congress (Washington, 1962).

[7] See for instance J. Rothenberg, 'Urban Renewal Programs', Ed. R. Dorfman, *Measuring Benefits of Government Investments* (Washington, D.C.: Brookings Institution, 1965); M. Clawson, 'Methods of Measuring the Demand for and

the United States, cost-benefit analysis, after its comparatively lengthy trial period, appears to be regarded as capable of performing the dual role of public accounting and providing a method of assessing the claims of competing development schemes. In Britain, on the other hand, where interest in such exercises is comparatively recent, it is currently one of the most fashionable offshoots of economics. There is a certain aura of sophisticated mystery surrounding it, and the implied promise that it can bring calculated precision to the task of allocating resources between land uses and can rationalize public decision-making has earned it, in the eyes of some, the reputation of a major 'break-through' in economic planning. It has been heralded as a new technique for the evaluation, in monetary terms, of goods and services for which no market exists.

An illustration of an extremely optimistic view of the potential efficacy of cost-benefit analysis (in quantifying the subjective) is inherent in the following statement made by Professor Peter Hall:

> . . . if a factory owner's chimneys pollute the air, that is a social cost. If he builds a beautiful house for himself, and that improves the view, that is a social benefit. In both cases society is not responsible, but it feels the effect. This leads to the revolutionary concept that we can actually add up the social costs and benefits, in money terms, by asking what value people would themselves put on them. We can then express them as a rate of return on capital, as an ordinary capitalist would, and so determine our investment rationally, from the point of view of the community as a whole, just as the capitalist can now do from his private point of view.[8]

Prevailing fashion would invest the subjective art of cost-benefit analysis with attributes which it does not possess—those of the

Value of Outdoor Recreation', *Resources for the Future, Inc.* (Washington, D.C., 1959); B. A. Weisbrod, *Economics of Public Health: Measuring the Economic Impact of Diseases* (Philadelphia: University of Pennsylvania Press, 1960); M. Blaug, 'The Rate of Return on Investment in Education in Great Britain', *The Manchester School*, Vol. XXXIII, No. 3, September 1965; T. M. Coburn, M. E. Beesley and D. J. Reynolds, *The London-Birmingham Motorway: Traffic and Economics*, Road Research Laboratory Technical Paper No. 46. D.S.I.R., H.M.S.O., 1960; C. D. Foster and M. E. Beesley, 'Estimating the Social Benefit of Constructing an Underground Railway in London', *Journal of the Royal Statistical Society*, Vol. 126, Part I, 1963; R. R. Nelson, 'The Simple Economics of Basic Scientific Research', *Journal of Political Economy*, Vol. LXVII, June 1959; R. N. McKean, 'Cost-Benefit Analysis and British Defence Expenditure', *Public Expenditure, Appraisal and Control*, Ed. A. T. Peacock and D. J. Robertson (Edinburgh: Oliver and Boyd, 1963).

[8] P. Hall, *Labour's New Frontiers* (London: Andre Deutsch, 1964), p. 173.

exactitude of objective science. To expect of cost-benefit analysis that it should perform, empirically, the role of a scientific analysis and follow specific and universally accepted rules is presumption.

There is no reason to suppose that one analyst's standards, criteria and evaluation regarding social costs and benefits will coincide with those of any of his colleagues. The basic reason for the singular character of each man's estimates is simply that value judgements which have to be made at almost every step in the calculations are the result of subjective opinion and cannot be tested against real evidence. Moreover, since the techniques of measurement are subject to no agreed consensus, no two exercises are likely to yield the same results.

As an illustration, let us consider briefly a topic which is relatively well documented: the quantitative assessment of recreational benefits. In that context, the authoritative Prewitt Report[9] of the National Park Service of America noted that virtually everyone who had given the problem careful consideration concurred in the tenet that primary benefits from recreation are personal and varied, and therefore not readily measurable in dollar terms. Nevertheless, it concluded that if it was decided that the interests of the National Park Service required intangible benefits to be expressed in dollars, such dollar values were to be based upon the best judgement of those most competent to evaluate such intangibles. The United States Forest Service, for example, has consistently refused to attempt to place monetary values upon the recreational use of the forests under its jurisdiction. The Forest Service was able to stand its ground because it was not required to resort to monetary comparisons to justify its programmes. Many other agencies, on the other hand, are engaged in active competition for the allocation of funds, and it was deemed necessary[10] that they should support and justify their claims on public funds by appropriate cost-benefit computations.

It may at first sight appear curious that the Prewitt Report should have made the obvious point that the judgement of the expert is preferable to that of the dilettante. It must be remembered, however, that exercises concerned with measuring social costs and benefits, by their very nature, cannot be entirely objective. The lack of unanimous agreement among analysts, the dangers of double counting,

9 Land and Recreational Planning Division, National Park Service, *The Economics of Public Recreation*, 'The Prewitt Report' (Washington, D.C., 1949), p. 30.
10 Federal Inter-Agency River Basin Committee, Sub-Committee on Benefits and Costs, *Proposed Practices for Economic Analysis of River Basin Projects* (Washington, D.C., 1950).

the risk of crediting benefits improperly, the constant need for subjective evaluations are among the factors which cause estimated figures to be viewed with grave suspicion. As credibility attaches to expertise, it would seem rational to expect that the higher the standing and reliability of an expert, the greater the degree of credence likely to be given to his findings. Hence the plea that the specialist's task should not be entrusted to the layman, and the implied hope that some consensus of opinion might obtain at higher levels of expertise.

Taking our cue from the Prewitt Report, we have sought to identify a common element in the approach of some of the leading experts in the evaluation of recreational benefits and looked for an expected similarity in the results they obtain. Their basic technique is one which enjoys the greatest currency and makes use of statistical demand curves. A demand curve would be built up by postulating a recreational facility priced at zero, recording varying quantities of the facility demanded at various prices up to the point where there would be no demand at a certain high price.

Trice and Wood[11] make the assumption that there exists a direct relationship between the distance that a consumer is prepared to travel to a recreational area and the benefit he derives from the recreation enjoyed. Visitors' starting points of travel are arranged in distance-zones with the area as centre and travel costs from each of the zones to the area are calculated. A measure of the area's recreational 'market' value is deemed to be given by average travel costs for visitors from the outermost zone. It is then argued that visitors from the inner distance zones would pay less than the 'market' value and therefore enjoy a 'free' recreational value or consumers' surplus measured by the difference between the average travel costs from the outermost zones and the appropriate inner zone. The sum of all such 'free' recreational values in respect of all visitors from the inner zones would give the value of the free recreational benefit for the area.

In using costs of travel as an index for the measurement of recreational benefits, Trice and Wood follow Hotelling's 'concentric travel cost zones'[12] and assign consumers' surplus to all visitors to the recreational area, except to those from the outermost zone. In other words, they assume that the recreational benefits are equal to the longest travel costs. In determining the value of the 'true' benefit to a visitor from an inner zone, his actual costs of travel are disregarded. Instead the measure of 'free' benefit to a visitor from an

[11] A. H. Trice and S. E. Wood, 'Measurement of Recreation Benefits', *Land Economics*, Vol. XXXIV, No. 3, August 1958.

[12] 'The Prewitt Report', *op. cit.*, note by H. Hotelling, pp. 8–9.

inner zone is taken as being the difference between the average cost of travel from the outermost zone and the average cost of travel from that inner zone. This procedure is justified on the grounds that using average costs rather than the actual costs incurred by each visitor 'avoids such questions as economic ability, personal tastes and appetites and forms of recreation enjoyed'.[13]

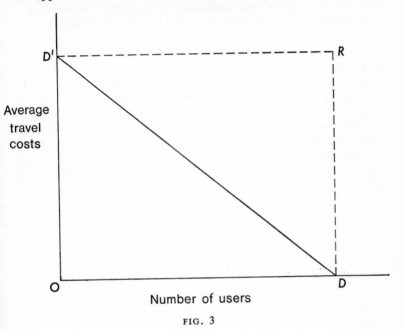

FIG. 3

The measure of recreational benefits is taken as being represented by the quantum of 'free' benefit. Thus in Figure 3, if $D'D$ represents the demand curve, the 'free' benefit supplied, given by the difference between average 'market' travel costs and average inner zones travel costs would be represented by area $D'RDO$ minus area $D'DO$, i.e. area $D'RD$.

Clawson,[14] on the other hand, uses data of the numbers of visitors to a recreational area and their starting points of travel to build a demand curve. Cost data are used indirectly as a means of determining prices which visitors are prepared to pay in order to enjoy the amenities of the recreational area. Costs in this context are deemed

13 A. H. Trice and S. E. Wood, *op. cit.*, p. 203.
14 M. Clawson, *op. cit.*

N

to be comprised not only of travelling costs as in the Trice and Wood method, but to include lodging, food and other costs in excess of those which would have been incurred had the trip not been made. Clearly such costs vary in relation to trip lengths.

If we now assume that visitors to the park emanate from population centres located at varying distances from the park, the rate of visits for each unit of total population of each centre would vary.

The relationship may be expressed in equation form as:

$$V = f(C)$$

where V represents the rate of visits in hundreds per thousand population and C represents the cost of each visit.

Alternatively, the data of consumer behaviour relating prices of trips and visits per unit of total population may be used to construct a demand curve. The next step involves the construction of a demand curve in respect of the recreational area itself, by estimating the quantity response to varying prices for the recreational visit, through the use of the data showing the relationship between number of visits and cost of each visit.

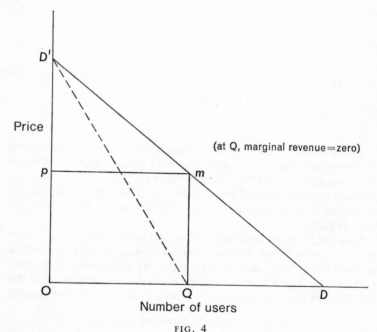

FIG. 4

Estimates are made by postulating various levels of an imposed entrance fee to the area in the form of an additional cost of each visit. The number of visits which would result from each cost group, under the increased costs, is determined by analysing the visit-cost data.

The assumption is then made that the recreational benefit of an area is the maximum revenue obtainable by a non-discriminating monopolist, and this maximum revenue is reached where marginal revenue is zero. Figure 4 illustrates the result. Knetsch,[15] commenting on the technique employed by Clawson, makes the point that it is unrealistic to suppose that the demand schedule is the same for all distance groups. Since the preference functions of visitors to the recreational area are likely to be different, the values of recreational benefits to various individuals should take account of such factors as incomes, ages, population densities, availability of other recreational facilities and other socio-economic variables. Substantial differences in any one of those variables as between groups would be likely to cause substantial variations in the demand schedules of those groups. Clearly, therefore, there is a need to incorporate all those factors into the analysis of the relationship between visits and total costs.

Moreover, the effect of the availability of close substitutes as well as the degree of congestion of people at the recreational area must also be considered. Account must thus be taken, not only of the number of alternatives, but of their location, size, the quality of the recreations they offer. Consequently, Knetsch suggests the following formula as an elaboration of the Clawson formula:

$$V = f(C, Y, S, G)$$

where V = rate of visits in hundreds per thousand population
C = cost of a visit
Y = income of population groups
S = substitute areas that might be relevant for any group
G = some measure of congestion

He recognizes that the model suggested takes no account of another important factor: time. The time value element varies greatly both as between different individuals in respect of the same lengths of time and for the same individual in respect of different time periods. However, he argues that although time is an important constraint on use, the time element in this context is little different

[15] J. L. Knetsch, 'Outdoor Recreation Demands and Benefits', *Land Economics*, Vol. XXXIX, No. 4, November 1963.

from the time element in the general context of the consumption of other goods and resources marketed in the economy. He therefore postulates that it is 'the amount of money involved which has a bearing on price and time value, and not how much time it takes to experience the result'.[16]

Unlike Clawson, Knetsch suggests that the measure of the benefits of the recreational area should be regarded as the total worth to all those who use it.

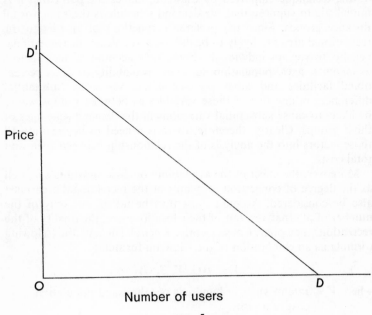

FIG. 5

Benefit = Total area $D'OD$.

Interpreted in diagrammatic form (Figure 5) the measure of such benefits would be indicated by the whole of the area under the demand curve, since the curve defines all the individuals who value the benefit at each price level.

Quite a different measure of benefit is suggested by Seckler.[17] He

[16] J. L. Knetsch, *op. cit.*

[17] D. W. Seckler, 'On the Uses and Abuses of Economic Science in Evaluating Public Outdoor Recreation', *Land Economics*, Vol. XLII, No. 4, November 1966.

defines an optimum price P' and use Q' at a point where marginal cost equals marginal utility (Figure 6).

In respect of all use to the right of the intersection of MC and DD', marginal costs exceed marginal utility. Therefore, the maximum gross benefit will be denoted by the area $OQ'm'D'$, costs by the area $OQ'm'S$, so that the net recreational benefit will be given by the area $Sm'D'$.

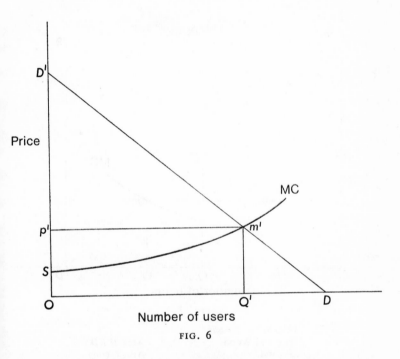

FIG. 6

In Seckler's opinion, this technique is most valuable on the assumption that the marginal utility curve is identical with the statistical demand curve. He then proceeds to question that assumption: 'We do not believe that statistical demand curves measure the utility functions of recreational facilities (or of anything else for that matter)'.[18] He makes the point that the rate of purchase of a commodity by an individual is determined both by the marginal utility of the commodity to the individual and the marginal utility of the income he must forgo in exchange for that commodity. He there-

[18] *Op. cit.*, p. 487.

fore suggests that a demand curve, corrected for the influence of a diminishing marginal utility of incomes, would have significant application to the evaluation of recreational benefits.

For ease of reference and comparison, the different measures of benefits in respect of a recreational area are illustrated diagrammatically together, in Figure 7.

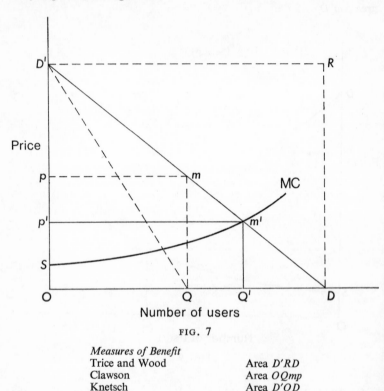

FIG. 7

Measures of Benefit	
Trice and Wood	Area $D'RD$
Clawson	Area $OQmp$
Knetsch	Area $D'OD$
Seckler	Area $Sm'D'$

The wide disparity in these results arises because of the general vagueness of the approach which attempts to measure the quantum of recreational benefits to an amorphous mass of people. The assumptions which are made are based on the analyst's personal judgement of how he thinks people will react. Users of the recreational amenity are seen not as they really are: people whose tastes, actions and individual peculiarities are as personal as they are varied; but as identical modular cells comprising a molecular structure.

198

Is it, in fact, true to say that all those who are able to enjoy a recreational facility without incurring the full expense of the most distant visitors invariably obtain a consumer's surplus in an absolute sense? Lessinger,[19] indeed, questions the validity of such propositions. For him, those living near a recreational area in the countryside are likely to be isolated from central metropolitan areas, while many visitors from urban areas travel long distances to enjoy the amenities of the countryside. Choosing to live in the countryside may imply a decision to forgo the advantages of urban accessibility. Those who have deliberately made the choice at the cost of urban proximity may well make frequent use of the recreational amenity because of its low cost to them. Clearly they could not use it so cheaply if they had to pay additional charges commensurate with the full travel costs incurred by more distant visitors. And it is cogent to ask whether in fact they have incurred in another form the costs of acquiring the proximity benefits in the higher prices they have had to pay to purchase residences in the favoured location.

On the other hand, it may well be that those living in the vicinity of a recreational area are insensitive to its charms, and use it far less than do visitors from farther afield. Beauty on the doorstep can be unappreciated—familiarity breeds contempt. The economics of the unfamiliar are real enough. The Tower of London is unfamiliar to many a Londoner and well-known to many an overseas visitor. Can it therefore be said that if the former were to visit it, he would be enjoying a consumer's surplus commensurate with his counterpart's travel costs?

It is illuminating to trace the origins of the notion of consumer's surplus. Dupuit's work on utility theory stemmed from his concern to provide a means of assessing public utility in terms of the utility of specific entities. In pointing out that the price charged for a particular scheme could not be relied upon to give a measure of its total utility, he was concerned with the identification of the amount which the particular users of the scheme would be prepared to pay in order to secure to themselves its advantages. The difference between that amount and the actual price charged for use, he called *l'utilité relative*,[20] and later, Marshall called it consumer's surplus. Dupuit illustrated his concept of 'utilité relative' by examples from railway tariffs and other analyses of pricing policies in respect of the private and the public monopolist. He showed how an enterprise

[19] J. Lessinger, 'Measurement of Recreation Benefits: A Reply', *Land Economics*, Vol. XXXIV, No. 4, November 1958.

[20] *De L'Utilité et de sa Mesure*, Ed. Bernardi (Turin, La Riforma Sociale, 1933).

which would run at a loss if it charged a uniform price could be made profitable by a method of discriminatory charges. Users of the facility would then come forward at different levels of payment, therefore displaying in the range of the differentia, the relative differences in the true values of the facility to each participant in its benefits.

The first major advance on the concept of *utilité relative* came from the investigations of Auspitz and Lieben[21] into price theory. They took the view that although it should be possible to measure small *changes* in an individual's feelings (satisfaction or dissatisfaction), his aggregate satisfaction or dissatisfaction cannot be measured. '*Les sentiments de l'individu ne sont pas susceptibles de mesures*', and further: '*encore moins saurait-on comparer les sentiments de deux individus*'.[22]

In the analyses of recreational benefits previously made, 'average man' is central; yet he, in the world of recreation is the make-believe of all make-believes. Each analyst formulates his own conception of average man, endows him with specific responses to various hypothetical market situations and assigns monetary values to his presumed reactions. Since at every step such subjective values pave the way, in association with assumptions which can never be appropriately tested, an agreed consensus of measurement between analysts can hardly be expected.

There also arise the questions of primary and secondary benefits[23] and the manner in which these should be viewed, enumerated and evaluated. But perhaps the most severe limitation on these methods of analysis is the existence of those benefits which admit of no direct quantitative evaluation in money terms. In the vocabulary of cost-benefit analysis, these are referred to as 'intangibles' and 'incommensurables', and their very nature precludes them from being mensurable and comparable with benefits which are quantifiable directly in money terms.[24] For example, scenic beauty and the relaxing atmosphere of calm and quiet countryside utterly defy mensuration and would be classed as intangible. The benefit derived from the availability of a new road link between a city and a recreational area would belong to the incommensurable class because it

[21] R. Auspitz and R. Lieben, *Untersuchungen uber die Theorie des Preises* (Duncker and Humblot, Berlin, 1889).

[22] *Recherches Sur La Theorie du Prix* (French Translation, Giard et Briere, Paris, 1914), pp. 8–9.

[23] A. H. Trice and S. E. Wood, *op. cit.*, pp. 196–7.

[24] E. J. Devine, 'The treatment of Incommensurables in Cost-Benefit Analysis', *Land Economics*, Vol. XLII, No. 3, August 1966.

cannot wholly be evaluated directly in terms of money, although some measurement of its worth to users may be obtained in terms of, say, user-hours.

Although, at first sight, it may appear a relatively uncomplicated procedure to translate incommensurables into other quantities which in turn may be evaluated in money terms, the transposition bristles with serious difficulties and incongruities. Take a particular illustration. In a cost-benefit study of the London–Birmingham motorway,[25] the list of benefits to road users included such factors as economies in travel times and savings due to the reduction of accidents. Work-time savings were estimated on the basis of hourly rates of pay of drivers and passengers, and the value of accident reduction was based on estimates of damage to property, the costs of medical treatment and the value of lives saved or lost.

In exercises of this kind,[26] it is assumed that the savings of one minute times a factor of sixty equals the savings of sixty minutes, and that an hour saved in travel time to and from work has a value commensurate with the hourly pay rate. Such fancy assumptions are wholly lacking in realism. Many short time savings are quite value-less and many long time savings will not necessarily be employed for economically productive work. A man who, by using a new road, would shorten his journey time to work might not work an hour longer but simply leave home an hour later. The assumptions made in estimating the value of lives saved or lost are even more singular. The basic premise is that the economic benefit of a life saved is given by the present value of the loss of production avoided through the life being saved. In order to assess this it is necessary to determine how much the average person whose life may be saved will earn during his life-span. The estimates which have to be made include those of average earnings in respect of various socio-economic groups, of the probability of survival to various ages, of the pro-portion of people employed at each age level and their appropriate contributions to production. Housewives' services are not forgotten; they are ascribed values in terms of their opportunity costs or through some other means. Weisbrod,[27] for example has devised a method of 'replacement cost' to take account of housewives' services in terms of payments to a housekeeper. However, since the supply of food previously needed for the deceased is no longer required, a

25 T. M. Coburn, M. E. Beesley and D. J. Reynolds, *op. cit.*

26 T. E. Kuhn, *Public Enterprise Economics and Transport Problems* (Berkeley and Los Angeles: University of California Press, 1962).

27 B. A. Weisbrod, *Economics of Public Health: Measuring the Economic Impact of Diseases* (Philadelphia: University of Pennsylvania Press, 1960).

gain is registered. Accordingly, estimates of various consumption costs in relation to age and income are calculated from family budget data, weighted, and incorporated in the cost-benefit analysis as a benefit accruing to 'society' as a result of the deaths.

In defence of such dubious sophistries, it has been argued that calculations of this nature are perfectly valid and that the judgements of the courts should 'make it possible in each country to obtain an average opinion as regards the sums to be spent to avoid the various effective losses'.[28] However, as Prest and Turvey have commented: 'These calculations are worth undertaking only if we believe that more resources should be devoted to saving a more "productive" life than a less "productive" life; for example, the average man in preference to the average woman of the same age, a white Protestant American in preference to a coloured one, the average Englishman rather than the average Scot, a young worker rather than a baby.'[29]

Although the expressions 'social cost' and 'social benefit' are used deliberately to denote the consequences of actions which reach beyond the parties to them and affect others, near and far, many and few, the inhabitants of a whole village or the members of some other grouping in society, they have no reality or identity in themselves and apart from the experiences of individual men and women. The suspicions engendered by analysis on the lines mentioned and criticized above derive from attempts, unavoidable by the approach, to imagine the reactions, value judgements and fate of average man, as if so hypothetical a being were real. There is no social experience apart from the experiences of individual people. Surely, therefore, if we need to measure costs and benefits of schemes and undertakings – smoking chimneys not excepted – the nearer we can get to actualities and the subjective views of the parties enjoying the benefits or incurring the costs, the less speculative and spurious will the estimates and conclusions be. Proprietary land use analysis can provide a framework within which an approach to actualities is possible. An elaborate and detailed examination of the claim would take the text beyond the compass set for this work. The following paragraphs, however, are intended to illustrate the principles implicit in it and to adumbrate the possibilities of the use of the analysis as a method of assessing and presenting costs and benefits.

[28] J. Thedie and C. Abraham, 'Economic Aspects of Road Accidents', *Traffic Engineering and Control*, Vol. II, No. 10, February 1961.

[29] A. R. Prest and R. Turvey, 'Cost-Benefit Analysis: A Survey', *Surveys of Economic Theory: Volume III. Resource Allocation*, American Economic Association and Royal Economic Society (Macmillan, New York, 1967).

Proprietary Structure: a Key to Benefits and Costs

The value of consumer's surplus to a particular consumer can never be known unless the recipient reveals voluntarily his own desires and satisfactions. By definition market prices, the only common form of customer revelations, are ruled out. It is pointless, if not presumptuous, for an analyst to attempt to estimate the social benefits of an undertaking in terms of consumer surpluses of which he can have no sure knowledge. To argue that, since A lives nearer to a place of recreation than B does, A's consumer surplus is the difference between the cost of making the journey as B incurs it and as A incurs it, is to discourse in a world of hypothetical conjectures—'*Oh! may we never, never doubt what nobody is sure about*'. B's longer journey may for him add the spice of adventure to the totality of the recreational enjoyment focused in the ultimate destination; an added enjoyment which is denied to A. A has no added benefit from living nearer—rather the reverse.

Consumer's surplus, like many other analytical tools from the workshops of pure theory, finds no ready acceptance in the world of real experiences. It would surely be exceptional and, indeed, somewhat absurd for a family on a day's outing to divide the totality of the day's experience into component parts, of the journeys there and back and in-between, the hours of rest and the hours of play and so on, and to think of the energies expended on one pursuit as a kind of debit or cost to set against the benefits of the others. Real folk in the real world do not analyse their actions, emotions and expenditures in this way. To do so would border on the neurotic and in any event would be likely to rob the activities of much of that total enjoyment whose birth-spring is spontaneity. Normal men and women are not analysts, either towards themselves or towards other people. They take their pleasures and other benefits in the round; or, if we can use the language of Martin Buber,[30] as a total impact or encounter. The householder enjoys the totality of his dwelling experience in the house of his choice. He does not analyse and quantify the contributions made to that total enjoyment by the shape of the bedrooms, the layout of the garden, the view from the dining room and so on; one element is the complement of the other. To analyse is to destroy. The value of the whole is so much more than the sum of the parts. The value of the house to him lies in his encounter with it as a home and dwelling.

A concept of value which those concerned to perfect the technique of cost-benefit analysis should come to recognize is value in encounter.

[30] M. Buber, *I and Thou* (T. Clarke, Edinburgh, 2nd Edn, 1958).

Like consumer's surplus and indeed all values it is subjective to the one who makes the value judgement and cannot be known to a mere observer or analyst unless revealed to him by the recipient of the benefit valued. The value of a proprietary land unit to the holder of it would be a measure of the extent to which at the time of valuation the holder of the unit had satisfied his motives for holding the unit or assessed the probability of his being able to do so. The value of the benefit of his proprietorship to him would be an entirety, defying analysis, the consequence of the encounter of the proprietor of the unit with the totality of the property owned, and in the light of the motive for which he held it. Costs incurred by the owner of the proprietary land unit as money outlays or resource expenditures would lend themselves to analysis and summation; on balance they would represent the costs to be set off against the totality of the value in encounter of the benefit enjoyed by the proprietor *qua* proprietor.

It is not too fanciful to envisage a cost-benefit exercise being carried out with reference to the proprietary structure of the area of a project and in terms of the costs and benefits peculiar to the holders of the respective proprietary land units. Whether we are dealing with a project involving the public ownership of interests in land or weighing alternative government plans for the use of land by private holders of it, the land over which the project is to be carried out must inevitably have a proprietary structure pattern. The project will alter that pattern and the costs and benefits of the project can, therefore, be presented as a schedule of the experiences of the proprietors of the land units before and after the execution of the project.

The incidence of costs and benefits would be far more precisely determined by such an approach than is possible by any interpretation of the relatively vague notions of social costs and benefits, while what is peculiar to members of the public will not be overlooked, but taken care of, by identifying points of actual public participation and assessing the consequences.

These general claims can best be illustrated by a particular example. In a citation we referred to earlier[31] the author pointed to a smoking chimney from a factory as the cause of what he called a social cost. The incidence of the cost is by no means certain. To wave the hand and say society at large, does not get us very far. In the real world, the nuisance from the smoking chimney will have a precise incidence: it will affect the use and enjoyment of specific proprietary land units in the vicinity of the factory. The units may be held by a private or a public body and be used accordingly. The effect of the nuisance

[31] P. Hall, *op. cit.*

cannot extend beyond the experience of each and every person who uses or is likely to use the resources distributed among the respective proprietary land units. If the effect of the nuisance is thus measured, the measurements will tell us all there is to know about the total effect of the nuisance upon everyone involved.

Consider for a moment the owner of a freehold proprietary land unit who had developed and used it for professional offices. The nuisance may incur him in higher cleaning costs or necessitate the reconstruction of cupboards on the premises. These outlays would be peculiar to him as proprietor and professional man and could be expressed as tangible costs. But the changes in office layout and administration, and the alteration of the environment in general could reduce in his eyes the total benefit which the offices in their original state conveyed to him. What he encounters now is of less value existentially to him than had been the unvitiated offices. To try and assess the reduction in total value by asking what drop, if any, might be experienced in the market value of the freehold would be a somewhat spurious exercise: market value implies a market transaction in which the holder of the unit is voluntarily relinquishing his title to it, and another, the purchaser, is voluntarily taking the unit with full knowledge of the nuisance. Neither party is in the position of the holder who retains the unit and suffers the nuisance. Members of the staff might have to be bribed in some way to stay and put up with the less congenial circumstances. The extra pay would be a tangible cost and benefit, and to the extent that for the staff member it was a form of recompense for having to work in less desirable surroundings, would be a degree of redress for the nuisance suffered by that person as a member of the public using the neighbourhood. But money is one thing and pleasant surroundings for work another; the higher pay might not go all the way to make good the inconvenience experienced by the staff member. Some intangible loss of value beyond the power of money to recompense might remain. The total experience of coming to and working in that office has undergone change—the value on encounter has fallen. Nevertheless, by focusing attention on the affairs of the proprietary land unit as such and upon those concerned with it, these costs and losses of benefit to certain members of the local society are identified. Each proprietary land unit throughout the entire area of the project could in turn be treated in the same way, and a composite picture of costs and benefits built up.

In this regard it should be remembered that services like roads are usually provided by public authorities who have to be proprietors of proprietary land units in order to provide the service required.

The effect of the nuisance would be determined by reference to its effect upon the realization of the motive of the public authority in holding the proprietary land unit. If the motive was to provide and run a hospital, an assessment of the degree to which the nuisance had adversely affected the realization of the motive by the holders of the proprietary land unit would reflect an impact of the nuisance on those members of the local society who used or were eligible to use the hospital; there would be no need in this case to take up the issue with each patient or potential patient, because unlike the case of the staff member of the offices, in the first example, the hospital's function is to perform a public service—and to the extent to which it fails to reach desired standards, the members of the public suffer.

While we have a hospital in mind, we may use it to illustrate another aspect of cost-benefit analysis based upon proprietary land structures. In considering the building of a hospital as an integral feature of a development scheme, all that should be done and needs to be done, is to compare the costs of different layouts with the entire functioning of the hospital for hospital purposes. The provision of the hospital as a hospital is the only form in which the benefit from the costs can be expressed and experienced in reality. To try and analyse the ramifications economically and socially of curing invalids, young and old, literate and illiterate, is a sophistry that loses itself in its own maze. The benefit of the hospital as a public service to each member of the public eligible and likely to use it, is the value it has as a hospital to each member as he encounters it as a hospital. The same can be said of roads and other public services and institutions.

The proprietary structure approach to cost-benefit analysis advocated here envisages the proprietary structure as a frame of reference for the systematic gathering and presentation of evidence, and the calculation of costs and identification of benefits. An investigation pursued on these lines would require the investigator first to identify the proprietary land units and the holders of them and assess costs and judge benefits from their viewpoints; and subsequently, to move from them to all who work with them towards the realization of the motives which sponsor the plans for the use of the resources of the respective units, whatever those motives may be—entreprenurial, residential, recreational, providing a public service or some other.

Chapter XII

A RURAL EXERCISE

By way of a postscript to the general theory of the foregoing chapters, this chapter provides an illustrative study of the application of proprietary land use analysis. It is focused upon the use of land resources for forestry within agricultural proprietary land units in England and Wales. The analysis was undertaken by Dr Derek Nicholls who conducted his research in 1964–7. A full text describing the work of Dr Nicholls and his conclusions was recently published by HMSO.[1] What follows here is an abridgement and adaptation of the original work so arranged as to exemplify some of the concepts expounded in the theory.

Preliminary Survey

The fieldwork was done by Dr Nicholls in two stages—a preliminary survey and a main investigation.

The preliminary survey was conducted for the most part in the southern region of England and Wales where the area given to privately owned woodlands was 8·6 per cent against a national average of 4·9 per cent. Its purpose was exploratory, to penetrate a relatively unknown world of decision-making so as to discover whether or not information could be gathered on a more comprehensive scale about the attitudes of the owners of rights in land towards forestry, the nature of the problems facing them and how they viewed the advantages and disadvantages of afforestation.

Inevitably, there was a certain arbitrariness about the selection of the sample for the preliminary survey. It was made up of twenty agricultural proprietary land units.[2] The units were chosen to cover a variety of different sizes and proprietary character forms. On examination it was found that four of these had no woodlands at all;

---

[1] D. C. Nicholls, *The Use of Land for Forestry Within the Proprietary Land Unit* (Forestry Commission Bulletin, No. 39, H.M.S.O., 1969).

[2] Above, p. 26.

two of the others did not practise systematic silviculture and the remainder in various degrees had what Dr Nicholls, in his original work, called productive woodland.

The preliminary survey was successful. Not only did its findings give a lead to the manner in which the main survey could be conducted but they also yielded interesting factual information on their own account.

Throughout the run of the agricultural proprietary land units of the preliminary survey an entrepreneurial purpose dominated the use of the resources for farming.

The agricultural land was not in hand necessarily; but it was managed so as to maximize the financial return. The woodlands, by contrast, were at best accepted as worthwhile amenity assets. Some felt the financial burden of upkeep of the woodlands more acutely than others felt it. But wherever woodlands occurred, the economic production of timber was of secondary consequence. There was no apparent correlation between the size of unit or the proprietary character form and the degree of attention paid to tending the woodlands. Everywhere, this was a matter of personal fancy, interest and enthusiasm.

Because the proprietary land units were agricultural and the financial purpose was dominant over the use of the agricultural resources, very little new investment in woodlands had been made over the twenty years since 1945. No appreciable area of land had been taken out of agriculture for forestry purposes and on the majority of units with derelict woodland nothing was being done by way of rehabilitation. The reason was financial. The motive[3] to manage the total resources to achieve the dual pursuit of reaping the highest financial rewards from the farm land while keeping the woodland primarily as an amenity asset meant that the transfer of land from agriculture to forestry was, in the short term, the swapping of a financial asset for an amenity one. In the long term, transfer implied a single financial motive, in so far as the planting of land to forestry could be done, and was likely to be done, as a financial investment. Duration[4] as an attribute of the proprietary land units, does not appear to have affected the general outcome. Criteria were financial. Many of the holders of units of long duration were unable to find capital to lock up in tree-growth for the benefit of generations yet unborn; and those with the necessary liquidity were dubious of the validity of the long term calculations and preferred the present enjoyment[5] of the amenity of a derelict woodland to the speculative return from newly set plantations. A prevailing lack of understanding

[3] Above, p. 57.   [4] Above, pp. 28–30   [5] Above, p. 177.

of the finances of woodland management seemed to work paradoxically, and to prevent old, amenity woodlands being converted to agricultural land. The amenity was apparent, enjoyed and accepted; the costs of conversion and the probable yields from newly made arable land so speculative that the owners were reluctant to change from their dual-pursuit motive.

Size of units seemed to have a bearing upon the nature of the woodlands. No unit under a thousand acres had any productive woodlands. On the larger units, the productive woodlands were either leased to the Forestry Commission at nominal rents where the owner had no ready cash to deploy on woodland management yet valued the woodlands for their amenity; or, there was a properly recruited woodland staff, supplemented perhaps by contract labour.

The preliminary survey read a clear lesson about the use of resources, motive and proprietary character form. Among the proprietary character forms contained in the preliminary survey, were those which were manifestly identifiable as either simple[6] or fiduciary.[7] The fiduciary units were held for charitable purposes. The units with simple proprietary character forms were more frequently given to forestry than were the charity units. Of the total acreage of the simple proprietary land units, 17 per cent was given to productive woodlands; the corresponding percentage on the charity units was 5 per cent. The holders of the charity units had alone sold woodland and invested the proceeds to enlarge the consociate wealth[8] of the units. The keener interest of the owners of the simple units in woodlands is in large measure explicable by the current tax concessions allowed to the owners of woodland. Charities do not pay tax and the fiduciary units therefore enjoy no tax advantages from investing in woodland. A similar clear pattern of land use was observed over an extensive area of rural land surveyed in 1952–6.[9] Unlike simple units, fiduciary units held by charities for investment are likely to be exploited to maximize monetary income, especially if the corporate body or the trustees do not live on or near the unit. The influence of proprietary character form upon current rewards is well illustrated by estimated rents and actual rents. Actual rents on the charity units averaged 94 per cent of the estimated rental income; on the simple units the corresponding figure was only 76 per cent.

The Main Survey

The main survey was made with a sample of seventy-two proprietary

6 Above, p. 31.   7 Above, p. 32.   8 Above, p. 184.
9 D. R. Denman, *Estate Capital* (Allen and Unwin, London, 1957), pp. 173 ff.

land units selected with a wide geographical scatter throughout England and Wales. Each unit was chosen deliberately as having woodlands systematically managed, usually on a plan approved by the Forestry Commission for grant aid. In total area the sample covered some 560,000 acres, approximating to 1·5 per cent of the land area of England and Wales. Of this total acreage, 78,000 acres were woodland; an average equivalent to about 4 per cent of the land devoted to private woodlands at that time in England and Wales.

The information from the main survey was collated in accordance with the following schedule:

General: land use pattern;
location and shape;
ownership characteristics;
management structure.

Agricultural: area let by number of holdings—including actual rents and estimated rental values;
area in hand by number of holdings;
predominant farming systems;
future policy, especially in respect of structure.

Silvicultural: area let—including rents and the reasons for
(forestry) leasing;
area in hand by geographical distribution;
determinants of present woodland sites;
history of management;
main species and age structure,
labour,
utilization and marketing of products,
finance and other economic factors;
woodland tradition;
determinants of policy;
principles of management;
future policy making.

Principal Component Analysis

The data were subjected to two methods of analysis, much in vogue at the time: a form of multivariate analysis, called principal component analysis; and a method in which emphasis was placed on the functional and not upon the quantifiable, known as association analysis.

The objective of the principal component analysis was to discover which of a number of variable characteristics of the proprietary land units surveyed were more responsible than others for the total 'variability' among the observed characteristics. It was a refinement upon the more orthodox and simple method of compiling a correlation matrix and, indeed, was approached by presenting the data as a correlation matrix as a first step.[10] Proceeding in this way, it was thought possible to avoid the necessity of studying all the variables in the correlation matrix, a preponderant number of which did not greatly influence total variability. The principal component analysis was a means of cutting out the insignificant from the start.

The survey data were arranged and quantified in the following categories, known as the nine original variables:

1. area of unit.
2. agricultural area.
3. agricultural area in hand.
4. agricultural area let.
5. estimated average rental values.
6. woodland area.
7. woodland area in hand.
8. woodland area let.
9. woodland staff.

The upshot of the entire statistical exercise was the discovery by Dr Nicholls that 82 per cent of the total variability was to be accounted for by the following variables:

  unit size;
  woodland area;
  woodland let;
  agricultural area; and
  estimated rental values.

As a result of this analysis, it was possible to concentrate attention over the entire sample upon those characteristics of the proprietary land units which had a significant bearing upon the total use pattern of the resources.

Size and Development Use Pattern. The principal component analysis showed sufficiently well to demand recognition that the size of the agricultural proprietary land units studied had a bearing upon the area of the woodlands. It was to be expected that as the absolute size of units increased the area of woodland would follow suit, not

10 See Appendix A, p. 223.

necessarily acre for acre. This was borne out by the evidence. But within this overall correlation pattern, two lesser patterns were discerned which were not deducible from natural logic. The sizes of the units ranged from 250 acres to 35,000 acres. As the size of units moved up into the thousands of acres, the rate of increment of woodland area accelerated; and a corresponding slowing of the rate of increment was observed among changes in the size of the smaller units. The other of the two lesser patterns showed a clear rise in the percentage of total area occupied by woodlands as the overall size of the unit diminished. Six of the units were less than a thousand acres each; and on these woodland occupied 26 per cent of the total area, whereas the average percentage for the 560,000 acres of the main sample was 14 per cent. The practical conclusion, borne out by other aspects of the principal component analysis is that on the comparatively smaller units, woodland, in relation to agricultural land, is of greater consequence in the allocation of land resources within the units than is the case on the larger units.

Duration and Size. Table VII shows the regional differences in the development use patterns of the units of the main survey. The largest proprietary land units tend to lie in the East Midland and North regions; the respective averages being 19,000 and 13,000 acres. In the Chilterns and the Far West, the average sizes dropped to the other end of the size range and were rather less than a third of the overall average size of just under 8,000 acres. The units in the North tended to display extensive areas of moorland; and in the East Midland region the large units were often burdened with expansive acreages of poor quality. These trends, however, were not uniform. Many units in both of these regions had liberal acreages of relatively high quality agricultural land. Quality of land, then, was not the sole explanation for the size of the larger units. There is reason to suppose that the explanation involved duration rather than the inherent qualities of the soil. There are traditions in the north and parts of the Midlands to hold land in family hands generation by generation. With one exception, the units surveyed in these two regions had in most cases a duration of centuries of descent or of at least three generations. In contrast, about one third of the number of the units surveyed in the South East and East Anglia had changed hands on the market since the turn of the century. Also in these regions the demand for country residences and small amenity estates exerts a pressure to break up larger units of long-standing.

Size and Derivatives. On 20 out of the 72 units surveyed all the agricultural land was held by the owners of derivative units in the

212

form of agricultural tenancies. The size of the units on which this happened was on average almost half that of the average size of the remaining units on which some of the agricultural land was in hand and used either for farming as a business enterprise, or for farming and residential pleasure; the average acreage of the former group was 4,600 acres and of the latter group 9,000 acres.

TABLE VII: *Proprietary Land Unit Area and Woodland Area by Region*

Region	Number of units	Average PLU area (acres)	Average Woodland area (acres)	Average percentage of woodland
Far West	7	2,221	531	23·9*
Mid West	8	5,883	1,074	18·3
South East	8	3,394	575	17·0
West Midlands	6	7,224	759	10·5
Chilterns	8	2,343	833	35·5
East Midlands	7	19,336	3,136	16·2
East Anglia	6	7,075	1,068	15·1
North	10	13,234	1,596	12·0
South Wales	4	9,983	510	5·1*
North Wales	8	7,386	489	6·6*
Total	72	7,808	1,057	16·0

* These average figures are distorted by one large estate which appears to be be atypical of the region.

Proprietary character form appeared to be correlated with the creation of derivatives; only 2 of the 5 charity units had any farm land in hand but on all units held by companies some portion of the agricultural land was being farmed in hand.

The estimated rental income per acre was distinctly higher on the units wholly given to the creation of derivatives than the average estimated rental income on the units with some part of the agricultural land in hand. The exact explanation for this was not investigated. It might be that the units which were wholly given to tenancies were managed in this way because of the relatively high rental value of the land. What is more likely, however, is the influence of the size of the unit on rental values and rents. In the correlation matrix it will be seen that there is a significant negative correlation between the size of unit and the estimated rental values—the larger the unit, the lower the rent per acre. A similar relationship was clearly seen among the rental evidence from two earlier and extensive surveys of estate finances and rental values;[11] and as just noted, the

11 D. R. Denman and V. F. Stewart, *Farm Rents* (Allen and Unwin, London, 1959),

213

units wholly given to derivatives and on which the estimated rents were higher were on average half the acreage of the other units. The average estimated rental value per acre was £4·70 on the units wholly given to tenancies and lower in average size, and £4·10 per acre on the other units.

Predisposing Function and Development Use Pattern. Change of land use from agriculture to forestry and vice versa was not much in evidence. The former movement – out of agriculture and into forestry – never exceeded 10 acres on over half of the units of the main survey and on many of these the acreage of change was of truly insignificant proportions. Change from forestry to agriculture occurred on only 2 of the units. Only seldom did the evidence suggest that in making and revising the plans for the use of the land and natural resources of the units serious thought was given to the economics, the advantages and disadvantages, financial and otherwise, of a change from one land use to the other. The existing land use patterns seemed on many of the units to be due to the influence of the predisposing function of antecedents, or of some prior decision which while not strictly conforming to the definition of an antecedent predisposing function given in the theory,[12] exerted a similar influence. Dr Nicholls' own summing up speaks for itself and points to this conclusion:

> Very often the traditional pattern had been accepted unquestioningly. It is possible that this pattern was the one best suited to satisfy all of the proprietor's requirements, including, perhaps, visual and sporting amenities. However, the impression was often gained that the sole reason for the current allocation of the land between agriculture and forestry within the proprietary land unit was that the same allocation had been adopted or accepted by the proprietor's predecessor in title.

Association Analysis

Two proprietary land units may be compared by observing not only the presence of similar characteristics but also by noting similarities in the absence of certain characteristics. Where the two are similar in all their characteristics and attributes, it can be accepted that so far as the two units under observation go, any one characteristic common to both has a propensity to associate with the others in

[12] Above, Ch. VI.

identical patterns of association to the exclusion of characteristics not present.

The aims of the association analysis were to discover which of the characteristics of the proprietary land units tended to exert an associative influence over others, so as to establish a homogeneous identity among groups of units, patent in the pattern of the presence or absence of specific characteristics. The analysis has a special relevance to proprietary land use analysis for it is reasonable to assume that a characteristic which exerts a strong associative influence over others, in so far as it and they are components in the capital order of the assets of the proprietary land units,[13] has in some way a functional complementarity[14] with those others.

Dr Nicholls' association analysis was based upon observed variations of 51 variable characteristics.[15] The result is shown at significant levels of the analysis in Figure 8.

Profit and No Profit. The characteristics around which factors clustered with the greatest degree of homogeneity were the two alternatives of a plus or a minus to the profit and loss account of the woodlands. This does not mean that the association analysis divided the 72 units of the main survey into those where the motive was entrepreneurial and those where it was not. Whatever the motives and purposes underlying the management policies, the fact emerged that on some units the woodlands showed yearly profits and on others the entreprise either struck even or showed a yearly loss. As Figure 8 shows, 52 of the units formed a relatively homogeneous group round profitable woodland enterprise and 20 units a homogeneous group round unprofitability.

Interesting observations were made of both groups. The 20 non-profitable units did not easily sub-divide into smaller homogeneous groups as happened with the 52 profit-makers. The best that could be done with the 20 was to observe that on 18 of them considerations of soil and topography had had something to do with the siting of the woodlands, and these eighteen on that account had a certain degree of homogeneity.

More important than the sub-grouping were the trends in characteristics and attributes of the 20 units in the unprofitable group. Less than one in four of the units whose proprietary character form was simple belonged to this group while the group had 3 of the 5 charity-owned units. Duration and the predisposing function of antecedents also seem to have something to do with the grouping. More than

13 Above, p. 111.   14 Above, pp. 60, 61.   15 See Appendix B, p. 224.

FIG. 8: *ASSOCIATION ANALYSIS—PRINCIPAL DIVISIONS*

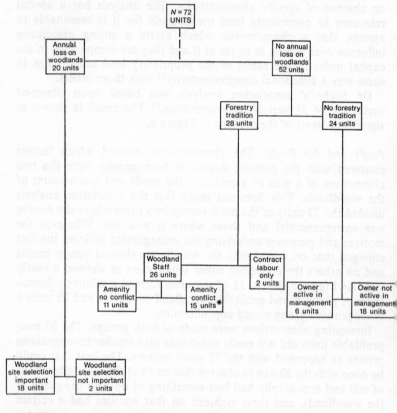

* This group contained two units on which amenity considerations were unimportant.

half of the units with a short duration, that is from the turn of the century, were found in the non-profitability group; a situation which has its counterpart in that no more than a fifth of the units with well established forestry tradition were in this group. The relative lack of tradition probably accounted for a good deal of the recorded non-profitability. With few exceptions the units were well-managed in respect of their agriculture. More than half of the 20 units had suffered from war-time clear-felling and again over a half had planted extra land to timber since 1945; and the majority of cases were without a long standing forestry tradition and continuous manage-ment bringing forward in rotation mature timber to offset the costs of planting. Indeed, it is open to question whether all the units recorded as showing a loss would have done so if the estimated ultimate return from the sale of mature timber had been discounted and offset against current yearly costs. This is borne out by the declared purposes of the owners of the units; all but one of the 20 were looking forward to the long-term creation of timber assets as a means of enhancing the overall value of the land and resources of the units. Tax benefits were also in mind but on only 2 of the units was tax advantage a conscious aim. Nearly half of the 20 placed a special importance on amenity and sport, and were prepared to give these aims the benefit if profit from the woodland had to be foregone for their sake. The use of woodland as shelter to adjoining farmland was also a significant determinant on half of the units and, again, profit was sacrificed in these cases to shelter if need required it.

Turning to the group of 52 units with profitable woodlands, it was found that 38 out of the 50 units in the main survey with a simple proprietary character form were in the group, and only 4 of the 38 had a duration less than the run of the present century. Long-standing forestry tradition also featured largely in this group; of the 35 units in the main sample with such a tradition, 28 were with the group. Right through the inter-war years the woodlands on nearly half of the 52 units had been consistently managed for commercial forestry; and only two in every five had had to alter plans to meet national demands and sacrifice timber to a premature clear-felling order. Two in three of the units had permanent woodland staff. The incidence of sporting amenity taking precedence over woodland commerce was proportionally the same as with the non-profitability group. A marked contrast, however, between the two primary groups was the predominance among the profit-takers of those who deliberately aimed at reaping yearly profits from the woodlands as distinct from waiting upon long-term capital growth with the natural maturity of the timber.

217

Tradition and No Tradition. Unlike the 20 non-profit makers, the 52 profit-making units sub-divided again into two smaller homogeneous groups, the key characteristic responsible for the sub-division being the presence or absence of a long-standing forestry tradition; in general terms we may say that the divide turned about what could in the main have been the predisposing functions of antecedents. On 28 of the 52 units with profitable woodlands a continuous tradition of forestry management ran back in the past over many generations; the other 24 units had practised forestry management for no longer than the twenty-odd years since the end of the Second World War. Here and there among the 24, were units on which woodlands had sometime in the past been well managed but had suffered from a discontinuation of systematic management; only on 4 of these was the last period of systematic management as recent as the inter-war years. Lack of continuous management showed on 14 of the 24 in the complete dislocation of the planting and felling rotation—hardly any timber would grow into maturity before the end of the century as two-thirds of the acreage was either already over-mature or recently planted.

Differences of proprietary character form and duration distinguished one group from the other. Of the 28 with well established forestry tradition no less than 85 per cent had a simple proprietary form; this form accounted for 60 per cent of the non-traditional group. In hard numbers, there were only 4 units of the 28 in the hands of either companies or trustees. All the units with traditional forestry practices had each a duration of no less a period than the end of the nineteenth century to the time of the survey. Among the 24 non-traditionalists, 4 had been acquired since the turn of the century. Tradition affected motive. One in every two of the traditionalists was prepared to place the provision and enjoyment of amenity from the woodlands above commercial profitability and to manage the woodland resources to that end; while only one in four of the non-traditionalists had a like motive.

Woodland Staff. The group of 28 traditionalists had within it two even smaller associations with a marked degree of homogeneity. One was much bigger than the other and accounted for 26 of the 28. The associative influence in this bigger group was the presence of a permanent woodland staff sometimes assisted by contract labour. On the 2 units in the other sub-group, the labour in the woodland was provided wholly by contract. Although the two units with contract labour had long-standing traditions of forestry, they were in themselves among the smallest of the units surveyed, too small in

218

fact to have estate staff of any kind; it was significant also that these small units were planned from an entrepreneurial motive which did not give amenity considerations prior place before commerce.

Amenity and Commerce. At a lower divide still, the 26 units with a permanent woodland staff fell into two homogeneous groups. The criterion on this occasion was the presence or absence of conflict between amenity and woodland profitability where these were the aims of a multi-pursuit motive. In all cases the dual-pursuit guided the planned use of resources. In one group, however, of 11 units, the double aim was accomplished without evidence of conflict; on 10 of these units the woodlands made a profit and the standards of amenity were not impaired. With the other group of 15 units, on all but 2 on which amenity was deliberately disregarded in favour of profitability, there was conflict. Here amenity considerations prevailed and there the dictates of commerce won the day. It is noteworthy that only 7 of these 15 units made a profit on the woodlands.

Principals and Agents. To turn back to the 24 units which had profitable woodlands but no forestry tradition, we find these 24 sub-dividing into 2 homogeneous smaller groups around criteria of management. A small group of 6 consisted of units whose management was in the hands of the owners of the units themselves who supervised the daily administration of management and policy. The larger group of 18 was composed of units whose management was in the hands of professional agents. Size had something to do with this sub-divide. The units in the small group were relatively small, and in size averaged 2,000 acres of which woodland on average accounted for 520 acres. The group was further identified as having only 1 unit with a sawmill, few had maintenance staffs and half of them, in contrast to the units managed by professional agents, employed the services of forestry co-operatives for the sale of woodland products.

Regional Distinctions. The association analysis revealed regional distinctions of interest. In the south east of England there were eight units and on these the predominant intent was to regard the woodlands as areas of amenity and game preserves; on two of them the woodlands were unprofitable and no one of the other six had a long, unbroken record of commercial forestry. Such forestry tradition as there was eschewed commerce and was wholly in line with the acceptance of woodlands as amenity and sporting assets. Charac-

219

teristic of these south-eastern units was a high level of consociate and adventitious wealth.[16] The tax advantages attending investment in agricultural land and forestry are not conditional upon the profitability of the respective enterprises; emphasis could be and was placed upon development for amenity and leisure pursuits without diminishing the benefits of the tax concessions, which meant more to units with high levels of consociate wealth than to similar units less well supported. In the eastern Midlands, a similar pattern pertained, although there, the average size of unit was well above average and differed from the average size of the south-eastern units. In the eastern Midlands also, while attention was centred upon the use of woodlands as features of amenity and as game preserves, there was more evidence than in the south east of conflict between amenity ideals and commercial aims.

In the north, by contrast, it was a story of profitable woodlands and long-standing commercial practice. Seven of the 10 units had permanent woodland staffs. And commercial criteria prevailed over amenity and sporting considerations when a choice of land use had to be made. The same was true of the units in the western Midlands. The climate was propititious for forestry and the soil most favourable to farming; while therefore the woodlands tended to be second favourites, both the agricultural land and the woodland were equally well managed. Not 1 of the 6 units had unprofitable woodlands and on only 1 was there no well established commercial practice in forestry.

The unprofitable units in the main tended to lie in Wales and the far west of England. Half of all the units in Wales, north and south, had unprofitable woodland and only one in four had practised commercial forestry over long unbroken stretches in the past. Only 1 unit in the far west showed any evidence of well established commercial forestry and sported woodlands to show a profit.

A Lesson in Motives and Management

Evidence from Dr Nicholls' surveys and analyses also renders examples of how motives behind the plans for the use of land and resources within proprietary land units influence management decisions in respect of tax policies. The greater volume of evidence exemplifies income tax decisions, although there is some relating to inheritance taxation in the form of estate duty.

In respect of woodland, the owner of a proprietary land unit can elect to be assessed to tax on actual income from commercial

16 Above, p. 146.

activity (under Schedule D of the statutory law) or on a notional income based on rental value (under Schedule B). Among the 72 units of the main survey, the owners of 67 were liable for income tax on the income from the units. The woodlands on 41 of the 67 were taxed partly under Schedule D and partly under Schedule B; on 17 units the woodlands were taxed wholly under Schedule B and on the remaining 9 units the woodlands were taxed wholly under Schedule D. On units like those characteristic of the far west, where the quality of the woodlands was poor or the land was recently planted, actual income would be low or non-existent, and the owners would elect to be assessed under Schedule D. Schedule D assessments were imposed on those units in East Anglia which belonged to the group in which the woodlands were not profitable. But in this region there were as equal a number of units with profitable woodland which was nonetheless managed with an eye to amenity and sporting. With this motive in the background, it was clearly wise to opt for Schedule B. Not only would the profits not be reflected in the nominal Schedule B assessments, but the consideration for amenity and sporting meant that the woodland would not be clear-felled on a regular rotation, and hence there would be no replanting costs to set off against revenue in a Schedule D assessment. A combination of assessments under Schedule D and Schedule B was the rule on those units with a strong forest tradition and well managed woodlands, as are found in the north, where new plantations are assessed under Schedule D and the maturing stands under Schedule B.

Estate duty liability only materially affected one of the 72 units surveyed. On 13 others it affected management policies to some extent. In the main it meant that mature timber was hoarded up and threw rotations out of balance. The object was not to build up a realizable capital asset to meet death duty so much as to possess a valuable asset which could pass at death to successors and legatees free of immediate death duty. This was possible, because duty is not payable on standing timber at death but only when subsequently it is felled and sold; also the value of standing timber at death is not aggregated with the principal estate to ascertain the rate at which estate duty is levied.[17]

In sum, it is interesting to note that of the 72 units of the main survey, only 2 were planned from motives entirely free of all entrepreneurial considerations and given wholly to the enhancement of

[17] For an account of Estate Duty provisions relevant to the period during which the survey was carried out, see, C. N. Beattie, *Elements of Estate Duty* (Stevens and Sons, London, 1952).

natural and sporting amenities. On the majority the motives meant dual or multi-pursuits. Financial gain in yearly income and tax concessions was the guiding motive of 18 units. The owners of 21 others planned for growth in capital investment and amenity values. Finance and amenity on another 18 meant management for income, capital appreciation and amenity. Owners of the remaining 13 had given up all thought of reaping a yearly income from them; they went for capital appreciation overtly and solely and developed forestry to that end.

APPENDIX A: *Correlation Matrix (half only) of the Nine Original Variables*

	(1)	(2)	(3)	(4)	(5)	(6)	(7)	(8)	(9)
Total area of unit	(1)								
Total agricultural area	0·988*	(2)							
Agricultural area in hand	0·587*	0·591*	(3)						
Agricultural area let	0·959*	0·941*	0·298†	(4)					
Estimated average rental value	−0·257†	−0·245†	−0·226	−0·225	(5)				
Total woodland area	0·592*	0·485*	0·274†	0·471*	−0·077	(6)			
Woodland area in hand	0·613*	0·518*	0·303*	0·500*	−0·024	0·921*	(7)		
Woodland area let	0·210	0·137	0·058	0·141	−0·142	0·589*	0·229	(8)	
Woodland staff	0·592*	0·523*	0·390*	0·470*	0·006	0·738*	0·821*	0·141	(9)

* Significant at the 1 per cent level of probability.   † Significant at the 5 per cent level of probability.

APPENDIX B: *Characteristics for Association Analysis*

Characteristic		Code	No. of Estates
GENERAL			
Shape	Compact	1	50
Ownership	Single person	2	50
personality	Company	3	10
	Charity	4	5
	Trustees	5	7
Duration	Established prior to 1900	6	62
	Established between 1901 and 1945	7	6
	Established between 1945 and 1965	8	4
Consociate capital	Substantial	9	62
Management	Owner	10	12
	Resident agent	11	39
	Firm of agents	12	9
	Owner and resident agent	—	3
	Owner and firm	—	9
Maintenance	Internal estate staff	13	51
Rainfall	Over 40 inches per year	14	16
	Under 25 inches per year	15	10
AGRICULTURE			
Farms	Definite amalgamation plans	16	34
Integration with forestry	Staff switched between farm and woods	17	2
FORESTRY			
Selection of sites	Soil and topography	18	31
	Shelter	19	0
	Amenity and sport	20	4
	Soil, topography and shelter	—	4
	Soil, topography, amenity and sport	—	24
	Shelter, amenity and sport	—	3
	Soil, topography, shelter, amenity and sport	—	6
1919–39	Consistent management	21	24
1939–45 War	Heavy fellings	22	30
Land use changes	To forestry	23	31
(post-1945, over 10 acres)	From forestry	24	2
Tree species (over two-thirds by area)	Broad leaved	25	37
	Coniferous	26	17
	Mixed—at least one-third of each	—	18

Characteristic		Code	No. of Estates
Age classes	Good age distribution	27	24
	All over 80 years old	28	0
	All under 20 years old	29	7
	Mainly over 80 years old or under 20 years old	—	30
	Otherwise	—	11
Labour	Contractors only	30	6
	Estate staff only	31	43
	Contractors and estate staff	—	23
Sawmill	Produce for sale	32	25
	Produce for estate use only	33	18
	No estate sawmill	—	29
Timber sales	All through a co-operative	34	12
	All direct to merchants	35	50
	Otherwise	—	10
Grant-aid scheme	Dedicated woodlands	36	51
	Approved woodlands	37	13
	Neither	—	8
Taxation	All Schedule B	38	17
	All Schedule D	39	9
	Schedules B and D	—	41
	Untaxed	—	5
Accounts	Profit	40	34
	Loss	41	20
	Neither	—	18
Tradition	Commercial forestry	42	35
	No such tradition	—	37
Estate duty	Important factor	43	15
	Unimportant	—	57
Shelter	Special importance	44	22
	Otherwise	—	50
Sporting facilities	Important: conflict with forestry	45	11
	Important: no conflict	46	42
	Unimportant	—	19
Amenity	Important: conflict with forestry	47	27
	Important: no conflict	48	36
	Unimportant	—	9
Policy objectives	Annual profit only	49	0
	Indirect economic benefits only	50	13
	Sport and amenity only	51	2
	Annual profit and indirect economic benefits	—	18
	Indirect economic benefits, sport and amenity	—	21
	Annual profit, indirect economic benefits, sport and amenity	—	18

Index

UNIVERSITY LIBRARY
NOTTINGHAM